KING JAMES VI & I
THE KING WHO UNITED SCOTLAND AND ENGLAND

Dedicated to Lorraine Dally

Great princes' favourites their fair leaves spread
But as the marigold at the sun's eye;
And in themselves their pride lies buried,
For at a frown they in their glory die.
      William Shakespeare, Sonnet 25 (lines 5-8).

KING JAMES VI & I
THE KING WHO UNITED SCOTLAND AND ENGLAND

KEITH COLEMAN

AN IMPRINT OF PEN & SWORD BOOKS LTD.
YORKSHIRE – PHILADELPHIA

First published in Great Britain in 2023 by
PEN AND SWORD HISTORY
An imprint of
Pen & Sword Books Ltd
Yorkshire – Philadelphia

Copyright © Keith Coleman, 2023

ISBN 978 1 39909 359 0

The right of Keith Coleman to be identified as Author of this work has been asserted by him in accordance with the Copyright, Designs and Patents Act 1988.

A CIP catalogue record for this book is available from the British Library.

All rights reserved. No part of this book may be reproduced or transmitted in any form or by any means, electronic or mechanical including photocopying, recording or by any information storage and retrieval system, without permission from the Publisher in writing.

Typeset in Times New Roman 12/16 by
SJmagic DESIGN SERVICES, India.
Printed and bound in the UK by CPI Group (UK) Ltd.

Pen & Sword Books Limited incorporates the imprints of Atlas, Archaeology, Aviation, Discovery, Family History, Fiction, History, Maritime, Military, Military Classics, Politics, Select, Transport, True Crime, Air World, Frontline Publishing, Leo Cooper, Remember When, Seaforth Publishing, The Praetorian Press, Wharncliffe Local History, Wharncliffe Transport, Wharncliffe True Crime and White Owl.

For a complete list of Pen & Sword titles please contact
PEN & SWORD BOOKS LIMITED
47 Church Street, Barnsley, South Yorkshire, S70 2AS, England
E-mail: enquiries@pen-and-sword.co.uk
Website: www.pen-and-sword.co.uk

Or
PEN AND SWORD BOOKS
1950 Lawrence Rd, Havertown, PA 19083, USA
E-mail: Uspen-and-sword@casematepublishers.com
Website: www.penandswordbooks.com

Contents

Introduction		vi
Chapter 1	Buchanan's Boy – *Early Years*	1
Chapter 2	The First Favourites – *Esmé Stuart and the Earl of Huntly*	14
Chapter 3	The Devil on the Forth – *King James and Witchcraft*	40
Chapter 4	Above the Black Turnpike – *The Gowrie Conspiracy*	55
Chapter 5	Two Mothers, One Wife – *Elizabeth, Mary, Anne*	69
Chapter 6	A Family Man – *The King's Children and Cousin*	87
Chapter 7	Shadows at the King's Right Hand – *Royal Associates and the Path to the English Crown*	104
Chapter 8	The King at Leisure – *Poetry and the Hunt*	114
Chapter 9	Lion Versus Unicorn – *The Ill-Made Marriage of Scotland and England*	124
Chapter 10	The Nation's Second Scotsman – *The Rise and Fall of Robert Carr*	138
Chapter 11	Steenie – *George Villiers, Duke of Buckingham*	159
Chapter 12	The Forerunner of Revenge – *The Death of King James*	178
Chapter 13	Solomon Weighed – *Reputation and Legacy*	192
Illustration Sources		200
Notes and References		201
Bibliography		214

Introduction

The title of this book may appear ironic in an era when the issue of the unity of Great Britain is again being raised. But, for James Stuart (VI of Scotland and I of England), the uniting of his birth kingdom of Scotland with his inherited kingdom of England was something he earnestly desired. Despite this, his two kingdoms did not legally merge into a United Kingdom until a century after he ascended the southern throne, and only then by a process that was characterised by underhand dealings and squalid compromises. In other things too, King James desired inclusion and the acceptance of opposing ideas. Religion was the most incendiary of these. Scotland's newly established Protestant Kirk did not want any mere monarch to stand as an intermediary between itself and its righteous dialogue with God. Some of its hardline leaders demanded a entirely religious state. Conscious of his own sovereignty, James despised the extreme sections of the Kirk and fought to establish a more moderate and Episcopal rule in the national church.

For all his desire to join the two nation states, and his wider self-proclaimed role as a peacemaker, on a personal level King James was no man of the people. This first king of Scots to become a king of England may have had his flaws exposed by contemporaries and later observers, yet he was convinced he had a divine right to rule and was answerable to God alone. The inheritance of this consequence had fatal consequences for his son and contributed to the fall of the house of Stuart as rulers.

In his personal affairs, James Stuart showed that he was all too human. He lavished affection of his close friends, and while he was a shrewd individual in some matters, he was vulnerable to the wiles

Introduction

of his chosen favourites, all of whom were attractive younger males. As a child, James was already a king, but he was alone and unloved and burned with an unfocused desire to succeed. He took refuge in learning, which remained a love of his for his entire life. The Frenchman Fontenay remarked on the character of the eighteen-year-old when he visited Scotland in 1584: 'He has a heart so big that there is nothing so wearisome that he will not attempt for the sake of virtue and in order to surpass others.'[1] This impetus to overcome rival contemporaries did not lead to James Stuart becoming an all-powerful ruler in traditional terms. He succeeded as king partly through good luck as well as good judgement, yet he was largely bereft of leadership qualities, and possessed little charisma. James was not physically brave, yet he survived a sterile childhood and repeated threats from enemies of his rule as a young man. During his Scottish reign, James successfully outflanked the nobility and the leaders of the Kirk using policies based on tactical awareness. The domain that the Scottish king inhabited was smaller and more personally deadly than that of the English monarch. His court was also less formal than the English one, and it was easier for the violent aristocracy to threaten and pressurise the monarch whenever they felt powerful enough.

This book does not attempt to tell the king's whole life story, but informally examines some key incidents, themes and major relationships in his life in an attempt to gain a better perception of the king as an individual. The lives of those he was closest to throw light on the life of the monarch they revolved around. Despite his conceit of his own learning and divinity, King James remained secretive in some aspects of his life. He acknowledged that being too transparent was unwise for a ruler. His book of advice for his eldest son, Henry, written at the very end of the sixteenth century, *Basilikon Doron* ('Royal Advice'), gave the following advice about those in the king's chamber, but also about the king himself:

> Let them that haue the credite to serue you in your Chalmer, be trustie and secret; for a King will haue need

to vse secrecie in many things: but yet behaue your selfe so in your greatest secrets, as yee neede not bee ashamed, suppose they were all proclaimed at the mercate cross.[2]

Elsewhere in the same treatise, James vowed to be open in all his actions in the eyes of the Almighty, vigilant that his actions may be viewed in 'the touche-stone of publike tryall'. It was a high-minded promise he sometimes failed to keep. Much of his regal paternal advice falls under the category of 'do as I say and not as I do,' and his lofty ideals were often sacrificed for the sake of his own pleasure, or when he indulged those closest to him. His lust for the English throne was a driving principle until he attained that goal. We can see the dissembling, chameleon king in his negotiations with the tiring and wary Queen Elizabeth of England, the incessantly aggressive factions in Scotland, as well as the double-dealing intrigues with European powers. But it is in his personal relationships that we can view a more vulnerable man behind the majesty. There are several key incidents in the king's life that helped to shape him, and they show more of James Stuart than he chose to reveal. The picture of the king which some people saw in his lifetime was unedifying. Based on unflattering propaganda from contemporaries who disliked him, a negative picture of King James has been carried down the centuries. Others broadly characterise his career in two parts: successful king of Scotland and incompetent king of England. His tarnished reputation lingers to the present day.

One modern, journalistic assessment of the king crystallises his inner uncertainty. If not the kindest view, it pinpoints the monarch's narrow shrewdness which arose from his hazardous early decades:

> Through wide-open, cold grey eyes, he distrustfully surveyed a world which, as early experience had taught him, held many surprises for a too distrustful prince. His portrait shows a dishonest man who does not expect others to be honest. Above all, James looked what he was, a Scotsman. You may see men of his general appearance

Introduction

behind many a counter and many an office between Berwick and Inverness. Not all of them have his mind, and, mercifully, very few of them have his character.[3]

So wrote a Scottish writer half a century ago, and it is a semi-humorous opinion that can be agreed with to a limited extent. The same author also notes that James in fact compared favourably alongside some of his contemporary rulers, such as the Holy Roman Emperor Rudolph II, Philip II of Spain and Henri III in France. For all his faults, James VI of Scotland and I of England was the right ruler for the right time for both his kingdoms, if only because there was no one better for his role. He was also the damaged product of his background, sundered from his immediate family by politics and violence, and in his boyhood forced intensive learning, hounded there by an aggressive tutor. Since he spent over half of his life in his native country, this book also gives due prominence to key parts of his earlier life.

James VI succeeded to the throne of Queen Elizabeth of England in 1603 after what must have seemed like an agonisingly long time in the royal waiting room in Edinburgh. He journeyed south with high hopes, solid experience of kingship, and an honest intention to rule effectively in the best interest of all the rival factions within his three kingdoms of Scotland, England and Ireland. He died twenty-two years later worn out by cares and with a reputation some way short of the glittering personal legacy left by Queen Elizabeth I. Elizabeth, to be fair, left James a kingdom that had ample signs of neglect hidden beneath the shimmering regal facade.

What did his English subjects see in their new monarch? God's chosen ruler, according to some detractors, was a foul-mouthed, slobbering, unhygienic, drunken, unintelligible buffoon. Some of the exaggerations spread by the king's enemies were based on genuine physical ailments, which seem to have affected his mobility and speech. Part of the animosity aimed at King James I was racial since many in England despised the Scots. Regarding this bias, it is illuminating to look at how woefully generous James was to a wide range of undeserving subjects, contrary to the stereotype of Scottish meanness. Several contemporary writers highlight the king's marked humour, which sometimes arose at inappropriate moments. King James possessed that cynical, ironic strand of Scottish wit formerly termed 'pawky', which tended to undermine his dignity in the eyes of some. But, if England misunderstood his humour, James overestimated his own intelligence and ability to easily rule England. Of all the king's faults, many can be seen to be caused by his willingness to be deceived by his own ambition. The prime example is his spending so long desiring the crown of England that he could never quite comprehend that England was not the boundlessly rich land of milk and honey he dreamed it to be.

The rot in James I's legacy set in quickly after his death, thanks to the character assassinations left by subjects like Sir Anthony Weldon, whose skilful written denigration of the ruler set a precedent for subsequent condemnation of James. Partly based on sourness for being inadequately elevated by the king, it was Weldon who probably first equated him with the title of 'Wisest Fool in Christendom', (though it is often attributed to Henry IV of France or his minister and cousin, the Duc de Sully), as well as painting a thoroughly unflattering picture of his physicality, morals, and intellect. Weldon was retailing a certain brand of incisive malice which only an upper-class Englishman could casually muster. But the damage was done by him was decisive.

Despite modern rehabilitation which sees James as a capable king who came to England after a thorough grounding in the difficulties of ruling, there are contradictions which can be placed alongside the obvious flaws in his character. It has been said, half-jokingly, that Elizabeth was a manly queen, and that James was a queenly king. This seems an unfair jibe both at the king's sexuality and his laudable wish for national and international peace. While Elizabeth could happily put herself on display and work a crowd of commoners, James avoided them as much as he shrunk from the sight of weapons.[4] Yet he happily raised up men with no standing into his court and made some of them favourites. Within his own court circle he was often an affable man

Introduction

who thrived in the company of others. Nor was he a great snob, despite his dislike of crowds. In a fit of temper, he once kicked a servant named John Gibb (a valet who served him for twenty-five years), blaming him for losing some papers. When he found out he was wrong, James went down on his knees and ardently begged for his pardon.[5]

Modern studies exploring the personality of James VI/I have the liberty of openly discussing the king's sexuality in a manner in which some historians, well into the twentieth century, felt unwilling to completely do. A discussion of this aspect of his life is important to assess the king's character and his relationship with a series of favourites he was involved with throughout his adult life. The most important of these men were, in order: Esmé Stuart, his own relative (who became Duke of Lennox); Robert Carr (Earl of Somerset); and George Villiers (Duke of Buckingham). Attempting to evaluate this aspect leads to a number of traps. The most formidable is the king's own secrecy. Secondly, there is an anachronism in the terminology and concepts of homosexuality, a term which did not come into being until the nineteenth century. Another risk is looking at the king's sexuality as if this alone can somehow unlock his multi-faceted personality. What bearing can the king's intimacy with other men have in the modern age? To some, it is a matter of vital interest which affects their deeply held beliefs. Some conservative Christians still ponder whether the sexuality of James VI/I, the man who commissioned the extremely influential translation of the bible, should be discussed in a theological context.[6]

While this book looks at the king's sexuality as an aspect of his personal relationship with others, there is little in-depth discussion of his theological thinking. His struggle with the Kirk in Scotland and his attitude to Catholics and Puritans is likewise not considered in any depth. This work has the more modest ambition of looking at the king's closest relationship to gauge whether they can tell us more about the man and the king. Also, I look at those crucial incidents like the Gowrie Conspiracy and the North Berwick Witch Hunt which tell us so much about this monarch.

Chapter 1

Buchanan's Boy

Early Years

It is easy to be sorry for this small, ungainly rag doll of a boy who took pitiful pride in always remembering that he had been a king from his infancy. In whimsical moments later in life he even styled himself a 'Cradle King'. The facts about his upbringing are doleful enough. Born on the morning of 19 June 1566, he was the sixth king of Scotland named James, heir of the Stewart (or Stuart) line that had governed Scotland since the late fourteenth century. His mother, Mary, Queen of Scots, had a tumultuous reign which lasted from 1542 until her forced abdication in 1567. Young James was deprived of her from early infancy, for she spent most of her later years in captivity in England until her state execution in 1587. The boy also lost his father, Henry Stuart, Lord Darnley, who died in highly unusual circumstances: murdered at the second attempt, being strangled by unknown killers after a botched assassination by explosion in 1567.

From both sides of his family, James was descended from Scottish royalty and, more alluringly, from the royal English house of Tudor. Despite being the great-grandson of Henry VIII's sister Margaret on both his mother's and father's side, the path to succession to the English throne was neither quick nor straightforward. His mother, even in captivity, remained a rival to King James. Yet, although Mary, Queen of Scots, remains the most iconic figure associated with Scotland in the wider world (apart, perhaps, from the foreign-born Bonnie Prince Charlie), even a sympathetic assessment of her reign could not term it a success.

The preceding reigns also contained themes which affected James in his early years and carried though into his adulthood. For a period, the pro-French and Catholic party in control of Scotland seemed unassailable following the premature death of the last adult king, James V, in 1542. This king's widow, Mary of Guise, ruled the nation as regent and engineered the marriage alliance of her own daughter, Mary, Queen of Scots, to the French prince who briefly became King Francis II. Following the death of Francis at the end of 1560, and her mother who had died several months earlier, Mary returned to a Scotland suspicious of her as a French-raised Catholic and a woman ruler. An already fractious society had been further polarised by a Protestant ascendancy widely supported by the populace. The nation's new religious orientation strengthened sympathies with Scotland's Protestant neighbour England, despite the fact that the religious change there had been instigated by the Crown rather than lower tiers of society. Following defeat and imprisonment, Mary was forced to abdicate, and the infant James went through his coronation as king on 29 July 1567, a ceremony that reversed the significance of his Catholic baptism (on 17 December 1566).

The birth of the heir to Scotland's throne was also prefigured by violence and uncertainty. The new prince's father, Darnley, was an immature, weak and drunken figure. He played a major part in the murder of his wife's secretary David Rizzio at Holyroodhouse and seemed to give jealous credence to the rumour that Prince James was the son of this Italian rather than his own offspring. It has been suggested that the jealous and suspicious Darnley's aim was to induce a miscarriage to get rid of this dubious unborn child. Indeed, one of the murderers threatened the unborn child being carried by the queen. Did this pre-natal trauma affect the king? We know that James feared violence throughout the course of his life, but there was trauma enough when he was young. The young king was potentially at the mercy of implacable Scottish nobles, so there was little permanent comfort during his early years. As the Frenchman Fontenay pithily put it, King James VI was 'nurtured in fear'. He hated the sight of naked steel and more than one source states that he wore a doublet which was overly padded as protection against the blades of would-be assassins.[1] The English observer Sir John Oglander said the king was the most cowardly man he had ever encountered, fearful of all strangers, and could not even abide the sight of soldiers or any talk of wars.[2] This is an exaggeration, but it's true that the king found violence unseemly and was inclined to pacifism. James honestly remarked that he was never bloodthirsty, and this is true to the extent that he would not personally indulge in bloodshed himself. But there were instances during his reign where he showed a taste for ruthless and cold-blooded action against his enemies, even individuals who happened to cross him in minor ways. The king was fine with extreme retribution on occasion, as long as he did not have to personally witness it.

When he was presented with the new-born James, Mary pointedly affirmed to Darnley that the boy was indeed his child: 'he is so much your owen sone, that I fear it be the worse for him heearfter!'[3] It was an undoubted blessing for the future king that he did not have to suffer from Darnley's influence as he grew up. Thankfully for James also, he did not inherit his father's apparently inadequate intelligence, though possibly his love of alcohol was a trait that was inherited. Allegations about the king's supposed base birth haunted him throughout his whole Scottish reign. It was brazenly bellowed by the enraged citizens of Perth following the death of their Provost, the Earl of Gowrie, in August 1600. The king, whose followers had slain Gowrie and his brother in his own house, was taunted as being a 'son of Seigneur Davie,' a reference to Rizzio. This slanderous nickname was widely known in Scotland before the end of the sixteenth century.[4] Even the mighty Henry IV of France (who ruled 1589-1610), allowed himself a snide comment on the subject, taking aim at James's supposed learning as well as his supposed low ancestry, 'He is Solomon. Is he not the son of David?'[5] Late into his life, James was still prey to scurrilous tales about his heritage.

More propitiously, the king was born with a membrane, or *caul*, covering his face, which was said to augur greatness.[6]

Another superstition said that a *caul* mask at birth gave protection from both drowning and witchcraft. This must have crossed the king's mind when he sailed across the tempestuous North Sea in winter to fetch his Danish bride home and was allegedly the target of witches in both nations who sought to destroy them both. Birth superstitions, as well as auguries concerning rulers, was ingrained in the contemporary culture, despite this period being on the threshold of the modern world. The proposed unification of England and Scotland under one ruler from either nation had been the subject of semi-supernatural propaganda for centuries, using prophecies and portents. When the future James VI was born, the River Tweed and the Powsail Burn in the Scottish Borders supposedly flooded and mingled over the spot which was reputed to mark the grave of the wizard Merlin. This fulfilled an old prophecy which said that such an event would foretell the coming of one monarch for the island of Britain.[7]

A more intriguing historical mystery surrounds the tale which suggests that Prince James was switched at birth in Edinburgh Castle for another infant. In 1830, after a fire in Edinburgh Castle, workmen removed a large stone block within Queen Mary's apartments and uncovered a cavity. Inside was a small oak coffin containing the skeleton of an infant wrapped in fine cloth. The remains were allegedly placed back in the hiding place, apart from several fragments, one of which was deposited in the Museum of Scottish Antiquities (and subsequently lost). According to the theory later written up by Lady Forbes and others, the royal child of Queen Mary died soon after birth and was swapped for the new-born son of the wet-nurse of the supposed heir to the throne. This was Lady Reres, wife of Arthur Reres of Forbes. It was also said that the changeling was the natural son of Lady Mar, wife of the Earl of Mar.[8] The strange discovery first appeared in print in the 1840s, but there was no mention in the first published reports that the concealed child was the rightful king.[9] And yet the slanderous changeling story was circulated, albeit in a slightly different form, during the king's own lifetime. An anonymous Flemish pamphlet entitled *Corona Regia*, which appeared in 1615, caused royal outrage by attacking King James on a number of points, including his drinking, slovenly behaviour and gluttony. It also made a sensational claim that there was an attempt by Protestant extremists to kill Queen Mary's child in her womb, a reference to the incident during the murder of Rizzio: when this failed, and unknown to the queen, her new-born infant was swapped for the child of an unnamed Kirk minister.[10]

In April 1567, Queen Mary saw her only son for the last time. He had been placed in the custody of the Earl and Countess of Mar at Stirling Castle and here he spent his early years. The fortress was chosen to keep him safe from any noble faction which might attempt to kidnap him. And though his household was chosen with care, it was no substitute for a family and there was disfunction around him from the beginning. Helen Little, his wet-nurse, was accused of being an alcoholic. It was a much be-tutored childhood, as his biographer David Willson put it. In 1570, he was placed under the dubious supervision of the brilliant scholar George Buchanan (1506-1582), who was renowned for his rhetoric and his writing of plays, poetry and history in Latin and Scots, including his highly regarded *Historia* of Scotland. The scholar had already enjoyed a long and varied career before he was appointed to govern the hapless king. Educated in Scotland and Paris, he had travelled in Italy, escaped the Inquisition in Portugal, became a supporter of the powerful Guise family in France, and at home became known to King James V, who appointed him as tutor to his illegitimate son James Stewart (not the later Earl of Moray, but a namesake who became Prior of Coldingham). His erudition placed him at the front rank of Protestant thinkers, respected throughout Europe, and his literary influence extended several centuries after his death.

By the time he took charge of the child king he was past sixty, ill-tempered and suspicious of the royal family, especially the king's mother, as he was a Lennox native, from the region associated with the earldom of that name and naturally of the kindred which included James's father. He was also an unsuitable overseer for any child, despite his intellect, as his temper worsened with age and the persistent bouts of ill health. Yet he did have a talent for terrifying formal knowledge into the brain of the vulnerable boy king. He used his own writings as a mechanism to drum into the royal lad the great responsibilities and limited rights of righteous rulers, recognising that his own writing was sometimes harsh. If James enjoyed little warmth, he soaked up learning from his tutor remarkably well, though he was not keen on Buchanan's lowly opinion of powerful monarchs. While George Buchanan despised the despotic tendencies he saw in the ruling house of Stuart, he was less staunch in his religion, advocating a milder form of Protestantism than some of the more zealous reformers.

James would have recognised the former trait without benefitting from his tutor's relatively moderate religion. Ill treatment and education went together for many children in this age, but the effect on James was significant and lasting. George Buchanan had a personal, pathological hatred of Mary, Queen of Scots and her supposed immorality, not to mention her Catholicism. He did not hide his loathing of Mary from her son, whom he once designated 'a true bird of that bloody nest'. Yet he had known Mary first in France and had been on good terms with her when she first returned to Scotland, acting as an unofficial court poet and classical tutor. Buchanan accepted a pension from the queen in 1564. Three years later, following Darnley's murder, he turned against Mary. His remarkable adaptability to conform with changing church and secular authorities in Europe and Scotland shows a keen, ruthless instinct. His tract *Detectio Mariae Reginae Scotorum* (1571) was a collection of foul rumours about the queen's behaviour and morals which did him discredit.

Hearing from his pedagogue that his mother was no more than a whore must have been profoundly disturbing for young James. Another broadside, to the monarchy as a whole, came in Buchanan's book *Jure Regni apud Scotis* (*The Rights of the Crown in Scotland*), which emerged when James was thirteen. Buchanan argued that a king must maintain rectitude and be the father of the nation, but he was also directly answerable to the people. Such notions ran counter to the king's own belief that he was accountable to God and no one else, though he surely kept such thoughts to himself. The king's second tutor was Peter Young, who was twenty-two years older than his young charge, and mercifully less fierce than the elderly Buchanan. King James rewarded the kindly Young with different roles and posts throughout his reign.

Foul tempered, brilliant, and occasionally brutal though he was, Buchanan also encouraged a natural cunning in the king. An anecdote tells how the old scholar taught him a lesson about granting favours too readily. He presented the boy king with two stacks of paper, which he told him to sign without reading. He then declared to the boy that he was the rightful king of Scotland, not James. When James queried this, Buchanan produced a written and signed statement stating that the realm should be transferred to the ownership of George Buchanan. Shrewdness was a natural instinct that James inherited from his mother, and he used it with better effect, since he could link it with intelligence, a trait that she lacked.

Buchanan, the king joked, made him speak Latin before he could speak Scots, and the figure of the elderly teacher haunted him throughout life. Decades later, long after he became King James I of England, the monarch would wince when one particular courtier came into his presence as his footsteps reminded him of his dreaded old master. As death loomed larger in the king's mind, it was personified by the figure of the fearful teacher in his visions. Once he dreamed that the old man severely scolded him, despite the fact that he vainly tried to pacify the angry apparition. In 1622 the Venetian ambassador, Girolamo Lando, related that James told him of a dream in which old Buchanan appeared before him and sonorously prophesied his doom in verse (probably in the most punctilious Latin). He would fall into ice, then fire, then endure severe pain and die after two years. hounded to his end by his ancient pedagogue, James stretched out his doom to three years and died finally in 1625.[11]

Despite or because of Buchanan, language, history, logic and theology were all readily absorbed and enjoyed by the king. He was educated in the company of other young aristocratic boys around his own age and excelled over them. There seems to have been little thought about teaching James etiquette or manners, nor would these trifles have appealed to the boy. Dancing and music were much loathed by him, though his retinue did contain four resident fiddlers (all brothers) and a dance-master or 'master balladine'. His manners were notably atrocious, and he spurned female company. There would be a lack of female presence at Stirling Castle anyway, but doubtless some of Buchanan's misogyny and James's own well-known preference for male company fed into his attitude. Buchanan's regime may have consciously tried to keep female influence to a minimum, as the Englishman Henry Killigrew noted in 1574: 'his schoolmasters are desirous to have him from the handling of women, by whom he is yet guided and kept, saving when he goes to his book.'[12] Buchanan also made the royal lad perform party tricks for the Englishman: extempore translation of bible chapters from Latin into French and then into English. The king was also made to dance before the guest, which he accomplished well, and this was probably the last time in his life that he was described as being a good dancer.

We know of one occasion when James played a game (called *trou-madame*) with some girls and petulantly refused to pay the forfeit when he lost. Doubtless this mixed-sex encounter was not often repeated. Annabell Murray, Countess of Mar, fondly known as Lady Minny, provided some measure of female influence, yet she was extremely conscious of her charge's position as God's anointed ruler, which prevented any overt shows of affection. She stepped in one time that we know about to protest against Buchanan's rough treatment of the boy, but her intervention was unsuccessful. Buchanan had been lecturing young James about an incident when his great-great-grandfather, King James III, had faced the retribution of his nobles after promoting some unworthy favourites. The low-born favourites of the monarch were rounded up in his presence and hung from a bridge by a group of noblemen who felt threatened by their influence. Rather than take the moral lesson intended by his tutor about the folly of kings, James answered back. Buchanan thrashed him for his impertinence and, when Lady Minny tried to stop him, the old man harshly retorted, 'Madam, I have whipped his arse, you may kiss it if you please.' It was the kind of crude jest the adult monarch himself might have appreciated. Buchanan's learning, or at least his accomplished Latinity, were remembered by James in England, but he naturally baulked at the man's ideas that monarchs should have limited powers. He warned his son Henry against the dangerous theories of George Buchanan, whom he placed in the same category as the Protestant firebrand John Knox in his book *Basilikon Doron*.

Following the abdication and flight of his mother, Mary, and the death of his grandfather, the young king of Scots was left without close family until the arrival of a dazzling French cousin in his early teens. Whether or not he thought himself hard done by due to these circumstances is unclear, but it was sadly far from unusual in the Scottish royal family. The last fully adult king to ascend the throne in Scotland was Robert III in 1390. The Frenchman Fontenay visited Scotland when James was eighteen and gives a picture of an adolescent who had not enjoyed robust physical health. Many of the king's physical and behavioural traits noted as an adult were seized upon by critics as evidence of his uncouth manner and habits. But his physical clumsiness, characterised by awkward gait, lolling eyes and difficulties with his mouth, may suggest a condition recognised in modern times as Lesch-Nyhan disease.[13] Added to his defects of ill manners and restlessness, 'his carriage is ungainly, his steps erratic and vagabond, even in his own chamber ... He has a feeble body, even if he is not delicate. In sum, to put it in a word, he is an old young man.'[14]

There are suggestions that the young king may have been afflicted by rickets as a child, leaving his legs weak and his right foot turned out.[15] However, Sir Anthony Weldon's assertion that the king's legs were so weak that he was unable to walk until the age of seven seems to be untrue.[16] More plausible perhaps, he suggested that this weakness was due to the traumatic scene when his heavily pregnant mother was threatened with violence at the time of David Riccio's murder. The king's slowness in learning to walk was noted with worry and blamed by some on the bad milk of his drunken nurse. In a medical report at the very end of the king's life his legs were reported as still slender and weak and had been so from childhood. His right leg had an odd twist when walking and had become misaligned and chronically painful, particularly around the ankle.[17] Always unsteady on his feet, with a tendency to physically lean on his associates, James may also have had mild cerebral palsy.[18] It is interesting that his son Charles also suffered from defects in his lower limbs when young, suggesting that this was a congenital issue within the family.[19]

Where James VI differed from his illustrious ancestors was that he had to rule in the shadow of his own mother until he was twenty years old. In a merciless age, James was not the only child who saw his immediately family brutally struck down by violence, and the cumulative effect must had been significant. Apart from his father, two other close male relatives came to an untimely end: his unloved uncle, the Earl of Moray, and his paternal grandfather, the Earl of Lennox. Overly familiar in later life with some favourites, the king had abandonment issues and did not demonstrate emotion at crucial times, especially with close family members. He did not attend the funerals of either his elder son or his wife, and cruelly ignored and locked away his female cousin until she died. He even abandoned his native country, Scotland, at a gallop when the English crown fell into his lap, returning home only once despite emotionally promising to go home every three years.

We might look further back to see whether dysfunction was indeed the birthright of this king. The last Scottish king, James V (1512-42), also became a ruler in infancy and spent a large part of his formative years being used as a political pawn, at the mercy of fractious and self-serving aristocrats. But where James V, on reaching maturity, wreaked revenge on those who had made his childhood miserable, his grandson had a more conciliatory approach with the lords of Scotland. Both James V and his own father, James IV (1473-1513), were conspicuously people's princes who would allegedly wander their kingdoms incognito and were beloved by the populace (especially James IV). James VI could never be accused of courting popularity with the people, and his failure to empathise or understand his subjects was remarked upon in England as it was in stark contrast to Queen Elizabeth.

Following the death of the Earl of Lennox, only one of the king's grandparents remained alive. This was the widowed Countess of Lennox who lived in England and whom he never met, though she sent him presents, chiefly books of history. There was one semi-spectral presence of his royal forebears close at hand. For part of his childhood his royal bedroom was in an austere tower room in Stirling Castle, where there hung an 'auld pictour' of his royal grandfather, King James V. More than any of his ancestors, James V crops up in the subsequent writings of the adult James VI and I. In one place James VI uses his grandfather as an example of someone whose rampant womanising spawned bastards like the Earl of Moray who betrayed his royal sister, Queen Mary.[20] James VI's natural romantic preference for men allowed him to smugly avoid the temptation of fornication with women. Elsewhere he criticised his grandfather losing support from his own nobility, though he acknowledged his great reputation as a 'poor man's king'. Much later, near the end, when his son, the future King Charles I, went on an ill-advised undercover jaunt to Spain, King James proudly said it reminded him of his own foreign adventure and of King James V. By default, and in spite of Buchanan's resolute denunciations of the divine right of monarchy, the prince was reaching back to the ghosts of his own family to find a way ahead for himself.

A series of regents had the perilous task of ruling the realm during James VI's minority. In chronological order these were: James Stewart, Earl of Moray; Matthew Stewart, Earl of Lennox; John Erskine, Earl of Mar; James Douglas, Earl of Morton. Of these, only Mar died a natural death. The first two were the young king's blood relations. Moray was the illegitimate son of King James V and therefore half-brother of Mary, Queen of Scots, and James's own uncle. Regarded by many Protestants as a competent administrator, Moray was known by some as the 'Good Regent', and regarded as the best king that Scotland never had, being ruled out of that role by his bastardy.[21] Others, including James VI, painted him as a traitor to the monarchy. Although initially trusted by Mary, he played a substantial part in her downfall. Towards the end of Moray's regency (1567-70), he had failed to capture Dumbarton Castle from supporters of Queen Mary, but eventually he was assassinated by a man named James Hamilton who had a personal grievance against him. It is a mark of one aspect of the adult King James VI that he singled out Moray for venomous spite, forgetting his own role in failing to save his mother from execution and disregarding the fact that Moray made it possible for him to be king. In his *Basilikon Doron*, he lambasts Moray as 'that bastard, who vnnaturally rebelled, and procured the ruine of his owne Souerane and sister'.[22]

The next regent was the king's grandfather (and Darnley's father), Matthew Stewart, Earl of Lennox. A different proposition from the supposedly upright Moray, evil rumour stated that he could not tolerate his own solitude because he had sanctioned the murder of children years earlier. His tenure as regent was event shorter than his predecessor; in 1571 he was also mortally wounded by an assassin's bullet by order of a member of the queen's party. Slumped on a horse, he was slowly taken back to Stirling Castle and brushed aside the comforting reassurance of his escort that he would be well. 'If the bairn [meaning the king] be well, all is well,' he muttered.[23] James was allowed to witness his dying grandfather being brought back into the stronghold and dying the same day. It was an image which stayed with him for the rest of his life.

One imagines that the king was also affected by the death of the next regent, his kindly guardian, Alexander Erskine, the Earl of Mar, who died in the following year. The fourth, and last, of the regents was James Douglas, Earl of Morton, a man with a reputation for being self-serving, whose rule did not directly impact on the daily circumstances of King James for a number of years. Despite his self-centredness, Morton was a man of staunch reformed religion and he ruled with an iron hand and with a great deal of success until he was inevitably challenged by his peers. A rebellion against Morton by two earls, Argyll and Atholl, in 1578, erupted into the king's life when these men came to Stirling and persuaded him to oust Morton. Aged twelve, James had his first practical taste in the running of government. But Morton was soon leading a counterattack, rabble rousing in Edinburgh under a banner that showed an image of the young king behind bars, replete with the legend, 'Liberty I crave and I cannot have it'. Following a banquet thrown by Morton, the Earl of Atholl died of suspected poisoning. To test the supposition, a dubious doctor examined Atholl's body, licked the contents of his stomach, and himself became gravely ill. The Earl of Mar, it was rumoured, had succumbed to the same fate.

As a young king, James VI tried earnestly to dampen the endemic feuding and other violence which the Scottish nobility were addicted to. On one occasion, which also seems comedic, he had the principal titled cut-throats parade together in a scene of forced bonhomie in St Giles Kirk in Edinburgh. He succeeded better with these recalcitrant lords than he did with the reformed Kirk, but both groups aired their disapproval and occasionally plotted against him, something that continued even after King James fled to the greener pastures of England.

Chapter 2

The First Favourites

Esmé Stuart and the Earl of Huntly

The arrival of a stranger into the life of King James VI when he was thirteen opened up a new world to him. This man was Esmé Stuart, first cousin of the king's deceased father Lord Darnley. Despite his Scottish ancestry, Stuart had never seen his ancestral homeland before; he certainly regarded himself, and was regarded by others, as thoroughly French. Stuart was asked to come to Scotland as a counterweight to the former governor Morton who retained a substantial following in the country. The Earl of Morton was still a disruptive threat in 1579, ruthlessly decimating the power rivals such as the Hamilton family and making sure that the king's influence did not extend beyond attending the occasional meeting of the Privy Council. The choice of d'Aubigny was not an easy one since there was always the powerful faction still loyal to the imprisoned Mary Queen of Scots to consider. Many in Scotland who were opposed to Morton were also opposed to the former queen.

The importation of this dazzling, foreign nobleman was possibly no great surprise to many in Scotland. The alliance with France had persisted, to varying degrees, from the end of the thirteenth century. Throughout the sixteenth century Scotland was often riven between pro-English and pro-French factions, though the balance tipped in favour of the former when the nation accepted reformed religion in common with its southern neighbour. Still, the king was one-quarter French himself, his maternal grandmother being the redoubtable Mary of Guise (1515-1560), widow of King James V. From 1554 to her death, Mary of Guise was a competent regent of the realm on behalf of her own daughter, Mary Queen of Scots, who was in France.

Esmé himself was descended from a branch of the Earls of Lennox, a title King James held after his father's death, which he later bestowed on his favourite. The decision to invite him to Scotland was nominally made by the king himself but was instigated by a group of courtiers headed by John Cunningham of Drumquhassle.[1] One faction loyal to the ex-queen viewed Esmé as a perfect import to influence the king, being both French and Catholic, and likely to be aligned with Queen Mary. Yet Queen Mary was no great fan of this d'Aubigny relative of her late husband, Darnley, even if he seemed to recognise her as the rightful queen of Scotland at first. His ability to lightly ally himself with various parties for the sake of his own convenience was a factor which caused Queen Mary and others to be doubtful of him.

The Scottish venture was attractive for Esmé, who was characterised as 'a poor and embarrassed man with an estate of not very great value'.[2] His family had been riddled with debt for many years, so prospect of possible advancement in Scotland was alluring. Not only was there hope of succession to the Lennox earldom, but he would also have been keenly aware of his blood closeness to the king (he was also a descendant of King James II). Aspiration to seize the throne was gleefully highlighted as a trait of this glamorous newcomer by the worried English authorities. In correspondence with Queen Elizabeth, Esmé pledged himself to be her loyal servant and went so far as to vow to fight a duel against anyone in her presence who spoke against him. He was not a simple opponent for the English to estimate.

Esmé's subtlety was partly instilled in him by his family background. His branch of the Stuarts kept a foot in two nations, with the French title being given to them in the early fifteenth century. Throughout that century they had been prominent participants in the large Scottish military contribution to France engaging in the wars against the English and others. Younger members of the

Scottish family often succeeded to the French title. Their French estate was centred on Aubigny-sur-Nère, a small town in the centre of France, where their chateau still stands. Esmé's father, John Stuart, 5th Seigneur d'Aubigny, was admittedly less illustrious than his predecessors. Described by his wife's cousin as 'a good stout gentleman, but not very wise,' he also had an unfortunate liking for persecuting Protestants. On top of that he was unlucky. His brother Matthew, Earl of Lennox, betrayed the French party in Scotland for the sake of the English, and the furious French king took his revenge on the unfortunate John, confining him to the Bastille for three years. He survived until 1567 after a middling career with the French army.

Esmé's mother, Anne de la Queulle, was related to the Bourbons and Armagnacs in France and the Scaligieri and the Visconti of Milan in Italy. Her son was linked with the French court and was encouraged to go to Scotland by the scheming Guise family (from whom, of course, the king was also descended). He was given 40,000 pieces of gold to spend as he saw fit at the Scottish court, on the understanding he would promote French policies. It was said that the Duc de Guise visited Esmé on board the ship which was to take him to Scotland and lectured him for six hours about the importance of his role while there. Stuart was also rumoured to have met the exiled Scottish Catholic bishops of Glasgow and Ross before his departure.

For the French, the bigger picture was tempting James back into the arms of the Catholic Church, restoring the old alliance between France and Scotland, and using Scotland once more as a hostile northern threat to England, which was under the heretical rule of Queen Elizabeth. The chances of bringing Scotland back into the Catholic fold was not so far-fetched as it may have afterwards appeared. Although the Protestant Kirk was in the ascendant and backed up both by resolute churchmen and powerful nobles, it had only been the established religion for two decades and its relatively weak infrastructure meant that it still had an insufficient grip on the nation. Some of those who disliked the Kirk's hardline stance were Protestants themselves. There was also a group of powerful Catholic lords, such as the Earl of Huntly in the north-east, who commanded significant power. James was young and possibly perceived as malleable in his faith; he had, after all, been baptised a Catholic and he was the son of the soon-to-be-martyred Mary, and his attitude afterwards proved he was amenable to lending an ear to Catholic doctrine, even if he did not seriously countenance conversion.

Many Scottish noble houses and lesser families despatched sons to give military service to the crown of France, a custom which persisted into the eighteenth century. Some of these Scots established permanent lines in that country, though they maintained powerful links with their homeland. Various minor branches of the royal Stewarts (whose name was Frenchified to Stuart by Mary, Queen of Scots) were resident in France and occasionally supplied high-ranking representatives to Scotland who usually ensured that French political policy was injected back into the core of its northern ally. While these imports may have been regarded cynically by some native Scots, those European Scots who had been accustomed to the comparatively polished lifestyles of the Continent may have regarded exile to their ancestral land as a penance. To characterise them as simply agents of the royal house of Valois or other noble families in France would be doing them a collective disservice. The most honourable of them who came back to serve Scotland was John Stewart, Duke of Albany (and Count of Auvergne and Lauraguais), who became regent of Scotland for several gruelling terms after the tragic death of King James IV at the battle of Flodden in 1514. Albany tried to hold together an unravelling nation, a task made impossible by the poisonous actions of the king's widow, Margaret Tudor, and her cohorts. But d'Aubigny was perhaps more in the mould of young knights who periodically dazzled the grey northern nation with their brilliance and courtliness. A prime example was the thoroughly French *Chevalier Blanc* (so-called from his flamboyant armour or his white clothing), Antoine d'Arces, Lord of la Bastie. First appearing in Scotland as a French envoy in the reign of James IV, he met a grisly end during the tenure of the regent Albany, his famed chivalry no match for the brutishness of the Scottish Borders. Ambushed by the locals, he was decapitated, and his head kept as a totem by the murderous kindred for generations. Another dazzling incomer was Esmé's predecessor, Bernard Stewart, Lord of Aubigny, who came to Scotland at the beginning of the sixteenth century, but who soon succumbed to the harsh Scottish climate. A figure of some accomplishment behind his foreign glamour, he was hailed by King James IV as the 'Father of War'. He was a famed military strategist and administrator who wrote a book on the subject. Despite his short tenure, he inspired the great poet William Dunbar to compose two poems for him, a welcome and an obituary.

The age of chivalry was of course over by the time that the latest Franco-Scottish prodigy Esmé d'Aubigny arrived at Leith in September 1579. His continental glamour was also anathema to the reforming party who remembered the French as an occupying force that had been thankfully expelled from the nation after the Treaty of Edinburgh was ratified in 1560.

More showy than knightly, Esmé was not a major player on the French political scene, as he had only been on the fringes of the royal court. From Leith, Esmé went to Edinburgh and a week later made his way to Stirling where he prostrated himself before the adolescent king. Like many major characters in this book, there are contrary evaluations of this French Scotsman. To many he remains a 'fascinating but sinister' figure who played the various factions and parties – the king, the Kirk, Morton, the Guises, Elizabeth of England – but who ultimately wanted to advance his own interests. A well-polished man of thirty-seven, he spoke only French and made no effort whatever to learn Scots. His arrogance in refusing to understand Scottish society certainly contributed to his own eventual downfall. Even the French Duke of Albany had immersed himself in written Scottish history through the medium of translation.

But the newcomer was handsome and eloquent, a bringer of light into a poor northern nation. Esmé had dark eyes, a red beard, auburn hair, black, Italianate eyes, and knew how to impress. Since he was also courteous and modest, he was a welcome contrast to the unadorned Scots surrounding the throne. King James was immediately entranced by his French cousin, one of his few surviving close adult relatives. For a youth deprived of both parents and any meaningful emotional component in his life, the appearance of this French cousin was cathartic. But in the shadows, there was immediate suspicion of the newcomer and his twenty French associates from the hierarchy of the Kirk and others. The arrival was sourly noted by the prominent minister James Melville, who said that d'Aubigny arrived with:

> manie Frensche fasones and toyes; and, in effect, with a plean course of Papistry, to subvert the esteat of the Kirk... He brought with him an Monsieur Mombirneau, a subtill spreit, a mirrie fellow, verie able in bodie, and maist meit in all respects for bewitching of the youth of a Prince. They within a few days insinuate tham selffs sa in favour of the young King.[3]

At first, Stuart declared that he was only visiting Scotland for a brief time and that he had arrived to witness his royal young relative enter public life, but the heaping of rewards soon persuaded him otherwise. The honours came thick and fast for the newcomer. He was made Chamberlain of Scotland and granted the earldom of Lennox, plus the abbey of Arbroath, Dumbarton castle, and lands formerly belonging to the Hamilton family. Within two years he was created the only duke in Scotland and became *de facto* the second most important person in the kingdom. When King James triumphantly entered Edinburgh on 17 October, resplendent in white satin embroidered with silver, he insisted that Esmé rode alongside him, with two thousand horsemen. It was no coincidence that the Frenchman's arrival saw the king abandoning the closeted schoolroom at Stirling Castle and taking on the mantle of kingship. It might have been expected that James would comply and return meekly to Stirling, but Esmé's immediate deference to his authority emboldened him. So too did the reception he received in Edinburgh. Not only had there been pageants and displays put on by the burgh authorities, but James was also genuinely received with joy by the inhabitants, who were weary of years of regents and civil strife. Through autumn and winter King James remained at Holyrood, with his French relative installed in apartments near to him.

The English ambassador Robert Bowes wrote to the Early of Leicester in May 1580 that the occasional absences of the Frenchman from the royal presence only increased the king's ardour. The following month he wrote: 'Lennox's greatness is exceedingly increased, and the King so much affectionate to him that he is only delighted with his company, and thereby he carries the sway.'[4] If this was an adolescent crush, or an over-exuberance of familial love long suppressed, it was a particularly intense and sustained outburst. Yet the exact nature of the relationship between the adolescent king and the middle-aged Stuart is still difficult to gauge, due in part to the extreme multi-faceted nature of d'Aubigny, which was perhaps his greatest lesson and gift to the king. In contrast with those male lovers who loomed large during his English reign, and who were actively encouraged by the king to find brides, it seems that James was jealous of his cousin's existing family. Esmé's wife was forbidden to enter the realm of Scotland on the dubious grounds of her Catholic religion, as if there were no Catholics in the country already. She was kept in a state of near poverty, causing her relatives to speak openly against her husband.

Esmé's relationship with his immediate family is hard to comprehend. Did he reciprocate the passion of his cousin and put his own wife aside, or was he playing a deeper game of sexual intrigue learned in his native land? The French court of Henry III (who reigned 1574-89) was known for sexual relations between that monarch and his servants, although Esmé was not a key political player in France. (By coincidence or not, the French ambassador to England, Christophe de Harlay, Count Beaumont, later wrote that the court of James I in England reminded him of the times of Henry III.) The offices of Lord Great Chamberlain and First Gentleman of the

Chamber gave Lennox formal access to the King's Bedchamber, meaning he had oversight of dressing the king, and also slept in the same room. This role, which linked physical access to the king to chosen favourites, was an innovation made by Esmé and James used it as a pattern throughout his life for other favourites.[5] By February 1580, the closeness between the two had been noticed and condemned, as noted by a contemporary observer in Scotland:

> At this tyme his Majestie, having conceavit ane inuaird affectioun to the said lord Obynnie, enteriit in great familiaretie and quyet purpoisses with him, quhilk being vnderstood to the ministeris of Edinburgh, they cryed out continually aganis atheastis and papistis that roundit in continually in the Kingis earis, saying it wald turne to his Majesties ruine.[6]

'Quiet purposes' is a telling phrase. The fact that the ministers' most vocal objection was the religion of this interloper goes a little way towards invalidating their suspicions. In an effort to neutralise the religious critics, and with prompting by King James, the new Earl of Lennox happily converted from Catholicism and embraced the Kirk, becoming a professed Protestant. Despite suspicions that he remained at heart a Papist, and to the dismay of his spouse, Lennox firmly remained a Protestant and died professing himself as such. This did not stop him intriguing with Spain and other Catholic powers, and in 1582 he was involved with two Jesuits in a supposed plot to replace James with Mary on the throne. Lennox gave his agreement, on the understanding that James would not be harmed.[7] In May the same year the Englishman Sir Henry Widdrington wrote that the king was led by him and could hardly bear to be out of his presence, 'and is in such love with him, as in the open sight of the people, oftentymes he will claspe him about the neck with his armes and kiss him.' In a following letter he speaks vaguely about 'carnal lust' which Lennox and the Earl of Arran are leading the king into.[8]

Much of the staunch religious opposition to the Duke of Lennox, as he became, was all encompassing and motivated by his personality and by disapproval of his cultural difference. So, in August 1582, the minister James Lowson delivered a thundering castigation against Lennox from the pulpit in Edinburgh, accusing him of uproars in the Kirk, introducing vanity in apparel, superfluous banqueting, deflowering dames and virgins 'and other fruicts of the Frenche court,' as well as introducing too much fancy music into the realm.[9] A lot of the damnation directed at Lennox from the ministry appears either hysterical or ridiculous. Other faults laid at his door included how much money he wasted on food, teaching his Majesty French and Italian swear words, and deliberately giving the king a wild horse, which threw him when they were out hunting. Whatever the truth, the legend of a physical relationship between Esmé and James lingered for a great many years, so that the English cleric John Hacket (d. 1670) could confidently claim 'Gratioso in the embraces of his great love above all others'.[10] A Scottish source stated, 'The ministers ... go up and down like masterless hounds, casting into the King's teeth the example of young kings in old time ruled by wicked counsellors, and menace the punishment of Sodom and Gomorrah to be poured over the realm.'[11]

If the king was immediately captivated by the Frenchman, many aristocrats were soon lured to his side by gold and the opportunity he represented in getting rid of Morton. The houses of Argyll and Mar became his allies, as did some of the Catholic lords. Lennox's continued prominence throughout 1580 was causing alarm for Elizabeth and her ministers in England who had favoured the Earl of Morton. Elizabeth formerly accused Lennox (whom she refused to call by this title) of being in the pay of the Pope and fracturing her own relationship with King James. The rumours against Lennox at this time, suggesting that he was plotting to kidnap the king and send him to France may have been invented by the English government.

Despite this, Elizabeth did not make an effort to save Morton. It soon became evident that he was doomed by dark forces. A mad seaman named Skipper Lindsey told Morton in the presence of the king and Lennox that his judgement was drawing near, and his doom was in dressing.[12] Years earlier, 'a lady, who was his whore' told him his fortune and assured him that the king would be his ruin. If Lennox was not the sole architect of the former regent's ruin, he was certainly involved. His chosen instrument was a fearless military man named Captain James Stewart. An accusation was concocted which linked Morton with the death of the king's father at Kirk O'Field in Edinburgh. The king played his part by keeping Morton close and hypocritically assuring him the day before his downfall, 'Father, only you have reared me, and I will therefore defend you from your enemies.' The accusation was sprung before the king and other lords, with the French monoglot Lennox happily feigning ignorance of the subsequent violent uproar.

James Douglas, 4th Earl of Morton, had his head removed by the Scottish version of the guillotine, the Maiden, on 2 June 1581. There is added irony in the tale, which may even be true, that Morton imported the Maiden into Scotland. Despite his self-serving nature, in death Morton was seen as something of a Protestant icon, one of the chief instruments of the Reformation of religion. Queen Elizabeth famously ranted deprecations against her royal northern neighbour, branding him, 'That false Scotch urchin!' She wondered aloud, 'what can be expected of the double dealing of such an urchin as this!' Behind the scenes, Mary, Queen of Scots recognised that Lennox's influence had moved her son to regard her more sympathetically, and she suggested an unwieldy and unrealistic constitutional pact, 'the Association', which sought to install her as a joint ruler alongside her son. James played along with her scheme, which had some backing from Lennox, having learnt the necessity for duplicity in his role, as Elizabeth recognised. The royal requisite of necessary ruthlessness was showing itself. Morton, shortly before execution, sent him a letter, but the young king refused to read it and worked himself into a worried frenzy, pacing up and down his chamber. He was perhaps troubled initially by the fact that Morton's death had been accomplished by treachery more than diligent legal process and that the death was all too obviously laid at his door. But the death of the earl did not leave a lasting mark on the monarch. King James gave the ex-regent's castle and lordship of Dalkeith to Lennox, and other of his enemies, Captain Stewart, was made Earl of Arran. There was already an Earl of Arran, but he was conveniently insane, so the cynical transfer of the title was accomplished without complaint. The moral slackness of the regime was evident.

While James and Lennox spent the following months at Dalkeith, the king was hampered by his inability to grasp real power, owing in part to his inexperience (despite the fact that he was learning statecraft quickly). The disparate groups who had hated Morton now drifted apart. James was able to show different faces to those he came across, both friend and foe, so that an English observer acknowledged in 1581 that this young king 'is in his tender years better practised than others forty years older than he.'[13] Lennox secretly suggested to the king that a Catholic based invasion of England, coupled with the freeing of his mother, might be an astute and achievable plan of action. But prominent Kirk ministers were circling around Lennox and were expressing doubt about the sincerity of his adherence to their religion. He was ill equipped as a new Protestant convert and a foreigner to face off against the growing stridency in the Kirk, which now adopted the doctrine of two estates, spiritual and temporal, with the spiritual unsurprisingly being more important. The Scottish Church repudiated episcopacy and Lennox drew extra ire by supporting a particular bishop for the See of Glasgow. The king had also grown fond of the dashing (and unscrupulous) new Earl of Arran, who presumed to pick a fight with Lennox, thinking he had the same standing. The two men later reconciled through the king's intervention.

The criticism of Lennox was kept up largely by clerical opponents, though he had a growing number of enemies in other places. Pressure from this unremitting criticism caused a deterioration in Lennox's amiable and unperturbed manner. He began to think that he was the subject of a murder conspiracy and was subjected to a haranguing from the formidable ecclesiastic Andrew Melville at Perth in July 1582, which reached such a level that a dual language shouting match ensued. On the secular side the rapid accumulation of titles and wealth by Lennox left those who might otherwise expect advancement obviously displeased. The king had no foresight about the danger this might cause among the nobles and gentry. Matters became grave when Lennox was granted the office of chamberlain, which gave him very great powers. As one anonymous author noted, 'invye [envy] is the great minister of popular heads,' and it became clear that there would soon be repercussions. Within a short while 'certane unquiett people of the nobillitye, were still devysing thair machinations againes the young King and the new Duik of Lennox, and the new Earle of Arrane'.[14]

With encouragement, but no material support, from Elizabeth of England, the lords and lesser nobles ramped up their plans to rid the nation of Lennox. Grandiosely calling themselves the Lords Enterprisers, their impetus came from the same Cunningham of Drumquhassle who had been instrumental in inviting Lennox to Scotland in the first place. Now he was apparently motivated by lack of advancement, which he thought he was his due from the ungrateful Frenchman. Another key participant was William Ruthven, first Earl of Gowrie, who was reluctant to take action at first, but was fed the rumour he was imminently going to be targeted for his part in the murder of Lord Darnley, just as Morton had been. He was only shaken out of his dithering by the assurance that Lennox had sworn to slaughter him when they met.

Near the end of August 1582 the king was out hunting and was invited by Gowrie to spend the night at his home of Ruthven Castle, just outside the burgh of Perth. When the king rose the following morning and proposed to resume his journey back to Edinburgh he was prevented by a number of the conspiring lords, including Thomas Lyon, Master of Glamis, who blocked the door. At first the king let loose a stream of curses and enraged threats, but he soon saw it was no use and, when his courage waned, he burst into tears. His captors laughed at his humiliation and one of them (probably Thomas Lyon, Master of Glamis) uttered the immortal put down, 'Better that bairns should greet [weep] than bearded men.' The king never forgot these taunting words.[15] Another callous wit suggested that a rocking horse might be procured for the king. The conspirators announced they were forced into actions by the misrule of Lennox and Arran, who had falsely accused them of many misdeeds. They released a document on 17 September 1582, accusing Lennox and his accomplices of 'craft, subtlety and treason,' leading the king astray and into misdeeds and away from friendship with England.[16] A primary concern of the self-proclaimed patriotic conspirators was the fact that government was concentrated in Lennox's hands and the other nobles were excluded. The unparalleled rise of this foreign favourite into a position of great power, second only to the king himself, sent tremors of alarm through the aristocracy and the religious establishment. Added to their justifiable fear there was suspicion about Lennox's Catholicism and the rumours that he was conspiring with foreign powers, specifically the Guise faction in France.[17] Such was the so-called Raid of Ruthven, which kept James under control for the next year, being moved first to Stirling and then to Holyroodhouse. Nearly fifty prominent men signed the bond that supported the coup. The rapid promotion of an untried favourite led to a crisis, but it did not deter King James from doing exactly the same thing with his English favourites when he inherited the southern realm.

In the wake of the king's capture, Lennox was unresolved about how to react. He moved from Dalkeith to Edinburgh, but his attempt to rouse the authorities there to raise a force to rescue the king foundered on the fact that he had been involved in recent disputes with the burgh and they had no goodwill towards him. His lack of any military experience left him at a loss of how to proceed and it seems he was incapable of acting decisively. The more action-like Earl of Arran was captured by those who held the king when he tried to liberate him. The king was moved several times, but a scheme to free him from Holyroodhouse failed.

In these last days in Scotland everything Lennox touched seemed to fail, even his first attempt to go back to France. He was incapable of raising sufficient support or coming up with any strategy that would have allowed him to regain power in Scotland. He fell ill during that first sea voyage and had to disembark again. Possibly this was the beginning of his terminal decline. His second attempt, on 21 December, took him away, never to return. He journeyed by land through England and gained an interview with Queen Elizabeth, who harangued him roundly. But Lennox survived the withering attack and, still intriguing with Spain and the Jesuits, assured Elizabeth that he might act in her interests if he ever made it back to Scotland. By February he was in Paris and became seriously ill. There were rumours that he had been administered poison by some party while he passed through England. He died in Paris on 26 May 1583. James had likely been making preparations for him to return and he did not believe the reports of his favourite's death for some time after news arrived in June. The loss of Lennox helped James resolve to rely on his own resources and engineer his own freedom in that month, since few seemed anxious to assist him escape. Gowrie had advised the king of his own reluctant involvement in the scheme of the Lords Enterprisers. He may have assisted the king's escape through well-timed inaction. He was later pardoned by the king but was later beheaded in 1584 for taking part in a further plot. Another casualty of capital punishment was Esmé's sponsor, Cunningham of Drumquhassle. James had experienced a steep learning curve on the subtleties of managing power and men both during and immediately after his period of confinement.

Within a few months he had sent for Esmé's son Ludovic, who came to Scotland in November and became a close and beloved associate of the king, though not in the same way his father had been. In March 1589 Thomas Fowler observed that 'the Kinge loves this Duke as him selffe'. The closeness lasted throughout their lives. One response from the king to Esmé's death was the composition, in the winter of 1583, of a long mournful poem, 'Ane Metaphorical

Invention of a Tragedie called Phoenix'.[18] In this he charts the tragic trajectory of Lennox, comparing him with the mythical bird which flew in from Arabia. The poet is captivated by the rare celestial beauty of the bird, 'Whose body whole, with purpour was owercledd, Whose taill of colour was celestiall blew.' Just as the poem has the bird being tamed, so Lennox in life conformed to Protestantism and the will of the king. And, just as the phoenix was sorrowfully sent back to its exotic origins in the mysterious east, Lennox was sent back to France. For those inclined to delve into its symbolism, it is interesting that James chose the motif of the asexual bird that could regenerate itself from its own sacrificial ashes, though he gave his phoenix the female gender in his work. As narrator, the king expresses sorrow for the destruction of his love and guilt because he could not protect 'her'. When the phoenix perched in his chamber, others grew jealous. When they attacked the phoenix, she fled, and took refuge 'betwixt my legs'. But the attackers continued the assault so violently that blood ran down James's lower limbs.

No other subsequent favourite elicited such poetic effusion from King James in his maturity. Such was the effect of first love. The impact of that love extended to the favour which King James extended to all the Lennox children. Beyond their direct emotional connection, d'Aubigny brought much colour, gaiety and actual love into the sterile life of the king and arrived at exactly the right time to free him from the narrow confines of his claustrophobic education. Liberating European ideas were fed directly into the power centre of the royal court. The Frenchman loved poetry and encouraged the already bookish monarch to explore this side of his creativity. The patronage of d'Aubigny helped to encourage the loose federation of poets that became associated with the king, the so-called Castalian Band (who were not known as such at the time). As a political participant motivated certainly by advancement, and to some extent by money and power, Esmé was little better or worse than those contemporaries who had the same opportunities dealt out by fate. His reorganisation of the government and clashes with the Kirk, burgh authorities and local legal matters happily lined his purse.[19] Beyond this, and judged alongside the similarly self-serving but rather more brutal Earl of Morton, he emerges a little better. Placed alongside the roistering James Stewart, Earl of Arran, he comes out favourably. If he corrupted the king with cursing, music and mirth, it was assuredly because the young king was ready for those things. One of Lennox's weaknesses was possibly not that he was promoted beyond his abilities, but that he was rapidly advanced beyond his own capability to cope with it.

But can we get nearer to the truth of the relationship between Esmé and the king other than admitting that James did display evidence of physical and sexual desire for him? The strength of emotion was naturally fuelled by James's own emotionally bereft upbringing and his need to connect with someone from his own family. We do know that Lennox admitted he had neglected his wife and child back in France for the sake of his love for his royal cousin, and that neglect was also noted by others. He may have colluded with the king in concocting the scheme whereby his religious wife would be allowed to join him in Scotland, but was forbidden to practise her religion, thereby ensuring that she would never agree to go there. On Lennox's part there was evidence of a great affection for King James (whom he called *mon petit maistre*), but it may not have reached the rampant passion felt by the monarch. The question has bearing on the king's subsequent obsessions with his favourite young men when he became king of England. Lennox, like many other men of his age and class, may have had a fluid attitude to his sexuality. Attempts to target his loose morality may be suspect, coming from those opposed to his Catholicism and foreignness. One account sourly claimed that 'The Duk is a verrey commen harlat and hes every weik iij whoores.'[20]

We will never know for certain if there was a physical relationship, though it appears likely. Rumour and insinuation about the closeness between them spread to England before James won the throne there. It is not hard to see a slightly veiled reference to the relationship in Christopher Marlowe's play *Edward II*, which appeared in 1594. In the play's opening lines, the king's young favourite swims from

France in order to be in the king's arms, a contemporary as well as an historical reference. In the fourteenth century the English nobles had driven King Edward's favourite abroad, in a parallel with the favourite of the Scottish king. (The historical fate of Edward II and his boyfriend was also used in France in the 1580s in relation to the licentious behaviour of King Henry III.)

Modern writers are divided as to whether James and Lennox had a full-blown physical love affair. One commentator at least believes that Stuart's course had begun as a French state sponsored mission, but was blown off course when genuine love blossomed within him for the king of Scots. He was indeed 'caught in circumstances beyond his imagination, swept along by the unvarnished, undiluted love of the king.' [21] This would explain his neglect of his wife and swift conversion to Calvinism. As for contemporaries in Scotland, they may have been suspicious about the closeness of the pair, but zealous kirkmen and others were perhaps ill equipped to recognise the traits of same sex intimacy and may not have wanted to look too closely at this type of behaviour.[22] Rooting out the prevalent evil of witchcraft was far higher on the moral agenda than examining personal sexual transgressions. One reason why a sexual relationship is sometimes discounted is because of the king's age at the time. There is so little remaining written evidence about the link between James and Esmé, especially in comparison to the later favourites Somerset and Buckingham. Much of the evidence of the relationship may have been deliberately disposed of soon after Lennox's death. The Frenchman instructed that his private papers, left behind in Scotland when he went back to France, were to be destroyed. King James asked to have some of these letters, but they had already been burnt.[23] So his secret words ended up in ashes, like the phoenix. Most tellingly of all, the embalmed heart of Esmé Stuart was carried back to Scotland after his death by a servant called William Shaw. Evidently on the instructions of Esmé himself, it was given as a silently eloquent and revealing gift to King James. His widow made it known that the deed was done without her knowledge. Within a few months of Esmé's death the king issued a proclamation forbidding people from speaking of the late duke as anything other than a true Christian. Despite his wild success and flamboyant appearance in Scotland, Stuart remains an opaque character and we can suspect that he appeared as such to those who encountered him, including men of the Kirk and the queen of England. An inscrutable man, his mystery was only compounded by the huge impression he left behind on the king of Scots, and whatever clues that once existed were destroyed by fire.

The tightrope which King James VI negotiated in the years of his adult reign of Scotland were beset with difficulties from untamed nobles like the Earl of Bothwell (whose wilder adventures will be covered in the chapter on witchcraft), the repeated challenge to his authority from the militant Protestant Kirk, not to mention the perceived personal threat from a malignant plague of witchcraft. England, France and other nations watched from the wings, ready to use Scotland as part of their wider regional power plays. With Esmé Stuart dead and no unassailable band of supporters to safeguard his authority, King James relied on powerful individuals to lend him their support, always aware that any alliances would come with a cost, which might be worthwhile if some counterbalanced or neutralised some greater pending threat.

One of the men whom the king came to rely on was George Gordon, 6th Earl of Huntly. Although Huntly was the king's closest associate in the early 1590s, the nature of their personal and political relationship is debatable. The king developed close friendships with male nobles which contained no sexual element in them. Huntly was a man of action and not the type that James was usually romantically attracted to, yet he was someone who could be mostly depended upon by the monarch for their virile support. More than Esmé Stuart, or any subsequent favourite of the king, George Gordon combined the virtues and the weakness of a hereditary Scottish grandee and a high-ranking courtier. He had a combination of glamour, intelligence and violence in his nature which made other Machiavellian Scottish peers (such as the Earl of Bothwell) appear like brutish thugs. Not for nothing was he lauded in contemporary poetry as *Surgundo*, the *Valiant Christian*. Had he chosen to (or been able to) follow King James to England, he may have been a key player in his administration.

Huntly was also a relation, by marriage, of Esmé Stuart, and this closeness was an ingredient in the royal favour he received. King James had a pronounced sentimental weakness for family, and even those who married his relations. An English agent remarked in 1579 that the young king favoured everyone who shared his surname and, though this was an exaggeration, he did value ties of kinship. Part of the problem in deciphering the relationships between these men is the distorting lens of James's effusive bonhomie. It was in his nature to gush at those whom he loved, and his nature meant that he genuinely loved many of those close to him.

Huntly would cause problems for the king through his political and religious waywardness, as did many contemporary noblemen, though their closeness ensured that his often unlawful pursuits made it uniquely difficult for the king to deal with him. Four years older than the king, Huntly was infuriatingly and stubbornly Catholic, despite expediently professing on occasion that he conformed to the Protestant faith, and his religion rang frequent alarm bells with the Protestant powers and Queen Elizabeth throughout the period. These forces saw Huntly not only flout Protestantism but take part and even orchestrate events that threatened the direct safety of the realm of Scotland. Many of the earl's followers were adherents of the old religion, including his uncle, James Gordon, who was an influential and embarrassingly active Jesuit. To the Kirk, Huntly was the most powerful agent of the Antichrist – the Pope – in his plans to turn back the clock and re-establish Catholicism in the north of the realm where magnates held more power than monarchs. Further to this, Huntly seemed able to flout the law when following his own feudal agenda, particularly in the murder of the Earl of Moray. Why did the king, they wondered, allow such a notorious enemy of the state religion to have so much power and to repeatedly escape from punishment? The answer is that the king shrewdly used Huntly as a counterbalance to those religious forces in his own realm aligned to the ultra-Protestant faction, and also used him as a channel to communicate with the Catholic countries of Europe with whom James had to warily maintain contact, despite England disapproving of this contact.

Was there more to the relationship of Huntly and James than this political one? On the surface a physical relationship seems unlikely. As already noted, Huntly was the kind of action figure who ran counter to James's chosen attributes in a favourite. But the evidence regarding their personal relationship is rather sparse. The king adopted a paternalistic manner with Huntly, as he did with his confirmed romantic favourites later, calling him 'my good son' and signing some of his letters to the earl 'your Dad, James R'. Huntly came into close contact with the monarch through association with Esmé Stuart, Duke of Lennox, the king's first favourite. Huntly formalised the relationship later by marrying Lennox's daughter Henrietta. Huntly's marriage to Henrietta was celebrated in July 1588 at Holyroodhouse in Edinburgh, an event of 'great triumph, mirth and pastime'.

Despite the looming threat of the Spanish Armada, with which Huntly was intriguing, the king paid no heed. He planned to write a masque to celebrate the union and give himself a starring role, though he did not get around to finishing it. Part of the ceremonies involved the newlyweds renouncing their Catholic faith. Although the king rejoiced at this, others probably saw the act as mere lip service. Henrietta was an astute lady who represented her husband's interests at court with aplomb, exerting a powerful influence at the centre of Scottish political life when Huntly himself was absent.[24] She was even credited with persuading the queen to convert to Catholicism. It was Lennox's downfall in August 1582 which spurred Huntly to take an active role in the political arena. Not only had the Francophile party been defeated by the coup, which was known as the Raid of Ruthven, but the lords who were behind the seizing of the king were strident Protestants who were implacably opposed to anything associated with the continued existence of the Catholic religion in Scotland. Huntly had returned to Scotland from a spell in France the previous year, aged nineteen. In the wake of James escaping from the Ruthven regime, the earl was able to underpin his freedom by placing a large number of armed men at his disposal.

Many of the Catholics in Scotland were concentrated in the north and north-east of the realm, which further complicated how the king related to them and to Huntly, since these peripheral regions were outside the royally controlled core of the kingdom. The king's campaign against the growing authority of the Kirk was long and hard, but necessary as far as James was concerned because it directly threatened his royal power. The Kirk's General Assembly had declared its ambitions for authority in 1574 by declaring it was responsible directly to God and not to royalty, conflicting with James's belief that he was God's appointed overseer over both Church and state. A decade later he enjoyed a major victory when he encouraged Parliament to pass the Black Acts, asserting his supremacy over the Kirk. Following this, some twenty hardline ministers fled south to England, including the zealous Andrew Melville. However, they returned several years later and the battle between king and church over the power of the state continued. The conflict between the king and truculent religious leaders rumbled on towards the end of the century, and though there was a brief alliance during the witchcraft panics in the 1590s the war between both factions continued. The king therefore looked for furtive alliances with both native and foreign Catholics to counterbalance those Protestants who opposed him.

George Gordon was also a feudal lord whose family had deep roots in Aberdeenshire and the wider region. The king relied upon him as his royal lieutenant to act as an effective surrogate to enforce royal writ in the Highlands. The deaths of the last two Huntly earls (in 1562 and 1576) had left the Gordons vulnerable in their own heartland and the 6th earl was determined to redress family influence as well as represent Catholic interests and become a national political figure. The king was aware of his significance in all these areas and valued him also as an intimate friend. Following his liberation from the Ruthven lords, King James set about carefully trying to balance the various factions in his kingdom, using Huntly as an antidote against the group who favoured unconditional alliance with England. The heavyweight pro-English force in James's administration was John Maitland of Thirlestane, who was Lord Chancellor. In the years immediately after 1583 Huntly was highly successful at integrating his own men into the inner circle of the court and relegating the influence of political outsiders with the king. There is no doubt that at one stage he was the closest in the kingdom to James, with one commentator asserting that the 'lord of Huntley is indeed ane greit curteour and knawis mair of the Kingis or ony man at this present doithe.'[25] Huntly also enjoyed the offices of captain of the guard and vice chamberlain and the revenues from the abbey of Dunfermline.

The English ambassador intercepted letters which seemed to show that Huntly was conspiring with King Phillip II, promising assistance to Spain if there was an invasion of Scotland. Huntly had first written to Phillip in May 1586 offering his services. Some incriminating letters were handed over to James VI on 27 February 1589. Huntly was imprisoned and wrote to the king begging for an interview. The king wrote him a reproachful letter, chiding him for his faults. Like a slighted schoolmaster (or a wronged suitor), James asked him to consider how he had offended, from what good royal opinion he had fallen, and told him to consider his present state. All his promises of obedience, James said, had been overturned. He was chastised for dealing with plotters and strongly advised to come to heel and 'remit fully to my discretion'.[26] Such laughable reproachfulness naturally had no effect on a man like Huntly. The good-humoured, forgiving king was soon dining with the earl every day and the Huntly was quickly released. However, Secretary Maitland engineered his removal from court in March 1589, which ended his period of pre-eminence in power. It was a step the king was unable or unwilling to take himself. Huntly allied himself in a northern uprising with the earls of Erroll and Crawford, but he surrendered when the king came north with a large force. He was held for a year and released on the occasion of the king's marriage. Further reports of him acting with foreign powers periodically arose, but he did not land in serious trouble for long.

The violent eruption that happened next sent shockwaves through the nation. It was a resumption of the blood feud which the Gordons maintained against the Stewart Earls of Moray. The Gordons were fully engaged in the violent regional dynamics of the north-east, in competition with other land-owning kindreds. No wonder they were nicknamed the 'gey' or 'wild' Gordons, which time and anglicization has transformed into the tamer (and misleading) phrase the 'gay Gordons'. Disturbing regional equilibrium, Queen Mary had made her own half-brother the Earl of Moray, infuriating Huntly's own father, who hoped to gain this title. Following Regent Moray's death, his son-in-law, James Stewart of Doune, inherited the earldom. Huntly and this 2nd Earl of Moray maintained their ancestral animosity. Important revenues in the north-east and control of the bishopric of Moray were closely contested between the two families. King James brought both sides to arbitration, but the situation was beyond his peacekeeping.

The violent eruption that came next was all the more shocking to the nation because it happened on the southern shore of Fife, almost in view of Edinburgh across the River Forth, rather than in the remote north-east. On 7 February 1592 Huntly crossed the Forth with forty men and besieged Moray in his mother's stronghold of Donibristle Castle. Moray refused to submit, and the house was set ablaze. Moray and a small party from inside attempted to fight their way free of the Gordon forces. One version of events says that his hair and the plume on his helmet were dramatically set alight as he fled along the shoreline, and it was this human torch that allowed his enemies to identify and track him. He was set upon and stabbed by the pursuing Gordons, and as the earl plunged his own knife into his rival's head, the dying man laconically remarked, 'You have spoilt a bonnier face than your own.' On the day after the outrage the king was hunting in Fife, some miles to the north, and saw the pall of smoke still rising from Donibristle.

The notoriety of the event was fuelled by his family's outrage, magnifying it in public consciousness. The slain man's mother,

Margaret Campbell, had her son's bloody corpse displayed in St Giles' Kirk in Edinburgh as an object to fuel public anger. The family later commissioned a gaudy portrait of the mutilated body to commemorate the outrage. A popular ballad, 'The Bonnie Earl o' Moray', highlighted the drama of the event, feeding on the key ingredients of the death of a young, good-looking hero. The fact that the young earl was an ardent Protestant who was slaughtered by a Catholic heightened the anger. Common gossip at the time also claimed that Moray was a lover of the queen. A rumour circulated that King James had either commissioned the event or was party to it, something he vehemently denied. One story says that the king had commissioned Huntly to capture Moray because he had been conspiring with the Earl of Bothwell, who was his cousin. Public disquiet was increased when Huntly went virtually unpunished apart from a scandalously short period of house arrest. Despite the propaganda and his pleasing looks, Moray was not the astute political heavyweight or fighter that Huntly was, and when he crossed the latter's interests there was only going to be one victor. In the wake of the Donibristle, the Gordons boldly recommenced their bloody consolidation of power in their traditional territory.

Huntly was soon afterwards implicated in a plot called the Spanish Blanks when his name was found on blank paper supposedly in preparation for a bond which Scottish Catholics were treacherously preparing with Spain. The conspiracy was by no means proven, though of course it was widely believed. When Huntly, along with the others involved, was excommunicated by the Kirk, the king furiously declared that there was no one he trusted more than Huntly. Even when the earl was not at court he remained in unbroken communication with the king.

Complicit or not, the king's reaction to the earl's death was a carefully judged act of cold expediency. The value of Huntly as an ally was clearly immense and James knew that he could disregard outrage and ride out any negativity that came in his direction following the murder. Although Huntly and other rebel earls were exiled in 1595, he returned unlawfully after a year. Countess Henrietta governed his affairs in Scotland, aided by her family connections, which saw Huntly elevated to become a marquis in April 1599. The king had written to him in 1597, ardently assuring him that he believed he had proof of his own feelings towards him at all times. 'And, if of my favour to you ye doubt,' he added sadly, 'ye are the only man in Scotland that doubts thereof, since all your enemies will needs bind it on my back.'[27] During these years, and into the new century, Huntly maintained a feud against several regional rivals, and also against the powerful Campbell clan of Argyll. James went to considerable lengths to broker peace between these northern opponents, part of his exhausting campaign to end all traditional blood feuds in Scotland. His effort in this area had included the notable occasion when he had made representatives of mutually murderous families drink together and shake each other's hands at Holyroodhouse in May 1586.

The personal reliance of King James on Huntly to provide him personal physical security is remarkable, but it was fortuitous for him that Huntly did not attain any of the great offices of state. Many of his enemies, and particularly those in Elizabeth's England, could not understand why the king repeatedly failed to keep Huntly (plus other Catholic troublemakers) in check or punish him for what they saw as his grievous misdeeds. While Elizabeth may have suspected that James's leniency towards Huntly and his fellow Catholics was a mark of weakness which detracted from his fitness to succeed her as monarch, some of her counsellors imagined that he was actively conspiring with England's Catholic enemies. For the forces behind the Catholic Counter Reformation, and particularly the power brokers in France and Spain, Scotland for a time looked like one key to reconnecting England and then other northern European states back to their former religion. Despite his perceived heresy, James was recognised by Catholic powers as the main viable heir to the English crown. Like the Duke of Lennox before him, Huntly was in contact with forces in Catholic Europe who were keen to bolster Catholicism in the British Isles. The question about how seriously

Huntly plotted with these parties can be answered by asking the extent of King James's contact with them, or how much he knew about Huntly's ongoing international Catholic contact.

The likely scenario is that James was inclined to give his Catholic noblemen considerable sway, as we have seen, as a political counterweight who could be used as a tool when dealing with England. With James's approval, Huntly was able to effectively keep himself at the forefront of politics until the middle of the 1590s when he stepped back and concentrated on his own estates and regional concerns. It may have been as well for the king that he did since his freedom and closeness to the centre of power was causing Elizabeth misgivings about the resolution of James to keep his house in order and may have caused her and others to take steps to actively block his chances of succession to her throne. Like Ésme Stuart before him, Huntly bowed to religious pressure and swore loyalty the Kirk in 1597, though few were convinced of his sincerity. He was excommunicated for a second time in 1608. Though he was never as close to the king as he had been formerly, he retained high favour. The king specifically requested that Huntly send his son as a chosen companion for his own young son Charles. When the king was nearing the end of his life he sent for Huntly and presented him to the future King Charles I, calling him 'the most faithful servant that ever serve a prince'. As long as Huntly was at his side, he told his son, he should not be concerned with seditious or turbulent men in Scotland. But Huntly continued to pursue his own feuding agenda right to his final days. In his last years the enemy was the Crichton family, and he was warded to his own house in the Canongate, Edinburgh. In 1636, sensing that death was impending, he hastened to return north to his ancestral homeland in Strathbogie, but death overtook him in the burgh of Dundee. He was buried with the full pomp of the Catholic Church. Four years later his widow, Henrietta, fled from the religious persecution of the Kirk, back to her native France, where she died in 1642. Only seven years later, Huntly's son, George Gordon, the 2nd marquis, was executed in Edinburgh, a fate that many would have wished on his father.

Chapter 3

The Devil on the Forth

King James and Witchcraft

For some people, the involvement of King James VI in the witchcraft outbreak centred around North Berwick and East Lothian in the 1590s is proof of his folly which saw him branded as a highly educated fool. Others viewed his immersion in the process of examining supposed witches as a by-product of his idiosyncratic personal theology. Either way, we gain insight into the beliefs and concerns of the king during this beleaguered period.

In the beginning, King James showed some scepticism about the truth of the confessions of the witches. The upsurge in national anti-witchcraft activity came during a period of tumultuous change for the nation's ruler as he made the transition out of his minority and took full control of the government.[1] National tensions in Scotland increased during this time with prolonged periods of failed harvests and famine, contributing towards an atmosphere where witchcraft allegations flourished. The last decade of the sixteenth century saw rising inflation, rebellions, feuding among competing kindreds, and intermittent trouble between the Kirk and the king.

The number of Scottish witchcraft prosecutions had increased after the Reformation for complex reasons. When it was a Catholic country, Scotland had been no more or less prone to seek out witches than any other nation. There had always been acknowledgement of the existence of the powers of healing through supernatural means, but, alongside this, was the darker knowledge of *maleficum*, the intentional power to cause harm through magic. In newly Protestant

Scotland local lairds and other leaders in the burghs had a new sense of moral duty to force the community to conform to godly standards. Witchcraft historian Christine Larner believes that the new elite used witchcraft processes as a mechanism to keep the peasantry in check and themselves in control.[2] Other authors believe that the trials were the result of Protestant zeal not only wishing to eradicate all traces of Catholicism, but all superstition which flourished under the wings of that idolatrous religion. Folk beliefs that were associated with healing began to be ascribed to sinister forces in the reformed nation, and even the old belief in the fairy realm became confused with a fictitious cult of Satan.

The groundwork for the severe treatment of witchcraft was laid out in the Scottish Witchcraft Act of 1563, and there were notable outbreaks of persecution in some areas within a decade. The Regent Moray burnt a company of witches to death in Dundee in July 1569, and a witch-hunt in the surrounding region led to around forty accusations. The outbreak in East Lothian, dangerously near the capital Edinburgh, towards the end of the decade, was different because of the scale, with more than seventy accused, and also because of the involvement of the king and the Privy Council. Although King James became interested in the East Lothian cases due to their proximity to Edinburgh, and the personal grudge the witches appeared to have against him, he noticed proceedings concerning witches shortly before. In April 1589 he interviewed an alleged witch named Marion MacIngaroch in Aberdeen, though, tellingly, she did not face further prosecution afterwards.[3]

Did King James's attitude towards women have a role in the Lothian witch-hunt? It is tempting to believe so, but the evidence is insufficient to back this up. Yet the traumatic life event for the king, the union of a likely gay man to a woman, may have fed into a crisis that affected the larger nation. The marriage of the king to Anne of Denmark in 1589 was a prominent focus in the evidence in the witch trials in East Lothian between late 1590 and 1591. Some of those accused allegedly sought to harm the king and his new wife through magic, and accusations were made about the involvement of his prominent enemy, Francis Stewart, 5th Earl of Bothwell. Following this outbreak, witchcraft cases rose in the years up to 1597. In the latter year, the king himself published his *Daemonologie* which sets out evidence for the existence of witchcraft and expounded his view that the punishment for diablery should be death. Both his involvement in the North Berwick cases and his subsequent writing afford valuable insight into the king's mind and beliefs.

At first, there seemed no supernatural element to the cause of the storms that delayed the king's new bride travelling from her native Denmark to Scotland in autumn 1589. After she was forced to shelter in Norway, James tried to join her, but was also delayed by the weather and could not depart from Leith until 22 October. The couple's eventual return was also hampered by storms, which raised no immediate suspicions in Scotland. However, Danish authorities quickly linked the gales to devilry and prosecuted local witches in April 1590. Links between disasters at sea and witchcraft had been made in Danish records for decades. Now, following the Scottish-Danish royal union, a woman named Anna Koldings was the main accused in the Danish trials and up to a dozen women were reportedly executed. The Danish process, as the Scottish trials would also do, involved people on the highest rungs of society. The Danish minister of finance was accused by Admiral Peder Munk of insufficiently outfitting the royal fleet that was provided for Princess Anne's voyage to Scotland.[4] The three vessels in the royal convoy were prevented from setting off by the most ferocious storms seen in living memory. Seeking a reason for this extraordinary weather, the admiral wondered whether witchcraft was to blame and at first cast his mind back to a Copenhagen man he had assaulted some time before. The man's wife was a notable, reputed witch, so Munk thought she may have been responsible.[5] But the minister blamed the storms that marked Anne's passage on the witchcraft of a woman called Karen the Weaver. Karen confessed to targeting the royal ship with dark magic and named other witches, including Anne Koldings, known as the 'Devil's Mother'.

Anne eventually named five other women as witches, including the wife of the burgomaster of Copenhagen. Whether this action was the seed that transferred over the North Sea and bore dark fruit in Scotland is unknown, and it has been doubted that the elements of witchcraft activity that were highlighted by Scottish authorities were recognised in Scandinavia.[6] However, it seems too coincidental to believe that the outbreaks, linked as they were with James and his prospective bride, were not indeed connected. Geillis Duncan, one of the accused, alludes to a meeting in the Firth of Forth and a witch from Copenhagen.[7] An international conspiracy of black magic was sure to raise alarm bells.

The contemporary pamphlet *Newes from Scotland* (written in Scotland but published in England in 1591) recounted that the first suspicion of witchcraft was made by David Seaton, a deputy bailiff based in Tranent.[8] He heard rumours that his servant, Geillis Duncan, was healing the sick through magical means. Duncan was tortured with 'pilliwinckes' (thumbscrews) and also had a rope tightly bound around her head. This failed to illicit a confession, so her body was examined to find evidence of 'Devil's Marks', which were found on her throat and near her genitals. She then confessed that all her healing was worked via the Devil and that she performed them by witchcraft. During the following months she was subjected to further torture.

Geillis pointed the finger at others who were practising witchcraft, including Agnes Sampson, Agnes Thompson, and Doctor Fian (a schoolteacher also known as John Cunningham). She also stated that Euphame MacCalzean (a daughter of Lord Cliftonhall) had cursed her godfather to death, and that Barbara Napier had cursed Archibald, the late Earl of Angus, with a disease that led to his premature death. Other men and women were soon implicated and detained. News of the growing supernatural crisis reached the king, who summoned two of the accused before him in Edinburgh. Agnes Sampson was unwilling to confess, but Agnes Thompson quickly stated that she had been in league with the Devil and practised witchcraft. She stated that on All Hallow's Eve she was in company with 200 witches who met near the sea.

The king was at first entertained by the testimony, and perhaps hoped to find some recondite knowledge, but he concluded that the women were 'extreme liars'. What rekindled his interest and catapulted him into full-scale belief about Satanic powers was when Sampson, now desperate to bolster her credibility, took the monarch aside and whispered to him the exact words which passed between him and his wife on their first night together at Oslo. Utterly convinced in her truth, James 'swore by the living God, that he beleeued that all the Diuels in hell could not haue discouered the same: acknowledging her words to be most true, and therefore gaue the more credit to the rest which is before declared.' Some modern writers have repeated Agnes Sampson's remote knowledge as actual testimony, but we only have this information from *Newes from Scotland*, a source which has its own political and religious agenda. What undoubtedly bolstered the king's belief in a devilish plot was the report that Satan had declared that he hated King James because 'the king is the greatest enemy he hath in the world'. The king's sense of self-importance guaranteed that he took this as gospel.

No more was this mere entertainment or an intellectual curiosity, but a treasonable, Satanic danger which threatened the very core of the state. Agnes Thompson delivered more incredible revelations. There were multiple plots to kill the king before his marriage, including one where a black toad was hung for three days, and its venom collected in an oyster shell. With the assistance of a royal servant, Sampson also hoped to procure a piece of his clothing to work a spell that would bring about an agonising end. When the vital piece of fabric could not be sourced, she and her fellow witches gathered for a third attempt. The coven christened a cat, bound to it parts of a male human corpse, then during the night they cast it into the Firth of Forth. This demonic act, when James was at sea trying to fetch his young bride home, initiated the greatest storm that had ever been seen.

Another murder attempt by witches involved using the king's stolen portrait during a ritual at Acheson's Haven near Prestonpans.

This likeness was passed from hand to hand, the witches muttering the king's name, until it appeared in the hand of the Devil himself, there in the likeness of a man. Agnes Sampson assured the gathering that there would be gold and silver aplenty from the Earl of Bothwell if the king was destroyed. Jane Stratton spoke of another meeting on Lammas E'en when a wax image of the king was employed to work harm on his majesty. Agnes Sampson asked Satan, 'Tak their the picture of James Stewart, Prince of Scotland, and I ask of yow ... that I may have this turne wrocht and done to wrak him for my lord Bothuillis sake.' Yet another demonic operation sought to use a concoction of toad and stale urine to be placed in the king's path and replace him in body with a Satanic doppelganger.[9]

Details of these assassination plots were alarming enough to prompt King James to have the rest of the witches brought before him to reveal their evil actions. John Fian was the register keeper at the meetings with the Devil. It was told how he caused madness in a rival for the affections of a lady at Saltpans. The king believed the testimony, and, because Fian would not renounce Satan despite intensive torture, he was sentenced to death. The method of execution combined the technique for those found guilty of treason (strangulation) and for witchcraft (being burned at the stake). Despite many documents surviving from the trials, we don't know how many supposed witches were killed.

The involvement of the Earl of Bothwell added credence that to allegations of a serious conspiracy against King James. Witchcraft was just one element in a life motivated by aristocratic arrogance, during which he indulged in blood feud with various rivals and gave ample opportunity for enemies to accuse him of all manner of evil doing. A nephew of the previous Earl of Bothwell, who was married to Mary Queen of Scots, shared a similar chaotic and reckless lifestyle. Cultured and well-travelled he may have been, but his motivations were as violently egocentric as any less-cultured contemporary. Bothwell's relationship with the king was even more tumultuous than those he had with the Earl of Huntly. Initially close to James, the earl made the mistake of several times personally threatening the king's person (or so James thought), something that Huntly never did. Following Huntly's murder of the Earl of Moray in 1592, Bothwell was cast in the role of a Protestant champion in some quarters.

Even the king recognised him as a useful counterbalance to northern Catholic aristocrats like Huntly (with whom he occasionally plotted), and a staunch ally of the Kirk. Bothwell was an important player in the court and a favourite of the queen, to whom he showed a degree of deference sometimes lacking from other lords. Whether or not he was scheming with supernatural agents, he was certainly capable of being a proven agitator against the king's interests, and continually dangerous, not only because of his talent to cause problems but also because he was a descendant of King James V (albeit via an unwedded union), and theoretically may have had a claim to the throne had James VI perished at sea while fetching his foreign bride home. A sinister characterisation of Bothwell was carefully woven into the evidence against the witches. There was, for instance, the dark insinuation in the testimony of Donald Robson, who heard Euphame MacCalzean say, in answer to the question of when they would get a ruler again when they disposed of the current one: 'The realm will not want a king.'[10] Bothwell had been placed high in the administration that controlled Scotland during the king's absence. As a result of the implications against him by the suspected witches, he was arrested in April 1591, but escaped from custody in Edinburgh Castle after a short time.

Bothwell blamed the charges against him on the political malice of Chancellor John Maitland, whom he despised for a few reasons, including the fact that he was not an aristocrat. Bothwell then prowled in various parts of Scotland with apparent impunity and mingled freely with his supporters. It is of interest that he was responsible, as Admiral of Scotland, in preparing the vessels which the impatient James took to Denmark in order to fetch his bride home. This is a parallel with the men involved in the Danish fleet, where witchcraft became involved. Following his acquittal, Bothwell remained a danger in the country. He and his accomplices battered their way into Holyroodhouse at Christmas and endangered the lives of the king and queen and Maitland. The next, wider crisis during this period of Bothwell's ascendant outlawry occurred in February 1592 when his friend the Earl of Moray was slaughtered at Donibristle Castle by Huntly.

At the end of June 1592 Bothwell launched another unsuccessful raid against the royal couple at Falkland Palace. The following July saw another raid at Holyroodhouse. The horrified king woke to find Bothwell kneeling before him armed with a sword. In the ultimate act of passive aggression, the earl was intending to signify that, although he had possession of the mansion, he intended no harm to his majesty. King James screamed at the raiders that they could take his life, but they would not have his soul, possibly referring to the powers of darkness which Bothwell was in league with.[11] The king had the presence of mind to argue Bothwell into withdrawing and keeping the peace until the time when he was due to appear in court on witchcraft charges.

If Bothwell was not the henchman of Satan, he still acted as the king's personal devil for a number of years, although his violent power seemed to diminish. During the trial, which took place on 10 August 1593, he staunchly defended himself against treason. Bothwell had been principally accused of plotting by the warlock Ritchie Graham. The latter advised that Bothwell had been given the magical prediction in Italy that he should have the favour of the king, but afterwards lose it. Graham swore he met with the earl twenty times to use magical means to regain that approval. Graham also gave evidence which said that he colluded with the earl for the king's destruction. Magic was also used to ensure that King James remained in Norway when he went there to fetch his bride home. Graham was put to death at the end of February 1592. To the end he insisted that Bothwell was conspiring against the king. But Bothwell's lawyers rightly tore his inconsistent evidence to shreds. Bothwell admitted meeting Graham a handful of times, firstly when the man asked his help for influence with the king. He also said he had encountered him once by chance at Kelso, when Graham showed him a magical, notched stick decorated with human hair and said he was at that time trying to heal the 8th Earl of Angus (who died in 1588, aged thirty-three). Bothwell knew nothing else, except that the chancellor and other of his enemies had concocted the charges against him; his evidence was believed, and he was acquitted.[12] We should also bear in mind that several of the accused, John Fian, Donald Robson, Agnes Sampson and Janet Stratton, mentioned his complicity in magical acts. Yet the idea that Bothwell was actively part of a magical group intent on doing harm to the reigning monarch finds little favour in the modern age. One who did support his complicity was the twentieth-century witchcraft writer Margaret Murray, who was convinced there was a witch cult active through the ages which chose divine royal victims as sacrifices. Her contention that Bothwell was a witch cult leader falls a long way short of believability.[13]

Following further schemes against the king and periods of outlawry, Bothwell fled abroad, initially to France, then made his way to Italy. Here his dark reputation persisted. The English poet and politician George Sandys had word of his legend when he travelled in Italy: 'Here a certain *Calabrian* hearing that I was an *English*man, came to me, and would needs perswade me that I had insight in magicke; for that Earle *Bothel* was my countryman, who liues at Naples, and is in those parts famous for suspected negromancie.'[14] It seems that Italians regarded the British Isles as a repository of the Black Arts just as some in Britain viewed Italy as being tainted by magic. Bothwell died in poverty in 1612, his final scheme at rehabilitation through the offices of Prince Henry dashed through the demise of that young prince.[15]

We can see how easily alleged treason and magical practices became interconnected at the behest of the state apparatus wishing to blacken its enemies who occupied the highest level of society. Whatever the truth of Bothwell's involvement in necromancy, the rumour of involvement was powerfully used against him by those close to the king. It was a tactic that James employed again within a decade, when black magic allegations were thrown at another enemy, the Earl of Gowrie, who was also dubiously accused of plotting against royal authority. Rulers were fearful of the effects of witchcraft and magic, which seemed to be an ideal weapon that could be against them, capable of targeting them in private where even assassins might not reach them. There were allegations from a former lady-in-waiting that Queen Elizabeth's death was hastened through the use of a magical coin and an impaled playing card found in her chamber.[16] The accusation of witchcraft collusion was a serious charge, and continued to be used as a highly effective propaganda weapon throughout the seventeenth century when targeted at the most powerful men in the land. George Villiers, the Duke of Buckingham, was the last of King James's favourites. Following the king's death in 1625, Buckingham was accused by multiple parties of poisoning the monarch. One accuser was the Scotsman George Eglisham who pointedly linked Buckingham with witchcraft, both in his association with known witches, but also in the quasi-magical powers he used to unnaturally enthral the ailing monarch.[17]

Witchcraft, both as a weapon and also as a beneficial tool, was recognised among all classes during James's Scottish reign. Some of the witches in the country around Edinburgh were from the middle and upper classes, which must have alarmed those authorities who saw them as a mortal danger. The infiltration of Satanic witchcraft into the aristocracy also gave that class the opportunity to weaponise it against their enemies. The family of Archibald Douglas, 8th Earl of Angus, likely used the connivance of Ritchie Graham to accuse his wife, Agnes Lyon, of causing his early death.[18] Rumour, poisoning and intrigue all played prominent parts in the political power games that swirled around the monarch. If we credit Bothwell's innocence of witchcraft, we are still left with the problems of whether the witchcraft was to any extent real, what was its relation to the king, and how he saw it himself. Despite the king's outburst on the occasion when Bothwell broke into Holyroodhouse, he was a more fearsome physical enemy than a spiritual one. Bothwell was a bit player in the schemes which the Devil directed personally against King James VI. The thinking of those who implicated Bothwell of witchcraft is unknown, yet it would be easy for prosecutors to slip that suggestion into the minds of those poor, tortured individuals. Evidence that such accusations were current and used more widely can be seen in the fact that the English ambassador Robert Bowes was rather clumsily accused of involvement by Geillis Duncan.[19]

The king can hardly be accused of beginning or even shaping the form of the witch-hunts that took place in Lothian and other areas in the last decade of the sixteenth century. Once his interest was engaged, however, via the realisation that he was a chosen enemy of the Devil, he energetically engaged in the legal process. While he may have voiced concerns at one stage about the truthfulness of confessions, by the summer of 1591 he was railing against the members of the assize who had found the accused Barbara Napier innocent. He argued that Napier was acquitted because of the influence of friends and family. More significantly, he explained his personal intervention on the troubling growth of witchcraft which demanded special legal action.[20]

There was a reason for the king's deep-seated belief that the problem of witchcraft was that it materialised evil which threatened the godly fabric of the world. His essay on the Book of Revelation, *Ane Fruitfull Meditation*, appeared in 1588 and states that this book of the Bible is most pertinent for study, 'for this our last age, as a prophecie of the latter tyme'. The world was entering into the end of days and Satan was making his final attempt to conquer the newly sanctified nation of Scotland.[21] The notion that the end was nigh was believed by some of the top rank in the Scottish Kirk – men like John Knox's spiritual successor, the Rev Robert Pont.[22] The king's considered view of the threat of witchcraft was issued in Scotland nine years later. His *Daemonologie* was a considered response, as he saw it, to the growing problem of witchcraft in his realm, informed of course by his first-hand experience in examining witches. It was also a refutation of Reginald Scot's *The Discovery of Witchcraft* (1584), a book which sought to expose those in power who pursued the poor, accused the simple and killed the innocent. While the king's own beliefs modified in later years when he attained the throne of England, he still had the book burnt by the public hangman. The book is not ground-breaking as a study of demonology, but it is unique in being a composition on the subject by a ruling European ruler. The work takes the form of a dialogue between a sceptic and believer about the existence of the supernatural, the reality of witches, and the correct measures which may be undertaken to safeguard against and prosecute those practising witchcraft. James attempted to bring his intellectual learning together with his religious beliefs to create a rational framework for discussing the scourge of witchcraft. One aim of the work is to reinforce the fact, as the king saw it, that magic and witchcraft are verifiable facts and a dangerous reality which needed to be punished with severity. The first of the *Daemonologie*'s three books discusses magic and magicians, while the second concentrates on female witches and witchcraft, and the last book mainly concentrates on the punishment of witches. But there is also a digression into other areas of the supernatural. The king explores four classes of recognised spiritual beings: ghosts which haunt places, spirits which trouble individuals, beings which possess humans, plus 'these kinde of spirities that are called vulgarlie the Fayrie'.

Events in late-sixteenth-century Scotland gave King James the impetus to write his work. His influences were previous works on demonology, the biblical treatment of the subject, plus the works of classical authors. Apart from any inherent merits, the book ranks among his most influential works in terms of the effect it had of shoring up the deadly waves of witch-hunting carnage which periodically engulfed Scotland for the next century. The book was a manifestation of the danger the king felt threatened him directly as God's appointed ruler in Scotland. While the level of personal threat from this supernatural source may have subsided after the early 1590s, it did not go away. The English ambassador remarked in August 1597 about the nation of Scotland being swarmed with witches, with their malice being directed against the king, and confessions obtained suggesting they were trying to harm both his majesty and his young son.[23] The top tier of Scottish society sincerely believed it was besieged by ungodly forces.

The king's experiences of witchcraft afterwards in England was never marked by the intensity of mania and personal struggle against Satan which occurred in the East Lothian cases. A new act was brought in under his reign in 1604 to punish witches more severely, but during the twenty-two years of his rule in the south there were no more executions for witchcraft than there had been under the last twenty-two years of Elizabeth's reign.[24] King James became aware that many supposed cases of possession and malefice were false. James wrote to his son Henry warning him about the dubious evidence of a 'counterfeit wench' alleging tales of witchcraft. In another instance he wrote to a nobleman warning him of the attempted deception of a 'bewitched' woman who alleged to survive without any food.[25] He took an active interest in the case of Anne Gunter, heard before the Star Chamber, when claims that the girl was bewitched were personally brought by her family to him. Suspicious of her lively appearance when she was supposed to be lethargic under the spell of witchcraft, James rigorously interrogated her in Oxford in 1605 and discovered her imposture, passing her claims onto an archbishop to investigate.[26] Under examination, her claims were found to be entirely fraudulent.

James developed a perverse hobby in debunking charlatans of all kinds. In April 1605 he heard of an Oxford doctor named Haydock who preached remarkable sermons on the Book of Revelation in his sleep. The king had him come to court and heard him preach, as if by divine power, during the night. Next morning, through probing questioning, he got the man to confess he was aware of his actions and of being a hoax. His motive was that his career was in the doldrums, and he wanted to do something spectacular which would lead to his professional advancement. Satisfied with his own detection, the king happily pardoned him. James wrote to Robert Cecil humorously mocking both Haydock and the 'strangely possessed maid'

Anne Gunter, along with other astrologers and people who claimed outlandish powers.[27] We are told that the king would make himself very merry by interviewing other men and women with similar invented afflictions which seemed supernatural on the surface.[28]

Thomas Fuller gives an example of the king's attitude to witchcraft in an incident of 1618, included in his *Church-History of Britain* (1655). The event reads like a folk tale, suggesting it may have reached Fuller via oral tradition. According to the story, King James determined to discover the truth behind some girls who claimed to be possessed by devils and the victims of witchcraft. To test how easily one maiden was aware of the normal currents of human behaviour, he sent a dashing courtier to make romance to her. Another lady, whose supernatural symptoms ebbed and flowed, was observed to be perfectly calm until the time when she was sent for to appear before the king. As soon as she stood before James, she 'instantly ran through the whole zodiac of tricks'. A third sufferer only displayed signs of possession when the first verse of St John's Gospel was read out to her. When the same verse was read in Greek the girl was unaffected.[29] Fuller took this as evidence that King James ceased to believe in the truth of witchcraft later in his life, but it is truer to say that he felt more distanced from it because these later cases were not directed at him. Some part of him believed that he defeated Satan himself before ever he set foot in England.

Other contemporary cases also had a touch of the farcical, such as the one in West Ham in the early 1620s, in which a puritan vicar sought to exorcise a local woman who claimed to have been possessed by two witches. The case collapsed, with one supernaturally afflicted woman charged with seeking to cause the death of one of the accused witches by laying false charges against her.[30] Although seven women had already been hanged, the king's intervention led to the freeing of five others.

Despite these debunked cases and an apparent attitude of scepticism, James still believed witchcraft was a reality and a danger. When the Earl of Essex was allegedly subject to the malefaction of witches in 1613, the king condemned the Archbishop of Canterbury, George Abbot, for daring to question the reality of witchcraft. While there was a rise of witchcraft trials in the middle of James's English reign, most infamously the Pendle witches of Lancashire in 1612, by the end of his reign the numbers were significantly down. In 1616 Judge Humphrey Winch was in ill-favour with the king after hanging some witches at Leicester. King James had found out that 'the juggling and imposture of the boy that counterfeited to be witches'.[31] But the indolent monarch who ruled England could afford to pay little attention to the world of darkness, unlike the younger king of Scots whose life seemed threatened by darkness all around.

Chapter 4

Above the Black Turnpike

The Gowrie Conspiracy

If the outbreak of witchcraft was a threat which King James had taken on and defeated, there were other deadly dangers present in Scotland. The events that happened on one summer afternoon in 1600 were not supernatural but were equally intriguing and presented another mortal peril. While the Gunpowder Plot is undoubtedly more infamous, the Gowrie Conspiracy set the precedent for personal plots against this most plot-prone king. James continued to commemorate his delivery from death on the anniversary of the occasion throughout his reign. No subsequent plot came so close to ending his life. The shady events also reveal something about the monarch's inner life.

Some believe the outbreak of violence in the burgh of Perth was sponsored by the king to rid himself of a troublesome earl and his brother. Others say the plot was manufactured by the Earl of Ruthven and his brother, who paid the price for their treason. Whichever is true, James VI was a central participant in the intrigue. On the afternoon of 5 August 1600, the king travelled from Falkland Palace in Fife to Perth at the invitation of John Ruthven, 3rd Earl of Gowrie, and his brother Alexander, the Master of Ruthven. Before evening arrived, both brothers were dead, and though the king proclaimed it was a botched attempt to kidnap him, the story was instantly doubted. Among the rumours about the event was a story that the earl's brother, Alexander Ruthven, was a lover of the king's wife, which prompted James to take deadly revenge on the family. Alexander was a young, handsome courtier and another theory states that the enraptured monarch may have been lured by him to Perth in the expectation of indulging in a sexual adventure. The reason for Ruthven's trap, if indeed it was one, is another matter for speculation.

The Ruthvens had long been opposed to the king and his mother and belonged to a staunch Protestant faction. There was also the fact that the king owed the family a large sum of money and getting rid of them conveniently erased this debt. The earl's grandfather, Patrick, 3rd Lord Ruthven, had rebelled against the widow of James V, Mary of Guise, and was a main player in the murder of Queen Mary's favourite, David Riccio, in March 1566. His son, the 4th lord, William, was created Earl of Gowrie in August 1581 and was foremost in the Raid of Ruthven the following year when the king was kidnapped. He later engineered another plot, but this failed, and he was beheaded at Stirling in May 1584. The earl's eldest son, James, succeeded to the title but died young and his brother John became 3rd earl.

John Ruthven had distanced himself from the tumult of Scottish politics to study at the University of Padua in Italy. In his absence there were unlikely tales that he had converted to Catholicism and that he was involved in magical practices. A messenger from the Kirk was urgently despatched to fetch him home, hoping his presence in Scotland would provide a strong focus for their agenda. On his way home, Gowrie first visited England and was favourably received by Queen Elizabeth, then in May 1600 he was back in Scotland. Still only around 23 years old, he and his brother Alexander, who was several years younger, were the heads of a large and influential family and both may have expected to lead long and full lives ahead of that day. Gowrie's return to bolster the cause of the Kirk was unwelcome to the king, who cast a jaundiced eye over the enthusiastic crowds which greeted John Ruthven when entered Edinburgh. More people had been present at Stirling, he caustically observed, to see the earl's father beheaded.

Despite some ill feeling between the Ruthvens and the king, there was no forewarning of the brutal events on 5 August. That fine summer morning, some time before seven, Alexander Ruthven arrived with two men in the town of Falkland just as the royal party was going out to hunt. He approached the king and told him a strange tale concerning a suspicious stranger he had accosted lurking in the countryside outside Perth the night before. The man was hidden under a cloak and was carrying a large pot of foreign gold coins. Believing him to be a possible Catholic agent, he was bound and locked in a secret room at Gowrie House. One version of the story says he did not inform his brother, the earl, about the stranger.

There was immediate doubt about the outlandish story. King James was 'stricken in great admiration both of the uncouthnesse of the tale and of the strange and stupide behaviour of the reporter'.[1] He rode off to hunt and later asked Ludovic Stuart, Duke of Lennox, to go with him to Perth. Later, the breathless king told Lennox, 'Ye can nocht guess quhat erand I am rydand for. I am going to get ane poise [hidden treasure] in Perth.'[2] Lennox said the tale was unlikely, but he and a group of around fifteen men went with James to Perth, a journey of around fifteen miles. The monarch was still in a mood 'twixt trust and misstrust', which begs the question: what else did Alexander Ruthven say to him in secret that made him risk a journey that he was so dubious about? Nearing the town, Alexander, Earl of Gowrie came to meet the king and accompanied him to the family mansion, Gowrie House, on the south-east side of the burgh. No preparations whatever had been made for the royal party. George Craigengelt, master of the household, had to rise from his sick bed and hurriedly prepare a meal. Alexander Ruthven gave him a garbled explanation of the king's unexpected presence.

King James dined with Gowrie in a small chamber, and while the rest of the party were fed, the king and Ruthven went up the main staircase. Part of the king's group went into the garden to pick cherries with Gowrie while others remained inside. The peace was shortly broken by a servant, Thomas Cranstoun, who came and announced that the king had mounted a horse and was leaving Perth. Gowrie then cried for his own horse, oblivious to Cranstoun's insistence that his steed was miles away at Scone. When the king's followers went to the outer gate, the Earl of Lennox asked the porter if King James had passed through and was told he had not. Gowrie angrily insisted that the king had passed through the back gate, though the porter said it could not be the case as he had the back gate key in his possession. Gowrie then affirmed he was sure the king had left and said he was going to find the truth of it.

While the group were debating what to do, the king's voice was heard and he was seen at an open window, red in the face, waving his hat. He cried out, 'I am murtherit! Treassoun! My Lord of Mar, help! help!' The window was in a turret room overlooking the Highgate. Sir Thomas Erskine and his brother grabbed Gowrie by the throat, accusing him of being a traitor. Proclaiming that he knew nothing, he was wrestled to the ground, but was freed by his servants. Meanwhile, Lennox, Mar and others rushed inside the house and tried to find the king. The door to the chamber was bolted and they tried unsuccessfully to smash their way in. They then sent for some hammers, but it took them half an hour to break through.

Another man, John Ramsay, was in the stable when he heard the king's voice. When he re-entered the courtyard he saw a winding staircase near the main gate of the house, referred to as the Black Turnpike. The door was unlocked, and when he rushed up and heard a struggle, he burst through and saw King James and Alexander Ruthven fighting. Ruthven was bent low, with his head grasped under the king's arm. The king called out for Ramsay to strike Ruthven in the lower part of the body since his torso was protected by a padded doublet. The king's knowledge of his under garments leads to the suspicion that there had been some intimacy between them. There follows a bizarre detail: Ramsay had been carrying a hawk on his wrist up to this point, which he then let loose. He drew a short sword and stabbed Ruthven in the face and neck. The king was then able to throw Ruthven down the winding stairwell. John Ramsay later swore that there was another man standing behind the king when he entered. He did not know the man and could give no description, nor even remember what he wore. The other man disappeared after he struck Alexander Ruthven.[3]

The identity of this strange figure caused huge speculation afterwards, even more so than the blatantly fictitious, gold-carrying stranger.

Three of the king's men ran up the stairs, and on the way encountered Alexander Ruthven, bleeding heavily from his wounds. One of the men, Erskine, shouted for the traitor to be stricken, and Ruthven was fatally stabbed. As he fell, he turned and said, 'Allace! I had na wyte [blame] of it!' In the meantime, the Earl of Gowrie, in the street outside, withdrew two swords from his scabbard and ran towards the building, declaring that he would enter his own house or else die. Seeing his dead brother's body lying at the bottom of the stairwell, he shouted on his followers to go up with him. In the turret room he was confronted by the king's men. King James had been locked away in an adjacent room for safety. Gowrie and Ramsay fought while his servants tackled the king's men. Astonished when he was told that the king was dead, Gowrie dropped his guard and was instantly slain by Ramsay. Men from both parties received minor injuries. When the king re-entered the room, he knelt and thanked God for his miraculous deliverance.

Word of the incident filtered out into the streets of Perth. An alarm was raised, and some officials and armed townsfolk arrived, hoping to assist. The king's party ordered them to disperse. A group of Ruthven retainers also approached, including another Alexander Ruthven, and tried to find gunpowder to blow up the house with the king's men inside. The threat fizzled out after some hours and the royal entourage departed for Falkland. The bright day of the hunt had evolved into a dark, rainy evening. Local tradition states that the first person that James told his dramatic story to on the way back to Falkland was William Moncrieff, Laird of Moncrieff, who wryly commented, 'A very wonderful story, your Majesty, if it be true.'[4] Such scepticism was unbridled in the days and months following. The king arrived at Falkland Palace around ten o' clock and immediately wrote an account of the day to the Privy Council.

Despite the number of witnesses whose stories emerged later, two crucial scenes are restricted to the evidence of the king himself.

These were his private conversations with Alexander Ruthven in Falkland and the full sequence events in the tower room above the Black Turnpike. An early account published in England gives much detail about the supposed events in Gowrie House. After dinner, the account says, the king followed Alexander Ruthven through many chambers in the house, with Ruthven locking each door behind them. In the final room there was a man whom James assumed had the treasure. Ruthven grabbed the king, drew a dagger, and said he had slain his father so he would now kill him. The king frantically argued for his life, promising him that if he stopped it would be kept secret and forgiven. But Ruthven tried to stab James. Both fell to the floor and the assailant called on the other man present to kill the king. But the mysterious figure answered that 'he had neither harte nor hand; and yet is a very curraigiouse man.'

On Monday, 11 August, the king's chaplain, Patrick Galloway, related the official story to the curious crowd at the Mercat Cross in Edinburgh, with King James beside him. This announcement was undertaken to counter rumours and general disbelief about the royal version of events. It did little to support the king's credibility. The statement included a claim from Andrew Henderson, Gowrie's chamberlain, that he was the mysterious man in the tower. Henderson first gave evidence on 20 August, implicating Gowrie by stating that, on the night of Monday, 4 August, the earl had ordered him to go to Falkland Palace.[5] On the fateful day, he went back to Perth at ten in the morning before either Alexander Ruthven or the king's group reached town, and was closely questioned about the company his majesty had with him.[6] Henderson's several statements contradict each other, but so do some of the other witnesses. The fact that, at best, he did nothing more heroic to help the king than open a window hardly warrants the leniency he was shown when several others of the household were executed. This must be due to the fact that he proved a pliable state witness. His testimony even strikes a pathetic note in many places, whether he is on his knees in a cupboard abjectly praying or frantically assuring the king that he was no more than a dog shut up in the confined space with him. His subsequent history, full of recriminations against employers and others, suggests he was an extremely untrustworthy individual.[7] Neither the king nor Gowrie would have chosen someone like him as a trusted conspirator.

Was the man in the tower the supposed owner of the treasure, an assassin, or a witness to an attempt by Ruthven to blackmail the king? Was he a passive, glittering figure in armour (as described by some) looking on while something passed between the king and Ruthven. Or was he a 'dark man' of uncertain identity? This strange, nameless figure is almost a supernatural presence. Although Henderson asserted on several occasions that he was the man on the tower, there were other candidates.[8] Sir Thomas Erskine spoke about a black-haired man present in the chamber after the fight, who he thought might be named Hugh Moncrieff.[9] The contemporary writer Calderwood said a proclamation was made stating that this third man in the chamber was one Oliphant, 'a blacke, grim man'. Yet Oliphant was not in Perth on 5 August, but twenty miles distant in Dundee. The other possible suspect was someone called Younger who was somehow slain by the king's men as he went to give evidence at Falkland.[10]

The first printed version of events came off the presses in Edinburgh weeks after the event, and rumours continued to proliferate. The Master of Gray wrote to Robert Cecil in England in September, stating that the Duke of Lennox had said he could not swear whether the deed had been instigated by Gowrie or the king. He also flippantly boasted that he knew where the mysterious pot of treasure was hidden.[11] When the king commanded the clergy to offer thanksgiving for his safety, five ministers in Edinburgh flatly refused. They had grave misgivings about the king's story and their refusal to be steamrollered by the propaganda was more to do with the flimsiness of official evidence rather than adherence to the Ruthvens as Protestant heroes. Four ministers caved in under government pressure and were dispatched to other places in Scotland to disseminate the official story and encourage thanksgiving. The Rev Robert Bruce obstinately failed to assent. The king made repeated, personal arguments to convince him that his version of events was correct. He even appealed to him on the basis that any suggestion of him provoking bloodshed would be entirely contrary to his nature. 'I see, Mr Robert,' he said, 'that ye would make me a murderer. It is known very well that I was never bloodthirsty. If I would have taken their lives, I had causes enough. I needed not to hazard myself so.'[12] Bruce was exiled and subject to strong pressure to accept the official version of the tale and was only eventually persuaded to give in by the persuasion of the Earl of Mar, a man he respected. Even then he confessed that he only gave the king's word a 'doubtful trust'. The record of an interview between Bruce and the king shows that he still had misgivings. Bruce asked James if he had intended to slay the earl and the king answered that he did not know that Gowrie was dying until he saw him in agony, and he prayed for him then. He did admit to being part of Alexander Ruthven's death, though said he did so in his own defence. When Bruce questioned him once more, asking if he had purposely intended to kill the Master of Ruthven, King James flew into a rage and started cursing.[13] Many others were still not inclined to believe him. Few seriously countenanced that a callow young nobleman would dare let such a hare-brained plot against the king take place in his own house, with the king's retinue in close attendance.

Action was taken almost immediately to target Ruthven associates. The Privy Council ordered that the two Ruthven brothers should remain unburied, and recriminations against their kindred commenced. William Rynd, the earl's tutor, was examined and tortured. He professed his own innocence, but attested that the earl had alluded to keeping secrets against those in high power. The wounded servant Cranstoun was denied any knowledge of criminal conspiracy, swearing that he reported the king's departure in good faith. A cousin of Gowrie's, James Wemyss of Bogie, had been hunting in Strathbraan on the fatal day. He too denied knowledge of any plot, saying Gowrie had not talked to him of this, yet he had said he had admitted practising magic while abroad.[14] At Perth on 23 August, Craigengelt, Cranstoun and John Barron were hanged, still claiming they knew nothing about any treason against the king. Between 23 and 27 September no fewer than 355 inhabitants of Perth were questioned by the magistrates about the affair. Andrew Henderson, the possible man in the turret, escaped recrimination and retained his office of chamberlain under the new owner of Gowrie House.

At the time of the Gowrie brothers' deaths their mother was living at Dirleton Castle in East Lothian. Two younger brothers, William and Patrick, were at school in Edinburgh. Their sister, Beatrix Ruthven, was in the queen's service, as was her sister Anna.[15] Queen Anne was unhappy when Beatrix was removed from her service. The day after the events at Perth, a party was sent to seize the two surviving Ruthven brothers, but they were tipped off and escaped over the border into England. The disembowelled bodies of the Earl and Master of Ruthven were transported to Edinburgh on 30 October. The corpses were hung and quartered and their heads impaled outside the Old Tolbooth, 'yair to stand quhyll the wind blaw yame away'.[16] The name of Ruthven was outlawed (a tactic the king later used with the clan MacGregor); their titles and estates were forfeited and the dark turret in Gowrie House was cast down, though the house remained standing for several centuries more. The over-the-top reaction of the authorities did nothing to dampen suspicion. Nor did the clumsy attempts to blacken Gowrie's reputation by accusing him of necromancy. Reports making out that he wore a secret purse containing magic spells, or that his servants believed him linked to magic acts, merely show that the king and authorities had learnt what good propaganda could be derived from linking noble enemies with the powers of darkness.

Of the two surviving brothers, William Ruthven avoided further controversy by fleeing overseas, and became a philosopher and alchemist. Patrick Ruthven was less lucky. Upon James's accession to the English throne, he was arrested and spent nineteen years in the Tower of London. He later practised as a doctor until his death in 1652. Five other sisters, apart from those named above, survived the fall of the family, and mostly married into the nobility.

The unconvincing, contradictory nature of the evidence about the event leaves room to doubt who was behind the extraordinary event. It seems inconceivable that the king, who was not physically courageous, would have purposely put himself in danger in an enemy's house. None of the motives about the king owing the family a fortune, or his distrust of them because of the treacherous first earl, hold much water. The most ridiculous claim about the Ruthvens' motivation to destroy James was the story that they were descendants of Margaret Tudor, queen of King James IV, and therefore had a claim to the Scottish throne. In fact, one of their family had married Margaret but the union was childless. Why would James VI bother to slay John Ruthven anyway? Despite being an earl, Gowrie was not a major political figure in Scotland, and there is absolutely no evidence that he was at part of any ultra-Protestant plot to harm the king. Neither was he a dangerous maverick in the mould of Huntly or Bothwell, both of whom stretched the generous patience of the king without deadly reprisal. Against the idea of a carefully conceived Ruthven plot, we have testimony stating that the household and the earl himself were unprepared for the king's sudden appearance and were genuinely confused as events unfolded. The actual scene of the action was in their most conspicuous property, situated within a busy town, and furthermore in a room which overlooked the public highway.

Some have suggested that the violence on that hot summer day followed Ruthven angrily rebuffing sexual advances from the monarch, while others wonder whether Alexander purposely lured the king into that turret room.[17] Either scenario is plausible, though it makes more sense to imagine that Alexander knew the king's proclivities and lured him into the room on the promise of sexual activity in order to blackmail him; the king sensed entrapment at a late stage and cried treason. James might have allowed himself to be led there by the false story of the treasure find, enticed by the tale and by Alexander Ruthven. Once things went wrong, he may have seized the opportunity to turn the tables and not only destroy

Alexander but quickly eradicate his own misconduct and the whole nest of Ruthvens. Even if this was so, it leaves the conundrum as to what motive Alexander might have had for playing this dangerous game with the monarch. Mental instability might have been a factor, along with a grievance against James for the murder of his father, the first earl. Yet his motivations are unfathomable.

If he was the sponsor of events, was Alexander acting alone? The earliest English version of events states that Alexander Ruthven told the king he had concealed the finding of the treasure from everyone, even his own brother. At dinner, the earl seemed anxious and unsure about the king's presence, and later when the king was upstairs, he appeared similarly disorientated. During dinner the king himself wondered whether there had been some dispute between the two Ruthvens. The only trace of such a private disagreement was reported in the tract called *The True Discovery of the Late Treason* where it is hinted that Alexander wanted the revenues of Scone Abbey which had been granted to his brother.[18] Yet there is too little known of the Ruthven brothers as individuals to be certain of the part they played that fatal afternoon.

English theories at the time favoured one of several variations: a sexual trap, the king making untoward advances, or simply a dispute which got out of hand. Whatever happened, King James called young Ruthven's father a traitor and Alexander became furious. Either alarmed at his rage or using it to his own advantage, the king went to the window, shouting that he was being attacked.[19] Another theory was that Alexander was conspiring with Queen Anne or acting against the king because of a romantic involvement. English agents made the most of suggestions that the queen was complicit in the bloody events. There were tales of Anne sending the Earl of Gowrie a bracelet and that the king proposed to keep his pregnant wife a prisoner after the event because of her connection with the Ruthvens.[20] The rumour that the younger Ruthven brother was Queen Anne's lover was the common stock of courtly gossip. This tale of an affair, or some jealousy on the king's part because he suspected this, was circulated in England at the time and taken as a possible reason for the two Ruthven deaths.[21] This gossip certainly mutated into a romantic tale in the eighteenth century which has the king discovering a ribbon worn as the queen's gift by Alexander Ruthven as he lay asleep in the grounds of Falkland Palace.[22] The same heedless tongues also linked her romantically with the 'bonny' Earl of Moray, who died young and in dubious circumstances.[23] It could be argued that James's liking for handsome young men would have made him unlikely to be jealous of any young man courting his wife.

Anne reacted badly to the deaths. Her comments that she hoped heaven would not wreak revenge on her family for the fate of the Ruthvens, and the documented fact that she was among many people in Scotland who doubted the king's story, is significant.[24] The court nervously tried to distract those in the inner royal circle away from harmful speculation. James Melville visited Falkland Palace and witnessed a show for the king and queen featuring a French *funambulus* (a ropedancer). 'This,' said Melville, 'was politiklie done to mitigate the Quein and peiple for Gowrie's slaughter.'[25]

The state-sponsored version of the events at Gowrie House, with its unlikely narrative and contradictory details, was widely questioned. Written accounts in France were mocked and withdrawn from circulation. Frenchmen who had encountered Gowrie before his return to Scotland could not believe that he was a malicious traitor.[26] The legacy of the king's supposed deliverance from death took on a darkly humorous aspect. Decades later, Francis Osborne wrote that many lies were annually told at the commemoration of the event and every Scot abroad laughed at the official version.[27] The king's enemy Sir Anthony Weldon also gleefully cited Scotland's disbelief in the official version and reported similar scepticism in England.[28] The event became notorious throughout Europe. One of the earliest works of literature on the subject was a long Icelandic poem composed by the priest Einar Guðmundsson in the early seventeenth century.[29] The Gowrie mystery became a staple in the educated Scottish imagination, obsessed over by that long-vanished class of Scots who vicariously relived the national past in a profound way during the centuries after the union with England in 1707.

We are still no nearer proving who initiated the bloodshed on that balmy August afternoon. If it was a planned conspiracy by either side, it was stunningly incompetent. Nor can we credit that England had any hand in a scheme to kidnap or damage the king. Later 'evidence' of a wider plot involving Gowrie and Sir Robert Logan of Restalrig proved to be based on forgeries. A man named Francis Mowbray appeared in London in 1602 and claimed he had evidence proving the Ruthvens were innocent. He was handed over to James and died in February 1603, allegedly having fallen from the window of his cell while trying to escape. Possibly his was the classically cynical 'accidental' death of an inconvenient state prisoner.

Although the accumulated and illogical details of the day add up to a mystery which is insoluble, the events on the surface seem wrapped up in absurdity, possibly 'a misconceived and farcical effort to woo a king', as the historian Jenny Wormald has called it.[30] If so, it was a farce which James immediately took charge of and used to his advantage. The coterie of doubting Edinburgh ministers was neutralised. By the time of the Gowrie Conspiracy, King James was no longer the callow, young king at the mercy of powerful adversaries, but a canny political player. His attitude had hardened by 1600, having faced a trial of strength during the last decade against the malice of witches, rebellious nobles and the malcontent Kirk. With his eye on the ultimate prize of England, he had become adept at turning situations to his advantage. He was certainly no simpleton who might be tempted by an imaginary pot of gold. Whatever the initial cause of the Gowrie Conspiracy, he used the events to his own advantage ultimately. At the event's annual commemoration in England on 5 August, the chief guest of honour each year was the king's supposed saviour, Ramsay, who was created Earl of Holderness. There was no appetite for commemoration in Scotland.

The supernatural shadow which the Gowrie Conspiracy cast over Scotland speaks not only about the misgivings wrapped up in the actual event and its aftermath, but also a wider darkness in the nation. On the day the Ruthvens died, the sea on the coast of Fife rushed upon the shore in a manner never before seen, then subsided again. The prominent minister James Melville dreamed that night that his wife was dead. He woke and realised that she was alive and yet mourned for her somehow all that day. 'And, indeed,' he wrote in his diary, 'thairefter sche was stricken with sic infirmitie, that sche could nocht be a wyff to mie.'[31] A peculiarity in the sea was noted when the king crossed the Firth of Forth to Leith on 11 August. It was a strange, black colour and there were unaccountable noises of gunfire nearby that nobody could explain. Earlier that day there was a mysterious sound of great mourning and wailing heard in Perth and witnesses saw agitated shadows moving around the murder scene in Gowrie House.[32] The king's second son was born at Dunfermline Palace on 19 November 1600. Soon after his birth, according to local legend, James was awakened by a loud scream from the baby's nurse in the next room. When the king asked her what the matter was, she said the apparition of an old man had crouched low over the cradle and cast his black cloak over the baby, as if to take him away. As the boy was constantly complaining, the king sourly said that he wished the fiend had removed his son clean away. Then he added the prophetic observation that, should Charles ever become king, no good would come of his reign as 'the deil has cussen [cast] his cloak owre him already'.[33] It was as if the forces of darkness which King James proudly thought he had quelled through the recent witch-hunt had gathered to make themselves known again.

Chapter 5

Two Mothers, One Wife

Elizabeth, Mary, Anne

By any standard of personality and form, King James VI and I pales in comparison with the two women who overshadowed the first decades of his life, his mother, and the queen of England. He still shared certain qualities with both these women, however. James was as much a survivor as Elizabeth of England and as much of a fighter, at times, as Mary, Queen of Scots. James had no means to maintain a normal relationship with his mother even if he had the inclination to do so. Separated from her forever when he was an infant, she was further distanced from him by her alien Catholicism and her interest in the throne of England, where she was at first a rival and then an obstacle to James's ambitions. Three years before his mother's execution in 1587, the Frenchman Fontenay remarked that the Scottish king displayed no feeling as a son: 'Of one thing only I am astonished; that he has never asked anything about the Queen, neither of her health, nor of the way she is treated, nor of her servants, nor of what she eats or drinks, nor of her recreation, nor any similar matter, and yet, notwithstanding this, I know that he honours her much in his heart.'[1] The fact was that James was led a dance for sixteen long years in his attempt to secure England's throne and his mother Mary, dead or alive, was a hindrance to his ambition.

There is doubt about the effect that his mother's execution in February 1587 had on James. He was ambivalent on two fronts, personally and as a king. While he sent special ambassadors to negotiate for Queen Mary's life, they were also instructed to do nothing that would imperil their master's claim to succession in the south. In his own letters written to the power brokers in England, he also had to walk a tightrope continually. Writing to the Earl of Leicester in December 1586, he advised that he hated his mother's religion and seems to suggest that he would never put affection for his mother before his ambition to be the English monarch.[2] It was said that the king could never stand to hear details about his mother's execution, but this may have been because of his general aversion to hearing about violence in any shape or form. On the other hand, we are told that he ordered the removal of a minister from preaching at St Giles Kirk in Edinburgh because he refused to denounce the English treatment of his mother. But that was quite possibly a staged reaction. Another report says the king was quite unmoved when the news of his mother's death arrived. He did not alter his usual routine and went out hunting. The cleric David Calderwood was more damning. He stated that the king could not hide his inner joy when he heard about the execution, although he wore an outward appearance of sorrow. That evening he allegedly expressed satisfaction to a small group of courtiers that he was now the sole monarch of Scotland. Chancellor Maitland was so ashamed of the remark that he ushered them out from the king's presence. On the other hand, David Moysie wrote that the king was in great displeasure and went to bed hungry. He rode to Dalkeith next day, wishing to be alone. When he later heard an account of the last moments from one of his mother's ladies-in-waiting he was crestfallen and once more would not eat that evening. Behind the scenes, an English agent reported, James was muttering about revenge and saying he wouldn't allow himself to be intimidated by the old woman of England.

James had to consider the aggressive gesturing of his nobles when it became known that Queen Mary was doomed. Outraged by nationalistic feeling that England should execute Scotland's sovereign, they pressed at James to be more belligerent in response. The Earl of Bothwell plainly stated that, should the king permit his mother to be killed, he deserved to be hanged next day.

King James merely laughed at this. Lord Claude Hamilton swore he would burn the north of England if Mary was harmed. The Earl of Angus observed that King James would be justified in cutting Elizabeth's throat. In the lead up to the eventual death of Queen Mary, James boldly reminded Elizabeth that her own father had greatly discredited himself by killing his own bedfellow and now Elizabeth was unworthily planning worse.

Rumours filtered down to England that the Scots were planning cross-border raids, which only bad weather prevented from happening. There was also whispering that there would be a renewed alliance between Scotland and France. For almost a year James did not communicate directly with Queen Elizabeth and he refused her envoy, Sir Robert Carey, to enter his realm. Elizabeth tried to distance herself from the final decision to execute Queen Mary, and assured James that his mother's treason would not disqualify him from being in the running to succeed her. Once he was securely on England's throne, King James dutifully moved his mother's remains from Peterborough to a lavish tomb in Westminster Abbey. He could afford to redesign himself as a loyal, doting son in retrospect. Never a day passed, it was noted, that he didn't make some comment lamenting the fate of his mother, and he frequently made those he thought had some part in her death fearful for their appointments, or even for a bloody end. But perhaps he chose to believe that it was a preordained tragedy in which he had no part. Having internalised the traumatic death, it resurfaced later in the king's life in odd ways. During a conversation on other subjects with Sir James Harington in January 1607, King James suddenly (and quite seriously) stated that there were gruesome visions of Queen Mary seen just before her demise and it had been 'spoken of in secrete by those whose power of [second] sighte presentede to them a bloodie heade dancinge in the aire'. He stated that he had investigated books which contained proof of this dubious supernatural ability but warned Harington not to do the same as it might lead him into evil consultations.[3]

The path to England's crown was uneasy and strewn with legal hazards. As long ago as 1351, an English law expressly forbade any foreigner becoming king of England. During the first half of the sixteenth century, King Henry VIII made it clear that he did not want foreigners, and specifically Scottish Stuarts, to rule his realm. In the absence of a firm stance by Queen Elizabeth to name the next in line, Parliament took it upon itself to state it had the power to name the following ruler, a power which King James strongly contested. Although there were a dozen possible runners in the succession race, there were far fewer likely winners. James, his English cousin Arbella, and one or two others, descendants of Henry VIII's sister Mary, were the front runners.

Elizabeth of England had been ambivalent about James from his birth, knowing that he, as well as mother, were rivals for her throne. In June 1566, when news of the prince of Scotland's birth was brought to Queen Elizabeth, she cried out in bitter acknowledgment of her own virginity and jealousy of Queen Mary, 'how that the Quen of Scotland was leichter of a faire sonne, and that sche was bot a barren stok'.[4] While Elizabeth resolutely refused to recognise James (or anyone else) as heir to her kingdom, to the frustration of all, it became ever more likely, as time marched on and she stayed single, that he was. The last serious chance of a marriage match, with the Duke of Anjou, evaporated in 1582, and the King of Scots must have been heartily pleased. The queen's pathological fear of admitting that she was not in fact immortal meant that she could not contemplate naming the next ruler. To do so would be like signing her own death warrant. 'Think you that I could love my own winding sheet?' she plaintively asked William Maitland, the representative of Mary, Queen of Scots, when pressed about that queen's claim to her crown. English subjects fared no better when they raised the subject. The English MP Peter Wentworth petitioned her to consider the succession in 1593 and was locked up in the Tower of London until his death four years later. Any mention of death was an affront to the ageing queen. A possibly apocryphal story tells how Roger Lord North made the mistake of serving a pie shaped like a coffin to the queen. 'Are you such a fool to give a pie such a name?' she roared at him.[5]

Elizabeth may have been grooming James, unconsciously and unwillingly, to be king. But it was no done deal and he had to be careful how to press his claims as the relationship between the rulers of Scotland and England was inevitably unbalanced. While James, with much to gain from keeping on her good side, was mindful to always respectfully address Elizabeth, she was not afraid to dispense advice, chastisement or unvarnished rudeness. On one occasion, she sent the king the gift of a clock, as if coldly advising him to bide his time. At times, she adopted the role of an exasperated, if distant, parent, fending off the wheedling demands of her needy child. James frequently played on the family relationship and called the English queen his loving or dearest mother, referring to her role as his godmother, and calling himself 'your natural son' and 'most loving devoted brother and son'. Elizabeth usually called him 'brother and cousin' (with James sometimes reciprocating this greeting too).[6] There was a fleeting idea early on to marry James and Elizabeth, but the match would have been disastrous for both, though entertaining for subsequent historians.

Differences between the two monarchs were keenly noted by observers. Sir Roger Wilbraham, a minor official who served both rulers, noted the king's generosity in comparison with Elizabeth's parsimony. While both were magnanimous in nature and not inclined to revenge, Sir Roger noted that the queen was slow to resolution while the king was impulsive in judgement. Elizabeth took and weighed expert opinion from her advisers (though she could be dangerously indecisive in later life), while the king was notably willing to exercise his own 'sharpest witt & invencion, redie & pithie speche [and] exceeding good memorie'.[7] Good nature aside, it was clear that James was a man who valued the sound of his own voice and opinions. He could also be sorely affected by personal slights from his English counterpart. When he sent Elizabeth a sonnet praising her in 1586 and received no reply, he was offended both by her silence and the fact that she did not appreciate his poetic talent. So, he wrote a fulsome covering letter and sent the sonnet again.[8]

The relationship between the monarchs improved in July 1586 when a treaty of mutual defence was agreed. This Treaty of Berwick ended decades of hostility and dampened English fears that the Auld Alliance between Scotland and France would continue to act as a security risk through the back door. James asked for a clause to be included which recognised him as Elizabeth's heir, and also requested an English duchy. He got neither, though Elizabeth consented that she would do nothing to prejudice his claim to the English throne. He also happily received a promise of an English subsidy and, more immediately, a stock of deer which he gleefully added to his park at Falkland Palace. There were subtle hints too in the communication from the queen at the time that she recognised his rights and, possibly, aspirations to occupy her throne.

Relations improved again during the Spanish Armada crisis in 1588 when James was exceptionally vocal about supporting Elizabeth and England in the face of foreign aggression. The panicked English ambassador in Scotland over-promised an array of gifts to keep the king onside: an English dukedom, larger pension, plus recognition of his claims of succession. Elizabeth vetoed all these promises, though James had chosen wisely in favouring England over Spain in terms of his likely future rewards.

Elizabeth opposed James's marriage arrangement with a Danish princess, preferring a French Protestant match. But she reconciled herself to his choice and took measures to provide support for the authorities in Scotland should there have been any trouble there during the king's absence for several months in Scandinavia. The next major disagreement between the monarchs came when the perennially impecunious king argued about the pension he believed he was due from Elizabeth. King James believed that he should be entitled to £4,000 per year. Elizabeth contended that the figure should be no more than £3,000, and further outraged James by deducting additional gifts from this total which he regarded as wholly separate. She regarded, for example, the plate worth £2,000 which she gave the king as a wedding gift as being part of that year's pension. He wrote to her in December 1591, complaining of his own needs: 'I weary to be so long time suitor, as one who was not born to be a beggar but to be begged at … remember, that as I am your kinsman, so am I a true prince. The disdaining of me can be no honour to you.'[9] Although Elizabeth did pay him considerable sums on and off, the argument rumbled on for several years. One point of contention was that James believed he was due money in lieu of receiving the English lands that had been owned by his father, Darnley, though Elizabeth denied this. On her part, she regarded the funds channelled north as reward for the continued good behaviour of her Scottish counterpart. She complained to him periodically about disruption on the Border and Scottish interference in Ireland.

There was further frustration on Elizabeth's part in the 1590s when she witnessed what she regarded as an alarming leniency towards an eternally plotting Catholic faction among the Scottish aristocracy. The activity of Jesuits and their followers, and the blatant intercourse between the Catholic nobility and England's primary enemy Spain caused alarm, especially as James seemed either unwilling or unable to effectively block the conspiratorial habits of some of the Catholic nobles, especially the Earl of Huntly. Finding James increasingly uncooperative, Queen Elizabeth put out diplomatic feelers to Huntly, and also gave encouragement to the Earl of Bothwell, who was the most destructive internal enemy of James within the nobility. King James complained to Elizabeth in April 1594 that Bothwell was being harboured in the north of England and went so far in his anger as to call Elizabeth a 'seduced queen'. Several months later he apologised. Relations were on the mend, and pension money was sent north. The English ambassador was accorded the primary place of honour at the baptism of the king's son Henry. James took steps also to quell the northern Catholic lords, sending the Earl of Argyll against Huntly while also himself leading a force against that earl. While there was some positive movement in relations, the suspicions of Elizabeth were reignited following Huntly's return to Scotland in 1596.

Even the naming the king's daughter Elizabeth did not lessen the queen's suspicions. James took offence at the publication of Spencer's *Faerie Queen* which denigrated his mother, forbidding its sale in Scotland, and made an angry speech in Parliament, blaming Elizabeth for the death of his mother, the non-payment of his pension and the attitude of the English Parliament toward his title. Shortly afterwards he engaged with leaders in the north of Ireland who were hostile to the English authorities there. Elizabeth was soon chastising him and accusing him of being possessed by evil spirits, and he was forced to backtrack and issue an abject apology to her.

In 1598 King James tried a wily ploy to influence Elizabeth into naming him as her successor. He sent messages to the leading Protestant leaders in Europe and asked them to support his claim as the pre-eminent Protestant claimant to the throne of England. But his plan did not result in active support from those who were approached. Following contact from the party of the Earl of Essex, who wanted to support James as heir apparent, the chances of finding high-level support among the English establishment seemed to be lost when Essex was executed. However, unexpectedly, James found support in the shape of Elizabeth's Secretary of State, Robert Cecil. Cecil started his discreet correspondence with the King of Scots in May 1601. He counselled the Scottish king to stop pressurising the ageing queen to name him as her heir. Following the advice, James was careful not to antagonise Elizabeth in his correspondence, and he also allayed her fears by informing her of contact and negotiations with foreign powers. He also emphasised his affection towards the queen in his letters and toned down any demands. It must have seemed to James that Queen Elizabeth would never die. She reigned for an astonishing forty-four years and had been in robust health for most of that time. Until a few weeks before the end, her sight and her mind were clear, and she danced, walked, and attended to what was spoken to her. The last illness came on suddenly and the queen would barely eat or take medicine throughout its dreadful course. She abandoned sleep because she was mortally afraid to take to her bed. Although she did not state that she wanted James VI to succeed her, one story states that she indicated by a movement of her hand, circling her head like a crown, that the king of Scots should also now become king of England.

Not long before her death she had informed Lord Nottingham that the throne was a throne of kings and that none but her nearest of blood and descent should follow her. Although this plainly indicated James VI, she would not directly name him. When Nottingham approached her death bed and reminded her of these words, she repeated them and added, 'I shall have no rascal to succeed; who should succeed me but a king?' Her Secretary of State, Robert Cecil, tried to press her further. After a lifetime avoiding this issue and many others, she allegedly answered with exasperation, 'My meaning was a king shall succeed me; and who should that be but our cousin of Scotland.' That, at least, was one version of events.[10]

Queen Elizabeth died in the early hours of the morning of 24 March 1603. James VI was proclaimed king shortly afterwards in Richmond and Robert Cecil announced his succession, 'by Law, by Lineall succession, and undoubted Right,' before the Privy Council at Whitehall at ten in the morning. But the legality of the Scottish king's right to England was not entirely robust. In the event, no challenge to his succession arose. It was supreme good fortune which let power pass seamlessly from the old queen to the younger king. Behind the scenes in England, few chances were taken with malcontents who might dispute the rights of King James. Vagrants, Catholics, and other suspects were either locked up or closely watched to prevent any disorder. Ports were closed and the navy was on standby. The courtier Sir Roger Wilbraham recorded during the last week of Elizabeth's life that the navy was braced 'in rediness against foren attempts'. People from outside London hurried into the city to hide away their valuables in strong places.[11] A watch was placed around the king's cousin and supposed rival Arbella Stuart, but no party made a move to carry her off and sweep her into power.

As soon as the queen passed, Sir Robert Carey immediately sprang into action, having rehearsed this historic moment. He mounted his horse and began the long journey north, anxious to be the first man to break the news to the king of Scots and therefore (he hoped) to be first in his favour. He reached the royal presence in Edinburgh on the evening of 26 March. Bloodied from a fall from his steed, he offered the sapphire ring that James had sent to Carey's sister in anticipation of the queen's death. (This was Carey's version; others say that James had the information from another source.)

Several observers in England noted the irony that one day it was treason to call James king, or even to say God save him, and the next day it was almost treason not to say so. Many in England made moves in advance to curry favour with their new ruler. Pictures of his deceased mother were brought out and prominently displayed. Some court followers scrambled to make early contact with James, as if preferment was on a first come, first served based, or via the 'footmanship of messengers', as one courtier sharply observed.[12]

The king's relationship with his wife, Anne, was less tempestuous than that with Elizabeth, but it had its own complexities. At the beginning of the marriage, James may have loved his wife, after a fashion, and even when they later became estranged, there was a lingering fondness between them. Anne, the queen consort of King James, daughter of King Frederick II of Denmark, is a figure who has suffered from the criticism of historians, as did her husband. Terms such as stupid, placid or frivolous have been assigned to her, in line with traditional misogyny and a misunderstanding of the difficult role she assumed.[13] Many writers have taken a dim view of the queen's interests and character, neglecting her sophisticated involvement in interior design and the visual and performing arts, which improved the standing of the new Stuart dynasty. For some, her love of childish games and jewellery marked her out as irrelevant to the new regime, yet she was neither incapable nor idiotic. She was multilingual, with a particular fluency in and a deep appreciation of the Italian language and culture.

The lack of involvement in the political life of Scotland and England has disguised her contribution to the arts, particularly the stage, where she consciously sponsored performances and enhanced the public image of herself and James. The reality of a queen in medieval or early modern times was centred around being marketable commodities and dynastic tools, sent away from home at a relatively early age, never to see their families again. The primary function of queenship was producing children, but life was often still unsatisfactory for those who did produce heirs. Anne of Denmark provided James with seven children, three sons and four daughters, of whom only Charles and Elizabeth survived both their parents.

King James was twenty-three years old when he dashed across the North Sea in Autumn 1589, in a burst of impatient romanticism, to claim his young bride. He would proudly remember the incident in a nostalgic glow, especially when his son dashed off on a similar, though ill-fated journey to Spain in search of love. The marriage negotiations had been convoluted, in line with all royal matrimonial matches. Elizabeth of England preferred that James should pair off with a sound French Protestant bride, and had also seriously considered trying to stop the Scottish king marrying anyone and therefore reducing his suitability for her own throne.[14] This, ironically, would have suited James's proclivities very well, if not his professional ambitions. A Scandinavian match potentially opened up lucrative trade for Scotland at the expense of England. Pressing ahead, the Scots had first enquired about the prospects for Anne's elder sister, Elizabeth. The king's old tutor, Sir Peter Young, and another emissary were sent across the sea to Denmark in 1587 to assess whether matrimonial negotiations could proceed.

James had been under pressure from his nobles and councillors to start looking for a wife and secure an heir for the kingdom. 'God is my witness,' he said later, 'I could have abstained longer nor the weal of my patrie [than the good of my country] could have permitted [had not] my great delay bred in the breasts of many a great jealousy of my inability, as if I were barren stock.'[15] His lack of interest in women is starkly revealed. One reason why discussions for the hand of the elder daughter faltered was that her father, King Frederick, thought that

King James was too faint-hearted a wooer. The agreement to marry the fourteen-year-old younger daughter, Anne, came after her father died and his widow agreed to the betrothal. When this arrangement was sealed an English observer also noted that the king was a cold wooer and not anxious for marriage. The pair were married by proxy and Anne set out for Scotland in September in1589. Beaten back by bad weather (and perhaps by witchcraft), she had to return home. Following James's impulsive journey to fetch her, the couple spent several months in Denmark and Norway and arrived in Scotland in May 1590.

Soon after the bride was back in Scotland, and certainly after the births of princes Henry (in 1594) and Charles (in 1600), it was clear there were growing differences between husband and wife. Their interests were also divergent, with the queen enjoying social interaction and the common entertainments of the day, and also having a distaste for books and abstruse debate which were meat and drink to James. The queen had no love of learning, nor any pretensions towards it. Religion also became an issue, with her Lutheranism running contrary to the tide of Calvinism in Scotland. Matters were made more difficult when she converted to Catholicism around the turn of the century. Her decision gives us a window into her character, and also gives insight into James's attitude. Following secret instruction by the Jesuit Robert Abercromby, James noted a new seriousness in his wife and expressed his suspicion she had received Catholic instruction. When she admitted this, the king responded, 'Well, wife, if you cannot live without this sort of thing, do your best to keep things as quiet as possible, for if you don't our crown is in danger.' This report came from Abercromby himself, who added that the king afterwards treated him with greater kindness and respect.[16] This is surprising in light of the king's later admittance to being somewhat tolerant of the Catholic laity (as long as they were loyal to him), but absolutely intolerant of Catholic clergy.

James and Anne were able to use her semi-secret conversion to their benefit in Scotland, and to make them a more attractive package to the still prominent Catholic faction in England. It was partly as a reaction to the prevalent Calvinism at Scotland that Anne favoured Catholicism, but was likely more influenced by her friend, the Countess of Huntly, Henrietta Stuart (daughter of Esmé Stuart).[17] Surprisingly, Anne's change in faith was tolerated quietly, not just by the king, but those around the Scottish court, in the face of extreme hostility by the Scottish Kirk. One member of court, who was engaged in a dispute with a kirk minister, joked when Anne took the minister's part that he would report her to Father Abercromby. Ironically, the closet Catholicism of the queen caused more of a problem at times in England since it was tied in with her pro-Spanish attitude, which flew in the face of prevailing national opinion. The queen wisely chose to be circumspect at times in concealing her religious view. She covertly maintained contact with significant Catholics in Europe, and her religious inclination was certainly known about, and covered up by, King James's loyal servant Robert Cecil.[18] By the end of her life, she may have reverted to Protestantism.

Queen Anne demonstrated a strong character, being well aware of her rights and dignity, and being the wise daughter and sister of kings; otherwise, she would have been more fully marginalised and neglected than she was. Soon after her arrival in Scotland she entered a dispute with the Chancellor, Maitland of Lethington, regarding land ownership in Fife, which she won – a victory made sweeter by the knowledge that he had argued against her marriage. She also showed marked reluctance to bow to the strict social protocols demanded by the Scottish Kirk. The latter sourly noted her fondness for dancing and other frivolous entertainment, regardless of her young age and the fact she had been raised in a more benign environment. Dubious rumours that the queen was romantically linked with the disgraced Master of Ruthven and the Earl of Moray rose from a deep suspicion of Anne in some sectors of society. While Scotland had no lack of strong women, independence was not a trait that the establishment looked for in a queen in a nation which had turned decisively against the king's late mother. Yet Anne also acted as an important bridge between her adopted and native countries, interceding for citizens of each place. Despite the love of entertainment and fine jewels and clothes, the tall, blonde, and good-looking Anne was still a pleasant contrast to the king and could have played a more active part in the national affairs. The first major, noticeable breach between the royal couple happened when the king insisted their first child be placed in custody of the noble Mar family in line with tradition, with Anne only being allowed occasional visits. Anne fought hard to retain custody of the prince, arguing with the king, and hatching her own plan to take him, but the king's will prevailed, and a distraught Anne suffered the consequences. She had a miscarriage in July 1595.[19] The next child born, Elizabeth (in August 1596), was placed in fosterage with Lord and Lady Livingstone. Prince Charles was placed under the care of Lord Fyvie.

Anne was likely unconscious that she was an object of suspicion as soon as her husband ascended the throne of England in March 1603. Secretary Robert Cecil for one distrusted Anne's ability to keep quiet about secret matters. He learned that Anne had been prying into the secret correspondence that he and James had been conducting, along with various others, prior to Queen Elizabeth's death and warned the king that she might be a source of trouble in the future. Later, however, the canny Cecil ensured he aligned himself with Anne. 'I cannot but be jealous of your greatness with my wife,' James told Cecil in 1608, though whether he was being flippant or serious is uncertain. King James had set off south to claim his new throne without Anne, who took the opportunity of his absence – despite being pregnant again – to go to Stirling with a band of followers and engage in a furious row with the Countess of Mar in an effort to retrieve her son. The trauma of the event resulted in another miscarriage. The king sent a conciliatory letter from England, and also despatched the Earl of Mar back to resolve the mess, though Queen Anne refused to see him. She wrote back angrily to the king and refused to leave Linlithgow Palace for Edinburgh unless she was accompanied by Prince Henry and without the Earl of Mar. Another responsive missive from James was a mixture of flattery and resentment, which did nothing to appease her. Her bold request for a public apology from Mar was met with a flat refusal. Further letters were exchanged. Then Anne played the trump card by refusing to journey to England rather than reconcile with Mar and would not even receive the prince directly from him. The boy was given to the Duke of Lennox and then returned to Anne via the Council.

Anne journeyed south with Henry, temporarily leaving behind the younger children, Elizabeth and Charles. At Berwick she incurred displeasure again from the king by rejecting those English gentlemen and ladies he had picked to be part of her entourage, instead favouring her existing Scottish and Danish companions. This struggle for control of her own household continued and the king raged at the Duke of Lennox for not preventing the appointment of a man he found unsuitable to a prominent position in Anne's household.[20] Yet the single-mindedness over the choice of household members did not always reflect well on the queen's judgement. A decade earlier a female member of Anne's household was implicated in a plot of the wild Earl of Bothwell to raid Falkland Palace, endangering the royal couple. King James was so furious that he threatened to export his seventeen-year-old wife back to Denmark. The same Danish servant may have been responsible for non-payment of debts to tradesmen several years later, casting some doubt on Anne's judgement and misplaced loyalty.

In the early phase of his marriage, King James was keen to portray himself in public with 'his Annie'. But he also put her in her place on occasion. Soon after they married, hearing that she was boasting about her status as a royal, he wrote to tell her succinctly, 'King's or cook's daughter, ye must be alike to me, being ance my wife.' Queen Anne also had an unfortunate knack of upsetting her husband by accident. A tragi-comic example, which shows an exception to the rule, was when they were both attending a deer hunt at Theobalds House in July 1613. Anne let loose a bolt from a crossbow and killed the king's favourite hound Jewel. The king learned of the death and ranted and threatened vengeance on the perpetrator. But when he learned that Anne had killed the dog, he said that 'he should never love her the worse'. Next day he gave her a jewel worth £2,000 which he said was a legacy from his beloved hound.

Coming from a royal family that was not the richest in Europe, Anne revelled in the fine clothes, perfume, and performance arts which England afforded, with little thought of the expenditure, and the king did not begrudge her spending, being similarly heedless of finances. Given their differing interests and personalities, it was no surprise that that the king and queen began to lead independent lives in England. Separate households were a convention among married royal couples, but there were of course degrees of disconnection. Disillusion was evident from the early years in the south. In 1604 Anne was telling the French envoy Beaumont that the king was drinking so much and behaving so badly that she expected a bad result. Nevertheless, there was some necessary continued physical relationship. In June 1606 the queen gave birth to her seventh child, Sophia, who only lived a few days. At the age of thirty-two she decided there would be no more children. The decision inevitable formalised the gulf between herself and James and from then on they were only together at Christmas and on state occasions. Prince Henry's death put a seal on the royal couple's choice to maintain wholly different pursuits, and Anne made a conscious effort to distance herself from James's court. The faction of Robert Carr and his Howard family allies was alien to the queen's tastes.

James was hardly heartbroken by the distance. The king felt free to seek the company of a succession of young lovers of the same sex. Disillusioned by the king's character and alienated by James's willingness to lecture her poor judgement, the attentiveness which he publicly displayed towards these young men must have been embarrassing. Evidence of her own possible romantic entanglements is less substantial than her husband's adventures. In England, a Dane in Anne's household is said to have been romantically attached to her, and two love rivals, both named Buchanan, are said to have fought a duel over her affections, whether reciprocated or not.[20] In a letter to Robert

Cecil, the king also refers to one man accusing another of being her lover. James was aware the matter had to be handled discreetly, or else there would be a scandal that would reflect badly on him. The queen had been informed of the tale, which was full of 'feckless scorn' and was hatched only from the malice the man bore the king. Anne discussed the matter herself with Cecil, but we hear no more of the details.[21]

Despite all this, the king continued to regard Anne highly and she remained involved in some aspects of court life and government. Strangely, she was initially fond of George Villiers, Carr's replacement as favourite, having been persuaded to get him appointed to the king's household by a group who wished to have Carr removed. Like many others, she was rather bewitched by Villiers' magnetism and was soon exchanging chatty notes with him and addressing him fondly. In the early days, Villiers was a good restraining influence on the personal excesses of King James, and it would take several years before he became a dangerously powerful figure in his own right. Some of those out of favour with James tended to gravitate towards his wife, although her household was an alternative rather than a rival court. Anne could still assert her opposition to the king in some matters. She may have consciously fashioned her elder son Henry into an ideal opposite of her husband: resolute and militaristic where her spouse was peaceable and pleasure-seeking. In the presence of the French ambassador, she once voiced the hope that Henry would one day overrun France in the manner of his ancestor, Henry V, and ensured her influence was paramount over the boy.[22]

Left to her own devices by the king, Anne became a noted patron of the arts and attended the theatre frequently. She also lent considerable support as a sponsor of the writer Ben Jonson and the visual artist Inigo Jones and had them collaborate, in a rather mutually jealous fashion, on elaborate masques held in the royal palaces. The first major production of Johnson and Jones, the *Masque of Blackness*, was too avant-garde for a conservative English audience who were confused by the players' costumes and movements and perturbed by displays of near nudity. Although she attended further masques, Anne did not have a hand in another production until 1608 when she helped stage Johnson's *Masque of Beauty*. This performance had to be postponed because of a diplomatic incident wherein the French ambassador thought foreign rivals received invitations before him. In the subsequent fallout the king took the default view and blamed his wife.

Anne's main concern, outside her love of entertainment, was her children. Charles was her favourite, which may be due to the concerns she and the rest of the family had for his early infirmity and her wish to lavish him with attention in compensation. But one contemporary stated that the queen's love for her firstborn, Henry, was so great that she could not bear him to leave him out of her sight. Her own health began to decline around 1611 and she was severely affected in the summer of the following year by the sudden illness of her son Henry, who died on 12 November 1612. Anne was naturally grief stricken and wept for days in a darkened room at Somerset House. Death did not bring the parents together and neither of them attended the funeral. King James was notoriously ill at ease around death and Anne was suffering from a bout of gout. The chief mourner, rather pathetically, was twelve-year-old Prince Charles. The queen took a greater part in the life of her second son following the death of Henry.

Following the queen's pivotal role in sponsoring George Villiers as her husband's new favourite, Anne's health worsened before she could capitalise on that victory.[23]. She developed pleurisy or congestive heart failure, and by the time James (and Villiers) returned to England from his only return journey to Scotland in November 1617, she was seriously ill. She remained gravely unwell for most of 1618 and died at the beginning of March 1619, attended in her last days by her son Charles. Her funeral was delayed for a long period, but not long enough to persuade her husband to attend. Ill himself at the time of her death, he remained at his favourite hunting seat of Theobalds House in Hertfordshire. A few days after the funeral, on 13 May, James decreed that mourning should be dispensed with at court, and when he returned to Whitehall on 1 June after his sickness he and his attendants were all magnificently dressed as usual.

Chapter 6

A Family Man

The King's Children and Cousin

The king's first child, and his great hope as the rightful ruler of the two island kingdoms, Prince Henry, was born in Stirling Castle in February 1594. The great hopes of the father were set down in the *Basilikon Doron*, the 'royal gift,' an extended missive to Henry which the king published when his son was five. As he grew, it seemed to some that Prince Henry was everything that his father was not: comely in appearance, attractive in personality, upright in morality. In later years, after the shady favouritism of his father's court and the weakness of his brother, Charles, as king, there was a retrospective urge to idealise the lost prince who died before maturity. He was widely mourned when he passed away at the age of eighteen, with contemporary commentator Simonds d'Ewes noting of the lamentation 'that even women and children partook of it'.[1] Prince Henry was tall for the period, around five foot eight. He had dark hair, a long face, and a full measure of princely sobriety and charisma which does not seem to have been inherited from his father. Another trait definitely not shared with King James was Henry's love of anything military from a young age, whether that was martial music or tales of battle strategy from old war veterans.[2] At one time young Henry spent five or six hours in armour and his mother encouraged these military leanings. Loving the sea and ships, he was given lavish model boats to command and employed the king's master shipbuilder, Phineas Pett. Balanced against his love of warfare was a pious, almost puritanical side. It is known that the prince kept a swear box in in each of his three houses, with all proceeds going to the poor. Henry was also lauded as a sound Protestant and an enemy of Catholicism, in contrast to his father, who was accused of accommodating the old religion at times. This prince was also reputedly an uncommon judge of character. 'He esteemed not buffoons and parasites, nor vain swearers and atheists, but had learned and godly men ... for the dear companions of his life.'[3] Sober, thoughtful, and disdainful of flattery, this paragon of a prince outshone his father from an early age, especially in the eyes of those who clearly saw the faults in King James. But did such staunch approval for someone so young signify that he would have become a hardline monarch, if not an outright tyrant? One member of the Howard family voiced this sour suggestion soon after the golden prince's death. Some historians have agreed, though others speculated he would have made an admirable ruler.

Around his siblings, we can see Henry occasionally as a mere mortal. Despite differing interests, his brother Charles and sister Elizabeth were devoted to him and there are records of his reciprocal love for them. But occasionally he let his pious aura slip and behaved like a normal teenager. In one incident he reduced Charles to tears by observing that his spindly legs made him look like a bishop in his vestments. He also had a habit of teasing Elizabeth by repeatedly reciting ghost stories before she went to bed. There was no such recorded banter between Henry and his father, who were notably dissimilar; so much so that there was a malicious rumour that Henry was actually the son of Lord Sinclair.[4]

Alongside his interest in all things warlike, Henry had no great love of studying, and even more disappointingly for the king, did not wholeheartedly enjoy the favourite royal pastime of hunting. The two had a heated dispute during one hunting trip in 1611, with James threatening to cane his son for not displaying proper regard for the sport. Rumours of their disagreements abounded, with some saying the king grew to be envious of his son's popularity. King James allegedly once said that Henry wanted to bury him before he was dead, a statement which he may possibly have regarded as chillingly ironic. Even if there was no outright jealousy, King James still kept a watchful eye on the growing popularity of his heir, aware that even beloved sons could be rivals. When he was made Prince of Wales, King James ensured his son's profile was not over-mighty by refusing to allow him to appear on horseback. Henry began to assume more power and even intrude into areas of his father's administration. He crossed over the line from being precocious to being meddlesome, pointing out the failings of the king's ministers. His famous comment about Sir Walter Raleigh, languishing in the Tower of London, was notably critical of the king. 'What man but my father,' Prince Henry said, 'would keep such a bird in a cage.'

The publicly known differences between James and Henry were not overly serious, such as their difference of opinion about the choice of tutor for Prince Charles, and the two were apparently getting on better by 1612. Cecil had done his best to stop the heir interfering with government decisions, though he characteristically told Henry it was the king's beloved Carr who had been responsible from excluding him from decision making. For the most part, the elder prince remained a dutiful son, whatever any enemies or idle tongues said about the relationship between father and son, though the gulf between them may have grown if he had survived. According to John Osborne, the Puritan faction pinned great hopes on the boy who might be the future king, some fondly imagining him as an apocalyptic hero who would utterly destroy Catholicism.[5] If he was aware of it (and he was so straightlaced that he may have remained ignorant), Henry would have been appalled by his father's sexuality. He certainly regarded the young Scottish favourite of his father, Robert Carr, with contempt and could not bear a moment in his company. It was an antipathy that his mother also shared.

During the latter part of 1612 Henry's health began to worsen. He lost weight, became pale, and complained of headaches, but he still pushed himself by exercising all day and into the evenings. The first crisis occurred on 25 October. That morning he heard a melancholy sermon from his chaplain, taken from the Book of Job: 'Man that is born of a woman is of few days, and full of trouble. He cometh forth like a flower and is cut down: he fleeth also as a shadow, and continueth not.' After dining with his father and his sister's future husband, he fell into a fever. His eyes became extremely sensitive, even to candlelight. Despite the close attention of doctors, he sank into delirium and convulsions by 31 October. The symptoms seem to be consistent with typhoid fever. He died on 6 November. Queen Anne was grief-stricken and locked herself away. King James, fearful as ever of anything connected to death, moved from Whitehall to his favoured house of Theobalds. Princess Elizabeth was beside herself and went two days without food. It was said that she had twice gone in disguise to see him at the end, despite orders to stay away in case he was infectious, but she could not gain entry to his chamber. He was prescribed a julep made of unicorn's horn, the 'bone of a stag's heart', and a split cock and newly slain pigeons were applied to various parts of his body. These useless treatments given to the boy add a grotesque dimension to his last days. Henry's last sensible words before the delirium set in were to enquire after his dear sister. The Archbishop of Canterbury visited the dying youth and harangued him to demonstrate signs that he acknowledged his Christian faith and hope of resurrection.

In death, Prince Henry was soon proclaimed as the paragon of all virtues.[6] The air also swirled with strange prophecies. It was said that 'a black Christmas would produce a bloody Lent'. The death of Henry was foretold by a famous Scottish astrologer named Bruce. Word of this prophecy was picked up by Robert Cecil, the Earl of Salisbury, who was so incensed that he had Bruce banished.[7] Before he went, Bruce dropped another prophetic bombshell. He foretold that Salisbury would not live to enjoy his banishment. The earl duly died within a short time.

Six doctors performed a post-mortem examination of Prince Henry. There were rumours that he had been poisoned (as there were with every sudden royal death). The seventeenth-century historian Arthur Wilson retold the many stories he had heard about the death. One tall tale said he was slain by the 'venomous scent' of a pair of gloves presented to him. A Spanish plot was spoken about.[8] One story (told by the contemporary Simonds d'Ewes) says Henry was poisoned by a bunch of grapes while he was playing tennis.[9] The queen is said to have suspected Raleigh, who had sent a cordial to the prince in the hope it would revive him. But there was a more favoured villain. The bad feeling between Henry and his father's intimate friend Carr aroused suspicion. Henry's hatred of Carr was so pronounced that his associate Sir James Elphinston once offered to kill him on the prince's behalf. Henry refused, saying if it came to that, he would do the deed himself. There were stories that Frances Howard, who later married Carr, had initially tried to seduce the young prince, which may have initiated bad feeling between the two men.

Speculation that Carr had murdered the prince surfaced several years later when he was implicated in the poisoning of his former friend Sir Thomas Overbury. Amid an upsurge of wild rumours, a lady named Mrs Susan Saul was examined by the authorities in November 1615 and remembered that Carr had employed her to prepare a banquet which the prince had attended in May 1612, months before Henry's death, yet she still believed she might somehow be blamed for poisoning him. No accusation was directed against her. Other tales said that Carr and his wilful wife wanted to wipe out the entire royal family and usurp the throne, which was an unlikely scenario. One associate of Carr's wife was said to have given a waxen image of the prince to a magical practitioner to cause him harm. The same person, a Mrs Turner, who was executed for her part in Overbury's murder, claimed that a doctor poisoned Henry. This spurious 'evidence' was rejected when Carr was brought to trial.[10] There was even a rumour among a Scottish faction in the royal court that Sir Thomas Overbury had used magical means to dispose of the prince because Henry was an enemy of his bosom friend Robert Carr. When Overbury himself was poisoned, it was taken as heavenly, if not poetic, justice.[11]

Rumours recirculated in 1629 when a Scot named Robert Melville was charged with treason for speaking against the king's favourite

George Villers, Duke of Buckingham, himself recently dead. He linked the supposed murder of King James by poison to the earlier murder of Prince Henry by the same method, accomplished by Overbury. This version of events was certainly long-lived and even lingered within the royal family. According to the Scottish cleric and historian Gilbert Burnet, writing in the late seventeenth century, King Charles I had informed an associate that Prince Henry was poisoned by Carr's means.[12] When the remains of Prince Henry were lying in state a naked young man burst in and announced that he was the ghost of Henry and had a message for the king. He was lashed and displayed naked for twenty-four hours at the porter's lodge. Then the king ordered that he be let loose into the world again.

The proliferation of bizarre tales surrounding the royal family possibly acted as a barometer for the unease of the nation about the king himself. Murderous rumours and stories about the estrangement of the saintly Prince Henry and King James were magnified by enemies of the king and proliferated as his reputation declined during the latter part of his reign. By his later years, and in the decades after his death, his children were sometimes held up as royals who had few of the defects of their father. The tract titled *Tom Tell-Troath* (published around 1622) reflected a prevailing attitude of militant Protestantism. Referring to the king's daughter Elizabeth and her husband, Prince Frederick, the author advised his majesty: 'In your Majesties owne taverns, for one healthe that is begun to your selfe, there are ten drunke to the Princes your forraygn children. And when the wine is in their heads, Lord have mercie on their tonges.'[13]

While Henry showed some precocious ability to rise to the challenge of government, Prince Charles, who became the new heir to the throne, was in awe of King James for much of his early life. He only managed to effectively counter James's policies in the last few years of his father's reign, heavily influenced by the support of the Duke of Buckingham. Like Henry, Charles also adopted a stringent sense of morality in his household, in contrast to the overindulgence of alcohol, food and favouritism which characterised King James's inner circle. But Charles lacked the charisma of his lost brother and the wily political instincts of his father. Apart from a short honeymoon period following the death of James, King Charles did not win widespread approval in any of his nations.

Besides the royal sons, who naturally became the focus of the dynastic attention, James and Anne also had three daughters. Princess Mary was born in 1605 and died two years later from a disease of the lungs. Sophia was born in June 1606 but died the following day. The daughter who survived to adulthood, and whose descendants provided the kings and queens of Great Britain, was Elizabeth. Notably, Elizabeth was the one member of the royal family whom the Gunpowder Plot conspirators planned to spare in 1606. Their scheme was to kill the rest of the royals, kidnap ten-year-old Elizabeth, then set her up as queen and rule in her name. When she later heard about this plot she declared, 'What a Queen should I have been by this means? I had rather been with my royal father in the Parliament-House, than wear his crown on such condition.' Lord Harinton, who reported this in a letter, added that Elizabeth had barely recovered from the revelation of the plot and remained very ill and troubled.[14] It is interesting to note the keen observation of her husband's factor, Colonel Schomberg, who pointed out a weakness that was all too obviously inherited from her father. Accusing her of being facile, Schomberg noted that Elizabeth allowed herself to be easily led, for fear of giving offence to anyone. Elizabeth was also constantly running into debt. Her generosity was problematical, possibly a token of a mind too lazy to weigh the worth of those people who came to ask things from her. 'Madam has no resolution,' wrote Schomberg, 'no consideration, is too liberal to the unfortunate, which I call rather fear, irresolution, pusillanimity than a virtuous liberality.'[15] He might as well have been making judgement of James VI and I.

Elizabeth married Count Frederick V, Elector Palatine of the Rhine (whom the English called the Palsgrave), on Valentine's Day 1613. She would be a queen later in her life, if only for a brief period. This was in 1619-20 when she reigned in Prague as the Queen of Bohemia.

Elizabeth and her German husband had been brought to Bohemia by Protestant nobles, but all too soon Catholic armies swept them from the country. Frederick's principal territory in the Palatinate was grabbed by the Spanish and Elizabeth was left with the bitter title of the 'Winter Queen' in remembrance of her brief ascendancy.

Although the king accepted the young man as a suitable match for his daughter, Frederick was not favoured by Queen Anne. One reason for her displeasure was the queen's adherence to Catholicism; also the prospect of her daughter being married to a Lutheran from a petty German dynasty did not accord with her desire to forge links with one of the great noble Catholic families of Europe. Anne saw too much of her husband in Elizabeth and there was an enduring indifference between mother and daughter, in contrast to the love Anne displayed for her sons. Queen Anne took to calling call Elizabeth Goodwife Palsgrave, while her daughter made it known that she would rather be that than the greatest Papist queen in Christendom.

Interested parties on both sides of the religious divide in England took a keen interest in the split within the royal family. It was due mainly to Frederic's political incompetence that he spent his later life powerless and in exile. But he also blamed the lack of support and unhelpful interference of King James for his predicament, and was heard ruminating that he should have married a boor's daughter rather than the king of Great Britain's, even though his marriage became a true love match. His wife (who was surely a royal daddy's girl) would come to share his bitter opinion. Soon after she had left British shores she had lamented, 'I shall perhaps, never see again the flower of princes, the king of fathers, the best and most amiable father, that the sun will ever see.'[16] But adversity and first-hand witness to the fact that King James's vain hope for a cooperative network of Protestant powers led by himself was mere folly had left her crestfallen. By 1622 Elizabeth herself was convinced that King James had done their cause more harm than good. Many of her later years were spent in exile in the Hague. She returned to England in 1661, the year before her death, and was remembered as the ancestress of the King George I.

We can see another side of James's character in his relationship with another female relative. Arbella Stuart was the first cousin of the king, with James and Arbella being children of two brothers in the Lennox Stuart line. Although born and raised in England (as was her mother), Arbella's Scottish connections also included the Douglas family. More significantly, she was also descended from Margaret, sister of Henry VIII, giving her a place in the running for the English succession. Being a woman made her claim to the crown weaker and she was overshadowed by James being a descendant of Margaret through both his father and his mother. Her royal descent meant she was used throughout her life as a political pawn by both Queen Elizabeth and King James. Although blessed with resilient female role models on both sides (maternal grandmother Bess of Hardwick and paternal grandmother Margaret Douglas, Countess of Lennox), fate and circumstance were against her. She possessed the charm, wit and intelligence of the Stuarts, but did not have the instinct or will to ultimately find a happy and fulfilled life. And she was entirely without ambition to attain the crown, whatever others may have thought. As one biographer noted, 'her royal blood rendered all her talents as nothing. Her inherited characteristics would bring about her eventual self-destruction.'[17]

Arbella was born in 1575 and her father, Charles, Earl of Lennox, died the following year. The government acting on behalf of the nine-year-old King James VI of Scotland refused to ratify the transfer of the Scottish Lennox lands to the infant girl, and the king himself inherited the earldom. James himself did not recognise Arbella's Scottish birth right and gave the earldom to other branches of the Stuart kindred. He also kept hold of valuable jewels which had belonged to Arbella's Lennox grandmother. Being brought up in her first years in the castle which imprisoned her tragic relative, Mary, Queen of Scots, may have given Arbella a repugnance of politics and royal power play. Her lack of personal ambition was a lifelong trait, but despite that, and because she was politically useful, she was advanced by Elizabeth as a possible bride for King James VI as early as 1585. Such a match would have neatly tied up two loose strands of the English royal lineage and would have been a major coup for James in his hopes to slide onto Elizabeth's throne after her demise. The fact that he turned down the opportunity shows poor judgement and how unwilling his was, at that time, to commit to any woman. Aware of the potential claim of Arbella to Elizabeth's throne, James later wrote to the English queen and requested that he was consulted over any marriage negotiations concerning the girl. He was not rebuffed, but neither was he given a straight answer.

In 1587 Arbella was invited to Elizabeth's court for the first time. The invitation was a cold reminder to James that there was another Stuart in the running for the succession. At the time, Elizabeth was considering arranging a marriage for her with the Spanish Governor-General of the Netherlands. This fell through, as did the suggestion of matching Arbella with Ludovic Stuart, son of his late favourite, Esmé Stuart, who was now Duke of Lennox. Even earlier than this it had been suggested that Arbella, when old enough, should marry Esmé himself, albeit that he was already married. The dubious information that the Franco-Scot 'longeth for Arbella' was passed south without having any effect. This was suggested as partial compensation for the fact that the girl had a competing claim to the Lennox title and Scottish estates. Elizabeth relished playing off the hopeful male Stuart contender against the female Stuart who was indifferent to the prize of the crown. The Scots also suggested the Earl of Arran as a potential suitor. An extremely dubious character, Arbella was lucky to avoid his attentions. In 1599, there was an equally unlikely match proposed between Arbella and the soon-to-be notorious (and prematurely dead) Earl of Gowrie.[18]

Doubtless dazzled, if only temporarily, by the magnificence of the court, Arbella caught the eye of Sir Walter Raleigh and others through her grace, learning and deportment. 'Look to her well,' Elizabeth remarked mischievously to the wife of a foreign ambassador. 'She will be one day even as I am and will be a great lady. But I shall be gone before her.' More educated than most of her female contemporaries,

Arbella was raised to be conscious of the fact that she was the great-great-granddaughter of a king. A second royal visit to stay with Queen Elizabeth resulted in some trouble at court and resulted in her being sent away for three years. A Venetian commentator long afterwards said the fault had been with Arbella being too proud and haughty. The reality of life there was not what she originally thought. She later commented, 'What fair words I have had of courtiers and councillors, and so they are vanished into smoke.' She may have realised that Elizabeth had sent her away from court the first time because changes in the domestic and foreign political tides meant she was no longer of any immediate use. In 1596 there was a rumour that the queen was offering her as a bride to Henri IV of France, supposing that he could manage to get rid of his current wife, Marguerite of Valois, which was certainly on his mind. There was a more unlikely rumour that Elizabeth's main minister, Robert Cecil (recently widowed), planned to marry Arbella himself in order to seize the crown after the queen's death. Arbella developed a friendship with Robert Devereux, Earl of Essex, the queen's favourite, and luckily was not tainted by the association when he fell from grace. Following his execution for treason in 1601, Arbella stated, 'I may well say I never had nor never shall have the like friend.'[19]

Another danger was that she was targeted by Catholics at home and abroad as a means to re-establish their religion in England. Some in that community hoped she would marry a Catholic prince and be the agent to depose Elizabeth from the throne. This threat was revived several times, even into the reign of King James I, yet Arbella herself showed no interest in abandoning Protestantism. Rumours of her dalliance with the old religion still troubled the king, however. In 1601 James wrote to his ally in England, Henry Howard, because a false story had reached him stating that his cousin had joined the Church of Rome. As he was:

> credibly informed, that she is lately moved by the persuasion of the Jesuits to change her religion and declare herself a Catholic, it may easily be judged that

she hath been very evil attended on by them that should have had greater care of her when persons so odious, not only to all good Englishmen, but to all the rest of the world.[20]

Despite Arbella's disinterest in these schemes, there was at least one credible attempt to kidnap her and spirit her out of the country when she was in her mid-teens. Arbella was not a prisoner, but she was closely watched and left unmarried in limbo in Derbyshire while Elizabeth's last days dragged out. Sick of the isolation and strict regime imposed by her grandmother, Bess (Elizabeth Hardwick), Arbella attempted to take control of her life at the age of twenty-seven. In a desperate move, she tried to marry herself off to Edward Seymour, son of Lord Beauchamp. She had never met the sixteen-year-old boy, nor previously had any discussions with his family, and it was a match that would never have been allowed by Queen Elizabeth as Seymour himself was in the line of succession, being descended from Henry VIII's sister Mary.

The marriage plot was inevitably discovered and Arbella's attempt to achieve independence was crushed. A measure of her distress can be seen in the behaviour she displayed in the wake of the discovery. Her conduct was usefully exploited by the authorities as confirmation of the rumour they had spread that Arbella was too mentally unstable to be considered as the next monarch. There were worrying signs that her years of solitude were taking a toll on her mental health. When the queen's examiner visited her, he found her responses to his questioning vague and erratic. Arbella played into the hands of the authorities by concocting an imaginary paramour to gain some leverage with them. The fantasy was fleshed out in some detail, with Arbella stating he was 'famous for his secrecy and had more virtues than any subject or foreign prince … and had done many things at her command.'[21] When this phantom lover failed to convince anyone, she went on hunger strike. She bitterly wrote to one of the queen's servants in March 1603. 'I told you there was no trust in man,' she wrote, and in another letter added, 'for all men are liars. There is no trust in man, whose breath is still in his nostrils.' For someone forbidden close contact with any man, it was a strange statement. Her domestic life deteriorated at the same time. Her grandmother Bess wrote a letter to London asking that Arbella be removed from her house. 'She is wilfully bent,' Bess wrote, 'and there is so little reason in most of her doings, that I cannot tell what to make of it. A few more weeks as I have suffered of late will make an end of me.'[22]

But Arbella kept plotting to escape, even with the authorities circling around her, though they were uncertain at first what to actually do with her. She was saved from immediate detention in the Tower by the death of Queen Elizabeth at the end of March. On his triumphant journey south, King James had been appraised of some of the facts about his cousin and made measures to separate Arbella from her long-suffering grandmother, who promptly cut her out of her will. Showing the same hard-headedness, Arbella defied royal protocol and refused to attend Queen Elizabeth's funeral. She said she had been deprived of the queen's company when alive, so she would not now be shown off for public spectacle.

When she was first invited to attend the court of James at Whitehall, both she and the king were understandably unsure of each other, though both were reassured about the other by the ever-resourceful Robert Cecil. The king had been briefed about the breakdown in communication between Arbella and Bess and arranged for the Earl of Kent to remove her to more suitable surroundings, writing to him in April 1603:

> Forasmuch as we are desirous to free our cousin the lady Arbella Stuart from that unpleasant life which she hath led in the house of her grandmother with whose severity and age she, being a young lady, could hardly agree, we have thought fit for the present to require you as a nobleman of whose wisdom and fidelity we have heard so good report to be contented for some short space to receive her into your house.[23]

At their meeting, King James is said to have been the more nervous and uncertain of the two and was inclined to send her back to the house where she had been warded following her recent trouble until Cecil persuaded him otherwise. James became fond of her in a lukewarm way, but Arbella was never regarded as an intimate family member. During the next few years, James kept his first cousin fairly close and made a point of declaring his affection towards her. Although he had not known Arbella's father, Charles (who died in 1576 and was not remembered by her either), one of his earliest memories was the death of his and Arbella's grandfather, Matthew Stuart, 4th Earl of Lennox, who had been assassinated in 1571.

But Arbella still struggled with her newfound freedom, and she was unable to adapt to the peculiar climate of the James's court. Intrigue and political jockeying were deadly pitfalls in the first period of the new king's administration. The self-serving competition there was hardly to her liking, and she did not have the instinct to thrive. If she once noted the treachery of men, she soon found that the women at the top level of society were just as perilous. The female world at court was summarised in a letter from the Earl of Worcester to Gilbert Talbot: 'First you must know we have ladies of divers degrees of favour: some for the private chamber, some for the drawing chamber and some for the bedchamber, and some for neither certain, and of this number is only my Lady Arbella and my Wife.' At the end of his letter he added that, 'the plotting and malice amongst them is such that I think envy hath tied an invisible snake about most of their necks to sting one another to death'.[24]

Although preferable to her previously isolated life, her new circumstances at court and in attendance to the queen meant that she was still closely monitored by the king. Nor did her bookish character align with Queen Anne's household. The women were the same age and though warm towards her, this never developed into deep friendship. The queen's frivolous pastimes, including children's games (which made some believe the queen herself was indeed childish), grated on the more serious-minded Stuart ladies.

Her love of study would seem on the surface to be more in tune with the king's interests, but he hardly approved of learning in women and Arbella did not indulge in his love of deep-seated pedantry. On top of her inability to find a comfortable place in society, she also faced a continuing financial struggle. Despite receiving an allowance and occasional access to other family funds, the cost of keeping up appearances at court was significant.

Arbella managed to sidestep involvement in the Spanish-backed Main Plot which planned to assassinate the king and put Arbella on the throne through marriage to Lord Grey. Although not in the proper sense an outcast, she had a tragic knack of being unfulfilled and unloved. Her character, or some inherent lack of self-confidence, meant that others regarded her coldly. At his trial for involvement in plotting against the king, Sir Walter Raleigh at least let Arbella off the hook from any involvement by coldly asserting that she was 'a woman with whom he had no acquaintance and one of whom all that he ever saw he never liked'.[25] She had no control over the tides of rumour and intrigue which surrounded her. There were stories that she was attempting to avoid her court entrapment by fleeing abroad to marry a Moldovan nobleman (who turned out to be a charlatan), but these were examined and found to be untrue. Another unsuitable candidate for a husband (in 1604) was Queen Anne's boorish younger brother, Duke Ulric of Holstein.

Arbella soon created another desperate matrimonial scheme by attaching herself to William Seymour, second son of Lord Beauchamp, and brother of Edward Seymour. On his side, the main reason why this twenty-two-year-old wished to marry a lady in her mid-thirties must have been financial and political. His family were the very definition of indebted aristocracy and even though Arbella struggled to fund her lifestyle, at least she had an income guaranteed by the king. But the marriage plot was discovered, and the participants were warned against proceeding. The couple pressed on with their liaison regardless and were married on Wednesday, 22 June 1610. By the following month the marriage was known about, and the pair were questioned. King James took a sterner view of the matter than Queen Anne or Prince Henry, aware that any children by the union of this princess of the blood could challenge his own line's right to rule in the future. While Seymour was put in the Tower, Arbella (also in confinement, in a house at Lambeth) wrote to the king and protested her plight, saying that James had done nothing in the seven years she was at court to find her an alternative suitable match. King James may well have placated her with promises to allow her to marry and have a normal life during this period, but Arbella did herself no favours in her missive to the king which contained no apology for her behaviour or any form of contrition. She may have been disappointed that her pleas were unheeded, but few others would have been surprised, even if they felt sympathy for her plight; she and Seymour had been warned more than once not to marry. Queen Anne tried her best to intercede on her behalf with the king, but he calmly and coldly proclaimed that Arbella 'had eaten of the forbidden tree'.[26] James could stand no suggestion of treason or assault to his majestic ego even by family members he believed he had treated with kindness.

By the early part of 1611 the decision was made to remove the troubled princess to the far end of England, at Durham, so she could not be near her husband. Before she was sent away, she penned more appeals to her cousin the king, ruefully signing herself once as his 'almost ruined subject'. When she proclaimed that a move at that time would probably kill her, she was given a month's delay, but no change in the sentence of exile. A further month's reprieve was granted. The next dramatic move might have gone either way: glorious freedom or further misery. Still in London, Arbella disguised herself as a man, walked out of the house in Lambeth and made her way to a river inn and eventually boarded a small vessel and waited in vain for William Seymour. They had plotted to escape abroad together aboard a French ship. William escaped late and the authorities were alerted. Despite the alerts, Seymour made it overseas, but Arbella was captured aboard the ship and brought back. Arbella was sent to the Tower of London, confined in the same chambers which had housed her grandmother,

Margaret Douglas, Countess of Lennox, when she was imprisoned as punishment for the marriage of her son, Lord Darnley, to Mary, Queen of Scots.

While Arbella undoubtedly played a part in her own downfall, the unyielding attitude of the king hastened her fate. She remained in the Tower, subject to a dwindling hope which led to melancholy, convulsions and, spiteful voices said, a 'crackt brain', until she died on 25 September 1615, having probably starved herself to death. The king was criticised for his ruthless punishment of Arbella Stuart. As in the case of Sir Walter Raleigh, the king showed a cold disregard and refused to intervene and save her. There was no royal pretence of sorrow at her death and no attempt to allay the circumstances of her tragedy. In her last, desperate bid to escape abroad the king might have relented and allowed her freedom, as one adviser suggested, but her affront to his majesty by marrying without his permission was deemed unforgivable, despite her lack of ambition, her adherence to the conformist religion, and the fact that she was not a dynastic threat to the newly founded English Stuart dynasty.

Chapter 7

Shadows at the King's Right Hand

Royal Associates and the Path to the English Crown

Apart from his favourites, King James VI and I had close connections with a number of other men, advisors and friends, whose influence strongly affected his mindset and course of action. Other figures, like Sir Walter Raleigh, came into his orbit and suffered as a strange exception to the king's usually inclusive nature. All these relationships reveal something of King James. He had few truly close associates with whom he was intimate through the whole course of his adult life. Trust was a commodity he could rarely afford to indulge in while he rose from adolescence and strove to stamp his authority on a nation that was ambivalent about his rule.

During the 1590s James skilfully managed a balancing act to keep himself in power in Scotland while always keeping a keen eye on his stake in claiming the future kingship of England. During that decade he had to neutralise the threat of the occasionally anti-monarchical Kirk which contested the king's view that church and state were separate. By luck and judgement, he managed to quell some of the endemic blood feuds that were damaging the social fabric of the nation, involving the extended families of the nobility and other kindreds. His own position was threatened by Catholic intrigue at home and by the domineering agenda of Elizabeth's England, which sought to impose a strong Anglo-centric policy on the king of Scotland. Added to his difficulties were the targeting of his own person by Satan himself through the agency of the witches who infested East Lothian, the possibly associated threat that came from the unbalanced Earl of Bothwell, and the mysterious, dangerous events of the Gowrie Conspiracy.

The goal of the English throne kept James VI going through the 1590s and his first powerful clandestine champion in his intended kingdom was the Earl of Essex. Robert Devereux, 2nd Earl of Essex, was the most powerful noble in Elizabeth's England. A courtier with a taste for military glory, Essex became the favourite of the ageing Queen Elizabeth in 1587 and gained much power in England in the following decade. A complicated and cultivated man, his influence was wide ranging, and he became a notable rival of Walter Raleigh. Essex achieved the pinnacle of his fame when he co-commanded a force which attacked Spain in 1596. His career took a downturn after that, with his commission from Elizabeth to lead an army against native forces in Ireland leading to failure.

His approach to James was not a mere act of cavalier desperation, however. He had maintained an interest in Scottish politics for some time, having been sanctioned by Elizabeth as early as 1588 to act as an intermediary between the northern and southern royal courts. He had also sensitively acted on the queen's behalf in 1593, opening up a diplomatic dialogue with the Catholic Earl of Huntly in an effort to persuade him to fall into line with English policy. His choice of James as preferred successor was based on his sex, royal status and the fact that he was thought likely to appeal to a range of people across the religious spectrum. While Essex was still in Ireland during summer 1599, his close ally Lord Mountjoy wrote to James VI, assuring him that both he and Essex supported James's right to succeed Elizabeth. Though doubtless music to the Scottish king's ears, he would have realised that Essex was no longer quite the favourite he was and had an agenda of his own. Mountjoy, who became Lord Deputy in Ireland, contacted James again with a more detailed proposal. He suggested that he bring 4-5,000 men from Ireland and combine these with troops raised by both Essex and James himself to establish the right of James to become King of England by force. James expressed vague and cautious support, aware that any recklessness might destroy his hopes, so the plan came to nothing.[1]

Essex failed to proceed with Elizabeth's aggressive campaign in Ireland and came to an accommodation with some Irish leaders. He retreated to England and fell from grace when he broke into Queen Elizabeth's chamber in an attempt to justify his actions. At Christmas 1600 Essex fired off a powerful letter to James, warning him that there was a plot brewing to thwart his succession among enemies of both he and the king. He urged the king to take action against his foes. These included the Spanish, with whom England was still at war. In answer to Essex's plea, the king made ready to dispatch Earl of Mar to enter discussions with him. But events took an unprecedented turn in February 1601 when the Earl of Essex instigated what appears to have been a coup to overthrow the queen in London. Although Essex denied that he meant harm to the monarch, he was found guilty of treason and executed on 25 February.

It is interesting to speculate how James may have got on with Essex had the latter survived to remain a prominent nobleman greeting the new king of England, expectant of his reward for smoothing the transition of power. Luckily for James perhaps, Essex burned some of his secret papers on the day of his uprising and other possibly embarrassing communication was destroyed by an associate. Whereas Essex was a man hamstrung by his own misjudgements, the queen's close associate Cecil was the opposite and it was King James's great good luck to have him pushing for a peaceful transfer of power after Elizabeth, especially since he and Essex were enemies. Robert Cecil was the younger son of Queen Elizabeth's great, long-standing minister William Cecil, Baron Burghley (d.1598). Utterly committed to Elizabeth and then King James in turn, he was a man who served James as well as Sir John Maitland had done in Scotland, although Cecil maintained his own cunning policies, hidden from the monarch. Nor was his great power based on his physical stature. A small man, with a deformed back and large, vivid eyes, he was called 'my pygmy' or sometimes 'elf' by the queen, who had a fondness for giving her minions nicknames. King James gave Cecil a half-affectionate, half-condescending canine alias: 'the little beagle that lyes at hoame by the fyre quhen all the goode houndis are daylie running on the feildis.'[2] Cecil may not have cared for the king's playful description of him, nor for the occasional condescending alternative 'my littill wiffe waffe', but both were preferable to his enemies labelling him 'Robert the Devil'.

For all his unprepossessing appearance, his great talent, as much as his family connections, ensured that he rose to power in the 1590s and comfortably took over his father's position as Secretary of State on his death. The Earl of Essex was strongly opposed to him and one of the aims of his uprising in 1601 was to depose him from power. There were suggestions that Cecil was directly responsible for arranging the fall of Essex,[3] but these seem mostly to be based on Cecil's growing unpopularity in the wake of the former favourite's execution. Essex certainly contributed in full measure to his own downfall.

James VI was singularly lucky that Cecil recognised him as the best possible (and only realistic) successor to the ageing Elizabeth I. He may have already considered the merits of backing Arbella Stuart, especially if her claim had been bolstered by marriage to another descendant of English royalty, but no English contender for the succession was closer in descent from royalty than King James VI. Foreign hopefuls were even more untenable, such as the Spanish infanta favoured by some Catholics, who would have been unacceptable to most of the nation. James's own Stuart cousin Arbella was not highly favoured because many people did not want another woman as monarch. James was possibly aware he was only the front runner by default, since there was no other viable Protestant ruler, though his ego may have obscured this realisation. Relations were complicated with Cecil since his father, Burghley, was the prime English agent responsible for putting Mary, Queen of Scots to death. On the other hand, Burghley must also have been aware that Cecil senior was strongly supportive of an Anglo-Scottish Protestant alliance, and even integration, and his son may have inherited this instinct to bring the two nations ever closer.

But there was still caution on either side of this delicate alliance. James had suspicions of Cecil in 1598 when an English Catholic named Valentine Thomas had rumoured that the Scottish king had asked him to kill Queen Elizabeth. Those who plotted against the monarch were ineligible for the crown, according to a 1585 law, and James believed that Cecil may have been behind the allegation. Although the queen advised that she did not believe the story, she would not issue a public statement confirming the king's innocence, leaving him fearful and insecure about the possible damage done to his position in the succession stakes. For his part, Cecil was paranoid about the queen discovering his secret correspondence with James. Great care was taken to encode the letters between the men. Cecil had at least one narrow escape from discovery when Elizabeth was walking in Greenwich Park and heard the post blow his horn. She asked that the bag of letters be brought to her, but Cecil knew that there would be letters from James and fell on his knees, begging her not to look at them. If she should do so, he said, people would think it would be out of suspicion and jealousy of him and he would be unable to work effectively for her any longer. Elizabeth luckily complied with his wishes.[4]

In the first letter that Cecil dispatched to James, he reassured him that the queen believed in dynastic legitimacy and would never 'cut off the natural branch and graft upon some wild stock'. However, any outright demand of James for recognition as heir would be taken by her as a threat. Taking the hint, the king's communications with the queen abruptly changed from nagging and petty to full of love and attentiveness. Elizabeth, in her prime, would have suspected there was something amiss in this new attentiveness of King James. As well as prudently taking Cecil's advice, King James recognised the need for further high-level support in England and forged links with two powerful Catholic noblemen, Lord Henry Howard and the Earl of Worcester. Cecil meanwhile began to consider moving against erstwhile allies in the anti-Essex faction, Lord Cobham and Walter Raleigh. Cecil informed Howard that these 'two hedgehogs ... would never live under one apple tree with him'. Cecil, like his father, was in the habit of carefully weighing his enemies and, where possible, setting up rivals against each other. Historian Thomas Wilson wrote in the seventeenth century that Cecil's father Burghley 'was like an aged tree that lets none grow which near him planted be'.

It was said that Raleigh had opposed the Scottish king's succession and favoured a Seymour to succeed to the English throne. The reality was that Cecil had turned against him, believing he was no longer a useful ally. His hatred was transmitted by King James. Howard was soon sending copious amounts of damning evidence against Cobham and Raleigh, and also the 9th Earl of Northumberland who was reported as having told his wife, 'He had rather the King of Scots was buried than crowned.'[5] Word also came from other sources that Cobham and Raleigh were speaking against King James. Accounts of the first encounter between the new king and the Raleigh are obscured by legend, though they provide an entertaining view of the homespun Scot and the sea dog whose every inch dripped with expensive jewels like an Elizabethan pearly king. Sir Walter's eventual fate was sealed as much by the personality clash as much as anything else. The writer John Aubrey (1626-1697) said of the charismatic Raleigh, 'He had that awfulness and ascendancy in his aspect over other mortals.' The meeting was made awkward by the king's horrible pun: 'O my soul, mon, I have heard *rawly* of thee.' It was even more embarrassing when the king boasted that he could have taken the English crown by force if he had chosen to. Raleigh observed that he wished that had happened, since the king would then have learned who his true friends were.[6] It was a response that James read as a veiled threat.

On the other hand, recognition of Cecil's continuing importance came quickly. Following the accession of James to the English throne, Cecil was quickly confirmed in his position of Principal

Secretary of State. Within several years he climbed up the ladder of nobility, becoming first a baron, then a viscount, and finally Earl of Salisbury in 1605. He was made Lord Treasurer of England in May 1608. Cecil's stabilising support was crucial to keeping the newly crowned king on track during the early years of his reign when he was profligate with the public purse, overambitious in his attempts to unite Scotland and England, and subject to deadly plots. The most notorious conspiracy, of course, was the Catholic Gunpowder Plot of 1605, which hoped to kill King James and his associates and install a more congenial rulership in the nation. The plot had begun to formulate in the mind of the premier instigator Robert Catesby as early as 1603, in reaction to James not delivering on the toleration which Catholics had expected under his rule and which he failed to deliver.

Although the plan to blow up Parliament with explosives stashed in the cellars was discovered by other parties, King James took full credit for finding out about and preventing the plot himself. In his egotistical relief at being delivered yet again from death, James may even have believed he had saved himself. Eight of the Catholic conspirators were eventually killed. Among those who watched the trials were the king and his family. There may have been a more subtle darkness at play behind the bold horror of the attempted regicide. There are suggestions that Robert Cecil himself was an *agent provocateur* involved in the plan, helping it on and then foiling it, to suit his long-term policies. Catesby's servant swore on his deathbed that Catesby and Cecil met three times, yet his story has never been substantiated. Whatever the truth of that, King James underestimated his right-hand man.

Not only was Cecil an indefatigable administrator and fiercely loyal to the crown, he also wisely accommodated (or suffered) the king's personality and sense of humour. James declared in 1609, 'I believe not a King in the world has such a Secretary as I have, both for earnest matter and great affairs and also for jest.'[7] During his last years, Cecil saw the danger of the influence that the king's favourite,

Robert Carr, was having. Cecil took offence at this untried youth rising too quickly in royal esteem, not through merit but because of the king's affections and 'cast out many mists before him, to hinder and damp his passage'. As Lord Treasurer he had every right to be alarmed by the amount of money the profligate king was throwing at the young man to win his love. To counter this and instil some sense of what was happening, he invited the king to dinner and showed him £5,000 in coin. When the king asked what such a huge amount was for, Cecil said it represented what James was going to reward Carr with. Shocked, the king changed his grant to less than half the amount.[8] Still, Cecil was ultimately unable to stem the tide of the king's profligacy, though he worked tirelessly to manage his government well. Defeated at last by overwork, he resorted to the healing waters of Bath in the spring of 1612 in an attempt to recover his health, but he died nearby. His death was pitilessly mocked by a number of people who said that he died of syphilis, comparing him to that other hated hunchback, Richard III.

If Carr was perceived as a minor problem, then Raleigh became a major one to Cecil and others. When James won England, he immediately replaced the English hero as captain of the guard with Sir Thomas Erskine. But while Raleigh was a popular hero, the public perception of the man and the reality were some distance apart. Early in his career he was regarded as an intellectual who used sarcasm against those whom he thought less clever, and he also took pride in being irreligious and arrogantly disregarded unpopularity. Even his close friend, the Earl of Northumberland, said of Raleigh, 'I knowe hem insolent, extreamly heated, a man that desirs to seeme to be able to swaye all mens fancies, all mens cowrses.'[9] His character was tempered later by the effects of long adversity, and he was redeemed by the bravery he showed when facing death. A man of undoubted brilliance and bravery, he came from a relatively modest background to carve out a place for himself at Elizabeth's court, attracting her attention because he was exactly the sort of decisive man of action she was drawn to. Ironically, it was just this characteristic that was an ingredient in him being mistrusted by King James I. James had seen quite clearly in Scotland the devastation that dynamic figures could wreak on peaceable governments, both while he was growing up and later when he was struggling with the complexities of being a king. Such men had taken him hostage for a year in the so-called Raid of Ruthven, and later individuals hellbent on pursuing their own agenda made it hard to maintain peace in the realm. The prime example of a chaotic maverick in Scotland was, of course, the Earl of Bothwell, who became the king's special nemesis. Even those unpredictable individuals like the earls of Arran and Huntly, who were largely allies, caused spectacular difficulties.

Cecil, as we have seen, instilled distrust of Raleigh before they had even met. James was easily misled by the opinions of those he valued, like Cecil, and his own judgement of people, particularly handsome men, was sometimes inadequate. On ascending the throne, James immediately dismissed Sir Walter Raleigh from his position of Captain of the Guard. He removed his primary sources of income and also took back Durham House, which Raleigh rented from the government. Worse was soon to come for Sir Walter when he was implicated on suspicion of treason and rounded up as someone supposedly involved in the Main Plot against the king. Charges against him were based on the confession and testimony of his friend, Lord Cobham, but were regarded as dubious by many. Raleigh's life was spared but he languished in the Tower of London until 1616.

Men like Walter Raleigh were not in the same mould as those who found favour with the king by means of flattery. Lord Henry Howard, who became the Earl of Nottingham, became a prime sycophant in the early days of the court of James I, and those who did not choose to overly praise his majesty often found the road to success barred. James himself professed to recognising this weakness. In his written advice to his son Henry, the *Basilikion Doron*, he tells him to choose servants 'free of that filthie advice of Flatterie, the pest of all Princes and wreck of Republicks'.[10] However, like much wise advice found in that book, he failed to follow it himself. One reason perhaps that King James fell so flat on his face in this regard is possibly that he was unused to the uncritical praise he attracted since there were few in Scotland, either noble or commoner, who chose to be so obsequious towards him. The inner circle at court were quick to spot the self-indulgent weak spot in the monarch and heap praise on him. Another Howard, Thomas, Earl of Suffolk, advised a petitioner on one occasion to praise the king's new horse. A nobleman who had recently failed to do so, he said, had been sent away with his petition not granted.[11] Henry Howard himself was a highly evolved political animal who was able to swim with the changing currents at the royal court. Possessed of a subtle and fine wit, he had a great store of reading and knowledge, 'excellent for outward Courtship, famous for secret Information, and cunning Flatterie'.[12] The Howards insinuated themselves with the king's first favourite in England, Robert Carr, and attempted to cement their place in the inner circle of the royal court.

Raleigh, on the other hand, was denied the opportunity to prosper. Pardoned by the king, he went on his last voyage to find the elusive treasures of El Dorado in 1617. Some of his men attacked a Spanish outpost, sparking outrage from Spain and even more outrage later when the Spanish demanded the former hero's death for violating a peace treaty between the two countries. King James betrayed Raleigh at the word of the Spanish ambassador, it was said. Raleigh's beheading, in October 1618, came not long after the scandal surrounding the death of Sir Thomas Overbury. The king's favourite Robert Carr, together with his wife, were found guilty of murder, but both were spared. The contrast between that leniency and the fate of Raleigh was stark.

Chapter 8

The King at Leisure

Poetry and the Hunt

The golden age of Scottish literature had long gone by the time that the aspiring young poet King James VI took up his pen early and published his first short collection of writing in his late teens. Published in 1584, the modestly titled *Essayes of a Prentise in the Divine Art of Poesie* did not convince anyone that a new poetic genius had emerged. In this endeavour, unlike in others, King James had some idea of his limitations. The young king included a treatise laying out the rules that should be used in poetic composition, but his motivation may have been more dictatorial than inspired by the tradition of poetry in his native land. His interest in verse may still helped to make the art of poetry writing fashionable among the upper classes in Scotland and abroad.[1]

While the king achieved some competence in poetry and could translate heartfelt sentiments and ideas to the page, he was never more than adequate in the art, being too fastidious in thought to be a good poet. Scottish letters had flourished in the early part of the reign of the king's great-grandfather, King James IV, and previously. Men like Robert Henryson and William Dunbar partly depended on royal patronage and in turn provided a unique perspective of the royal court, even if they observed from the margins of that world. What would the humorous and sometimes cynical eye of the great Dunbar have made of the character and behaviour of King James VI? Dunbar and his associates had vanished by the time James started to dabble in poetry. The Scottish Reformation had a deadening effect on Scottish poetry, stifling a rich tradition which was, for a brief period at least, more advanced and original than contemporary poetry in England.[2]

King James VI had contact with some fellow poets in Scotland as a young adult and was long reputed to be the guiding force behind a group of writers later termed the Castalian Band. This loose group faded from prominence after the king swiftly shifted south following the death of Queen Elizabeth. Even before this date, in a bid to promote himself to the English masses, King James had begun to anglicize his published writings. Among the very loose group of the Castalian Band artists was the poet Alexander Montgomerie, William Fowler, and the English brothers Thomas and Robert Hudson. The very name Castilian Band may come from one of the king's own poems, an epitaph on Montgomerie, who died around 1598. But the existence of this group seems to be more a construction of modern scholarship than a cohesive band of artists that really existed.[3]

Delving into the king's poetry for clues about his inner life is not a rewarding task. While the subject of his love for Esmé Stuart can be seen clearly in his poem about the phoenix, the meaning of others is unclear. The group of twenty poems called the *Amatoria* are also complicated because some of them have been edited by the king's son Charles I and some may also have been written in collaboration with the king's friend, Sir Thomas Erskine of Gogar.[4] The subject of most of these poems concern friendships within the king's close circle, though none are outright love lyrics. Most of the material can be seen as intellectual exercises than as the result of actual experience. There is a series of poems that concern the king's marriage to Anne of Denmark, but the language is centred around the symbolic and stately aspects of the union rather than the king's own deep desire for love.

A tantalising clue about a little-known aspect of the king's private life, however, might be glimpsed in his poem entitled *A Dreame on his Mistris Lady Glammis*. The subject of this poem is thought to be Anne Murray, daughter of the king's companion Sir John Murray, who was later created Earl of Tullibardine. Anne married Patrick Lyon,

Lord Glamis, in 1595. The verse speaks of the lady being magically transported to the writer while he dreams, and undoubtedly has erotic overtones. Sir John Carey mentioned Anne Murray in a letter to Lord Burghley in May 1595 and referred to her explicitly as the king's mistress, but there is no trace anywhere else of a relationship between the two. Elsewhere in his poetry, James wrangled with the complex issues of politics and faithfulness to God. He stirred up some controversy by his translation of *Lepanto* in the 1580s, which was a celebration of the Spanish victory over the Turks in 1571. Recognising that it could be seen as a glorification of Catholicism, he carefully used the word Christian in the work, reflecting his own ecumenical inclination (which was always present when he was in a tolerant state of mind).

The king's serious interest in poetry dwindled towards the end of his Scottish rule as he began writing prose on a broad range of other subjects including kingcraft, witchcraft, religion, and tobacco. The range and depth of his writing show that James was confident with his own intelligence, though he was not a highly cultured man. Although he presided over (and partially sponsored) a range of cultural heavyweight artists such as Shakespeare, John Donne, and Inigo Jones, the blooming Jacobean arts flourished in parallel with the king and had little influence on his thinking. He had no abiding interest in the arts, fine or otherwise. His tastes contrast notably with his son, King Charles I, who amassed a great collection of European paintings. Charles, a ruler who often seemed like a flip side of his father's character, did not often turn his hand to writing, though he edited King James's work and probably composed the sorrowful, religious meditation *Eikon Basilike* shortly before his execution.

Attendance at a masque or play occasionally bored King James to the point of yawning, though consumption of alcohol may have been a factor. After he nearly fell asleep during Ben Johnson's *Pleasure Reconciled to Virtue* in 1618, he crudely complained at the lack of spectacular choreography: 'Why don't they dance? What did they bring me here for? Devil take you all, dance.' His favourite, Villiers,

Above: Gowrie House, Perth, showing the building after the Black Turnpike was removed.

Right: Witches' sabbat from *Newes from Scotland*, 1591.

Above and left: Officially sanctioned image of James I as huntsman and noble ruler.

Above left and above right: Henry, Lord Darnley and Ésme Stuart, Duke of Lennox.

Right: James Douglas, Earl of Morton.

Above left: Portrait of King James VI and I in private collection.

Above right: Depiction of the fight in Gowrie House (*c.* 1700).

Above left and above right: King James as ruler of Great Britain. Robert and Frances Carr, Earl and Countess of Essex.

Above left: George Buchanan.

Above right: Thomas Overbury.

Above left: Henry, Prince of Wales.

Above right: Prince Charles.

Rev. Robert Bruce.

Elizabeth of Bohemia.

Right: Hearse of King James in Westminster Abbey.

Below: George Gordon and Henrietta Stuart, Earl of Countess of Huntly.

Above left: Arbella Stuart.

Above right: Anne of Denmark.

Left: Mary, Queen of Scots.

dully responded by jumping up and performing a few capers. The king was equally impatient when it came to posing for portraits. His patronage of the arts was no more than might have been expected from any monarch (with conspicuous generosity enhancing his own esteem), and much less than more artistically minded kings and queens. The King James Bible may have been sponsored by James, but did not have much input from him beyond the commissioning process.

James was altogether more at home outdoors, pursuing his passion of hunting, which he gleefully followed in England and Scotland. Perhaps because of his early infirmity and continued awkwardness with mobility, James was addicted to the speed and danger that hunting on horseback could bring him. The thrill certainly compensated for the inadequacy of other parts of royal life and gave him the opportunity to avoid his subjects in the company of a small band of followers. During his younger days he was only held back in his outdoor pursuits by his inadequate means. An observer in 1579 noted his delight in hunting and riding, although his relative poverty meant that he had only a handful of horses to ride. The Earl of Arran slyly distracted him by encouraging his interest in hunting in order to distract him from everyday government. An Englishman observed in 1588 that the king loved hunting better than religion. Soon after James came to power in England, the amount of time he spent in the field as opposed to dealing with matters of state was seen as a problem. In 1607 an Italian observed that the king was passionately devoted to hunting, which he treated as medicine as much as exercise. He neglected government and left it in the hands of his council and ministers, a charge which had been made by others as far back as his early personal rule in Scotland.[5] In contrast to Elizabeth, who spent only a few days a year in hunting, the king's preoccupation with it gave him a frequent chance to vacate London, a city which he loathed.

The image the monarch hoped to present, as a virile, outdoor huntsman, was not always viewed in a positive light by others.

He would dress all in green, with a feather in his cap and a horn at his side, not a sword, which some thought would have been more manly. This image of the king in his sporting garb was enough to inspire secret contempt in some. A ballad which portrays him as a roguish hunter may have found favour with him, if he had heard it, though it only seems to have become popular long after his death. This song, 'King James I and the Tinkler', tells of 'a pleasanter monarch sure never was known', who is encountered incognito by a poor man whom he later knights.[6] The storyline is stolen wholesale from a ballad which recounted an escapade possibly undertaken by his more genuinely adventurous grandfather King James V.

While the chase was a standard part of an aristocratic lifestyle, there were some who thought the king's single-minded hunting mania pointed towards a concealed cruelty. One foreign observer noted that the king was merciful except when hunting, and he would become furious when he could not corner and kill a stag. After the kill he would delightedly plunge his arms into the belly and entrails of the beast.[7] This observation possibly derives from a misunderstanding of the gruesome but commonplace practice of taking the assay of a stag. This involved the leader of the hunting party formally cutting open the slain deer in front of all assembled. In his bloodlust, King James took the already grotesque ritual to extremes due to his ravenous appetite for the sport. The king's heedless nature in the field was also noted by Sir Roger Wilbraham, who wrote in 1603, 'The King hath a magnanimous spirite, venturous to hazard his owne bodie in hunting especiallie & most patient of labour cold & heate'.[8]

Many nobles, including Queen Elizabeth herself, favoured a more genteel form of killing wild creatures whereby they remained immobile and shot at the animals that were driven past. But James despised this 'theevish' form of killing and preferred galloping after the hounds as they careered across the countryside in hot pursuit of a stag. Only when he was incapable of chasing after animals himself would he resort to the sort of hunting he despised. One instance of this was when he was recovering from serious illness in 1619.

Too weak to get on horseback, he had a herd of deer driven past him in Theobalds Park and targeted them with his crossbow. In later years in England, he would pick out a chosen stag from a large herd, let his pack of thirty or so hounds latch onto its scent, and then pursue the unfortunate beast to its doom. Yet he was not always such a purist in his lust for killing. In 1605 it was observed that he took a delight in catching larks, which surely his companions would not have thought of as a noble sport. Bear-bating, fox hunting, cock- and bull-fighting also occasionally featured in the king's leisure time, as well as the more decorous sport of watching horse racing.[9]

The king's advice to his son Henry in *Basilikon Doron* strongly advises that mastery of horsemanship is a kingly attainment. He recommended to the price his own practices in hunting with dogs as being the most honourable and was a connoisseur of killing, according to his own tastes. 'As for hawking,' he added, 'I condemn it not, but I must praise it sparingly.'[10] He likened his hunting to warfare, which made a man hardy and kept him alive to the vagaries of mischance, though he admitted that his chosen sport was 'an extreme stirrer up of passions'. Despite his lifelong devotion, he was at times inept in the saddle and suffered mishaps on numerous occasions. There was the time in 1580 that a loose seat and poor hands led his mount to fall upon him. He had a similar accident near Newmarket in November 1614, escaping with only bruising. Other ignoble accidents are peppered through the official records, such as the time he toppled from his mount when hunting near Falkland Palace in May 1601 and hurt his left shoulder. Few would have ventured to criticise the king's competence in country sports, especially when the weather or some other distraction prevented him from pursuing prey and sent him into a rage. Observers acidly noted his lack of prowess, such as the Lancashire gentleman Nicholas Assheton, who observed the king shoot at a stag in August 1617 and entirely miss. He only managed to find his target when the beast was twice shot by a companion.

The king's devotion to his hobby nearly proved fatal on his journey south from Edinburgh in 1603. James had heard that every

English gentleman maintained a well-stocked park for hunting, and he announced that he intended to use as many of them as possible on his way south to London. Among the many places he stopped was Widdrington Castle, where he killed two deer and feasted royally in the evening. On the estate of John Harington, he fell heavily from his horse, but was so excited by the hunt that he continued in the pursuit. The next day he was obliged to travel by coach when it was clear that he had broken his collar bone.

Heated enthusiasm led the king to take risks during his outdoor expeditions and he was careless of his own safety when seeking his prey. A Venetian reported in 1617 that he never held the reigns in his hand and relied on the support of grooms who rode on either side of him. Every now and then he had falls, but this was blamed on the hot temper of the breed of hackneys he rode, rather than his own clumsy impatience.[11] He also jealously safeguarded his own pleasure grounds, making a proclamation in 1603 forbidding hunting in royal forests. He later decreed that no one outside the royal family could go hunting with hounds within four miles of London. Important officials from foreign countries were banned from going to see him in the countryside because he wanted no distractions from his leisure activities. But the king did keep a line of communication open with Whitehall and had a system of receiving important news and information from his servants, and, during his later years, from trusted favourites like George Villiers. Despite this, it is doubtful that he expended as much attention as necessary on government. An anecdote is told of how his favourite hound, Jowler, once went missing and the king was extremely upset. Next day, Jowler appeared among the other hounds when the king was out hunting. Someone had mischievously tied a note around its neck which read, 'Good, Mr Jowler, we pray you speak to the king (for he hears you every day, and so he doth not us) that it will please his majesty to go back to London; for else the country will be undone; all our provision is spent already, and we are not able to entertain him longer.' Despite the blatant message in the jest, King James dawdled in the neighbourhood for another fortnight. In 1605 the monarch humorously characterised his interests as 'witches, prophets, puritans, dead cats and hares', though not necessarily in that order. If he had some insight that his priorities were misjudged, he did not say so.

King James enjoyed the escape from the pomp of the court and more particularly enjoyed the security of being enclosed with a small group of followers, usually all male. A favoured set of hunting bases was endlessly frequented around southern England. These including not only his mansion of Theobalds, but more primitive hunting lodges at Newmarket and Royston. The queen refused to use these establishments and preferred to stay at local villages on the occasions when she joined the king. Neither of the king's sons were as enamoured of the chase as he was, though Princess Elizabeth was keen on the sport and was known as the 'Diana of the Rhine' after her marriage and relocation to the Continent. Prince Henry did have a love of horses and would go hunting, but took greater pleasure in seeing his own animals enjoying their exercise. Once Henry was out hunting when a stag he was pursuing was killed by the dog of a butcher in the area. The prince's huntsman was incensed, but the prince himself was calm. When the huntsman observed that his royal father would have sworn so much that no man could have endured it, Prince Henry piously stated that no pleasure in the world was worth an oath.

The cost and the carnage caused by the king's obsession was another matter. The hunting pack was prone to indiscriminately trample crops and disturb grazing beasts when they passed through. Some were brave enough to tackle the king about his own disregard of farming. A farmer from Thetford was so enraged about the ruin of his land that he threatened to sue the king for trespass.[12] Hunting in general was criticised by some as a destructive enterprise, with the queen's chaplain in 1616 remarking how harmful it was to the poor farmers. In parallel with this was the cynical enclosure of common land by upper-class landowners, which further alienated the rulers from the ruled. In June 1607 a law was enacted to stop protests about enclosures. This followed the Midland Uprising, in which around fifty people were killed. While he was in pursuit across the fields, the king was liberated from the petty troubles of the court, but also isolated from the necessary concerns of government; free from troublesome crowds but fixated on pursuit of his own pleasure while trampling over the rights and the land of the people he ruled. Part of him perhaps also enjoyed the separation from his own family and his favourites. Neither Robert Carr nor George Villiers, his two principal male loves, were massively involved in hunting. Only Philip Herbert boasted a love of hounds and horses, which temporarily endeared him to the monarch.

Even as he approached his final years, the love of the hunt did not diminish for the king. In 1620 a courtier anxiously sought out the ruler to tell him about troubling developments on the Continent and eventually found him walking down a country lane in the midst of 'beagles, spaniels, greyhounds, sparrow-hawks and goshawks'. He was the very image of a 'Grand Cazador,' or great huntsman. The king struggled to keep physically active in the last years but was loathe to give up his favourite activity. As early as 1613 it was noted that he could not participate in hunting without some pain. His lifelong weakness in the lower limbs made him also very clumsy in riding and hunting, as his physician once observed, and in later years he had to be awkwardly trussed in the saddle. In 1623 it was noted that he went hunting nearly every day, and in the following year he was out hunting six days a week when it suited him. Despite physical decline, accidents and grumblings from some underlings, it is clear that the king associated the outdoor life (or his version of it) as healthy, in comparison to the stifled courtly existence he was sometimes forced to endure in London. Being in London, he observed, took years off his life. In 1605, to counter criticism, he wrote to his council in London that hunting was the only means by which he could maintain his own health.

The year 1619 was one of evil omen for the king. A comet seen streaking across the sky early in the year did not bode well. The king was struck by a serious illness, during which the queen died. He was too ill to attend her funeral (not that he would have done so in good health anyway). Loose tongues said that he would soon follow his wife to the grave. In June of that year, he was still badly afflicted by gout, but went hunting anyway and devised a bloody remedy for his illness. On a Saturday hunt in Eltham Park he slew a buck, slit open its belly and bathed his bare feet and legs in the hot blood, thinking this would cure his illness, and indeed was nimble ever since.[13] It was a strange belief and practise for the self-proclaimed man of peace who disdained all superstitious practise.

Chapter 9

Lion Versus Unicorn

The Ill-Made Marriage of Scotland and England

The proposed formal joining of England and Scotland under King James's benevolent, fatherly eye did not happen in his lifetime, to his profound disappointment. Like his own personal relationships, this proposed pairing of nations had elements of love and hate, distrust, and comedic misunderstanding (which lingers to this day). Despite the eventual union of countries in 1707, there was something slightly grotesque underlying the forcible joining of these two intractable nations.

The king who sought to forge Great Britain experienced the underlying tension between Scots and English in his infancy. In the sumptuous surroundings of the Great Hall of Stirling Castle on 17 December 1566 there was an unseemly cultural and diplomatic incident during the baptism celebrations of Prince James of Scotland. An elaborate entertainment was devised by a Frenchman named Bastian to entertain the noble guests who had come from various nations for the event. During the feast an array of nymphs, fauns and other apparently inoffensive woodland spirits pranced among the tables, carrying food and generally frolicking. But when the satyrs waved their long tails at a contingent from England, those noble guests took offence. One of their number, a man named Hatton, was only prevented from stabbing the French master of ceremonies by the appeasement of the English ambassador, and Mary, Queen of Scots herself.[1] The English assumed that the tail wagging was a reference to a widespread racial slur common in many European nations which insisted that Englishmen had tails. The Scottish version of this slander (published in the *Scotichronicon*, 1440) states that in the sixth century St Augustine was so badly treated by pagans in Devon that he cursed them and all their descendants with tails. Here as elsewhere, the Scots were part of a mainstream European current of thought very different to English thinking.

Tensions between England and Scotland were never far from the surface. In the decades before the union of crowns there was a hope that the conversion to Protestantism in both nations might end centuries of mutual suspicion. But this did not happen. If there was gentle mockery of the English during that joyous day at Stirling, there was also another element in the celebrations which made the visiting southerners uncomfortable. This was a Latin poem composed by Patrick Adamson which recalled a supposed prophecy of Merlin to claim that this son of Queen Mary was fated to catapult the house of Stewart (or Stuart as it was becoming known) to even further greatness: 'The fates will grant you to extend the territory of your realm, until the Britons, having finished with war, will learn at last to unite in one kingdom.'[2]

The claim of James VI to rule a united island of Britain was therefore present from his very birth. The grand idea of a British state to recreate ancient Britannia was James's grand plan which he promoted enthusiastically as soon as he set foot in England in 1603. The fact that he was able to step into the vacant shoes of the departed Queen Elizabeth so easily perhaps gave him false confidence that he could re-engineer the British Isles according to his own ideal. His failure to politically unite Scotland and England was not only due to the antipathy between the nationalities, but to practicalities like the difficulty of replacing centuries-old English law with new legislation applicable to a new British state. Francis Bacon met the new king soon after his arrival and conveyed his shrewd impressions to the Earl of Northumberland. He noted that the monarch 'hasteneth to a mixture of both kingdoms and nations, faster perhaps than policy will conveniently bear'. Yet Bacon himself favoured the union and promoted the name of Britain for the enlarged nation, though others fancied the grander ancient alternative of Albion. When the newly enthroned King James I of England enjoyed a stately procession, he was lauded by an oration at the Tower of London which boasted that the partition between the two kingdoms was gone; there would be one king, one kingdom, one land of Albion.[3]

The idea of one island nation had been promoted by James before he became king of England. On the day when Queen Elizabeth died the Scottish minister and lawyer Robert Pont went to see King James and enthusiastically greeted him as 'King of Great Britain, France and Ireland'.[4] In his *Basilikon Doron* he advised his elder son, Henry, that union might be accomplished through the natural mingling of citizens from both countries, though he recognised the traditional enmity that existed:

> in the times of our ancestours, the long warres, and many bloodie battels betwixt these two countries, bred a naturall and herediterie hatred ... the uniting and welding of them hereafter in one, by all sort of friendship, commerce and alliance, will by the contrary produce and maintaine a naturall and inseparable unitie of love amongst them.[5]

Even earlier, the birth of Prince Henry, in 1594, bolstered James's claim to the throne of England. And he sponsored concepts that this heir was not merely Scotland's king, but the fated ruler of a new Britain. The churchman Andrew Melville wrote a poem which dared to speak of Henry as a prince born to rule a Scoto-Britannic state. Queen Elizabeth became infuriated with the insinuation and even accused King James of treason, an accusation he shrugged off.

By 1604 the newly installed king of England was envisaging a future that would see the merging of separate churches, legal systems, privy councils and all the rest in one seamless system. Following his move to London, the English Parliament debated the creation of a new island political entity in early 1604 and it became quickly obvious that there was serious doubt about the project. Some went along with the king's optimistic nation-building venture, such as the Welsh member Sir William Morrice, who made a long speech in the House of Commons, expounding on the king's pedigree and calling him an emperor. Those opposed to the merger in England could see no economic gain or other benefits from shackling two nations together. Well-reasoned arguments about safeguarding the English economy were linked to a sense that the country would suffer from an influx of foreigners. Sir Henry Spelman's tract *On The Union* (1604), voiced native concern:

> The English ar our family; shall we then give awaye their breadde, which is their freedomes and libertyes, unto straungers? Mak the Scottes free of Englande, what will be the sequele? ...But our houses, our lands, our livings shall by that meanes be bought upp in all places. The citty and country shal be replenished with Scottes.[6]

Francis Bacon countered the fear with the observation that many Scots had migrated to France without overturning that country's culture. England was not overcrowded and could accommodate an influx of people. He also echoed the sentiments of King Henry VII, over a century before, when he said that any formal partnership between England and Scotland would always mean that England would predominate over Scotland as the major partner. The king assured the English there was no chance of being overwhelmed by a vast horde from the far north. Scotland, he mischievously observed, had abundant waste territories which might be utilised for the resettlement of unwanted English subjects, if needs be. Yet parliaments in both states were against political union. On the religious side, Scottish clerics feared integration under Canterbury and some English religious figures felt integration might lead to a Calvinistic influx which would bolster Puritan power south of the border.

An anonymous satire in 1605 predicted that King James would meet his death for using the name of Britain. King James suspected that the work had been composed by Guy Fawkes. In the same year the king hardened his attitude toward those who opposed his union. 'He that doth not love a Scotsman as his brother, or the Scotchman that loves not an Englishman as his brother is a traitor to God and the King.'[7] Scottish noblemen and councillors petitioned the king in 1607-8 to drop the whole plan for national integration.[8] Although there was little anti-English fuss (and some pride) when their king claimed the English crown in 1603, the Scots did not want to be conjoined with a country which obviously held them in contempt.

To safeguard the link with the crown, some Scots suggested that either the king himself or his eldest son, Prince Henry, should reside in their country. In a speech to the English Parliament on 31 March 1607 the king disingenuously denied the 'alleadged ... aversenesse' of the Scots towards a political union. He urged for a perfect union of laws and persons, and strangely cited the ancient union which allowed for the creation of the proto-Scottish kingdom of Alba, when the Picts and Scots conjoined in the mid-ninth century. Few English parliamentarians would have had time for that historical analogy. Again, with his eye on the concerns of his native nation, he said a new union would not be a political conquest, but a conquest cemented by love.[9] But the Scots remained vocal in expressing their fears about being turned into a slavish province ruled over by a viceroy or other functionary. In fact, the prevalent Scottish opinion on unity was remarked as early as 18 September 1603, when the Venetian ambassador stated that, 'The Scottish have already let it be known that they will never consent to abandon their name.'[10] Scottish suspicion about an English takeover refused to die down. In 1610, the Scottish Privy Council had to take measures against spoken and written anti-English sentiment.

In 1607 King James admitted he had underestimated the strength of feeling against union: 'The errour was my mistaking; I knew mine owne ende, but not others feares'.[11] Speaking to Parliament in May, he announced that he was the embodiment of the perfect union, an esoteric concept inextricably tied to his own ego. Stung by the continuing delays by politicians over his cherished ideal, he threatened to remove the royal court to somewhere equidistant from London and Edinburgh, not only to show equal favour to both his nations, but to discomfit the London establishment.

If the Scots feared being swamped by the English and losing control of their institutions and identity, the English fear of being overrun by Scots was less easy to understand. Sir John Harington recognised the irrational fear of his fellow Englishmen as early as 1602, when he wrote that the dread of Scottish conquest was 'foolish fears of men that commonly draw on by fearing that which they most fear'.[12] Notable among the Scottophobes was Sir Christopher Piggot who made an anti-Scottish rant in Parliament on 13 February 1604, calling the Scots thieves and murderers and regicides, which landed him in the Tower of London, though he was freed after a short while. Although the main aim of the Gunpowder Plot in 1605 was not racially motivated, Guy Fawkes was recorded as stating that he hoped to blow some of the Scots back to their homeland. Intellectuals joined in the game, with Sir Roger Owen theorising that the word Scot derived from '*scotios*, darkness in Greek'.

While national antipathy was real enough, actual violence was rare. At the Croydon races in May 1611, a Scot named Patrick Ramsay (brother of the hero of the Gowrie Conspiracy) assaulted the Earl of Montgomery (a former favourite of the king) with a riding rod after being insulted by him and sparked a brawl. It was thought that loss of life was only prevented because none of the participants had deadly weapons. The king had to spend several weeks sorting it out.[13] There were ongoing incidents of anti-Scottishness among the general population, with several violent incidents between Scotsmen and Englishmen occurring in London in 1612. Most notable was an inter-ethic argument at Inns Court which resulted in so much anti-Scottish feeling that 300 Scots fled back north within ten days.

Scot-hating was a nationwide phenomenon. John Tawte, a Chichester cobbler, got drunk one night in October1603 and ran up and down the street shouting that the Scots had brought a plague into the nation. In 1608 a Newcastle man named John Bacheler was heard wishing that his wife would have a son so it would be a counterbalance for all the Scots dominating the country. In the previous year an expansive Londoner ranted to his nephew in a letter, 'Away with Scots and Danes and English atheists, their complices or woe to England forever.'[14] There was a broad suspicion of many foreign countries in England at this period which shows a lively xenophobia. Spaniards, people from the Low Countries, and Catholics in general were cast in the same suspicious category as the Scots.[15] It has been pointed out that the overriding English interest in Scotland up to this time was a desire to colonise it, but by the time the Scottish king came south to rule, the English aspiration had evaporated and largely turned into apathy towards Scotland.[16]

For James, who was most pedantic and forensic when it came to matters of theology or kingship, the woolly notion of Britishness was a fantasy hatched from his genuine wish to extend amiability far and wide over those realms which he ruled. The imperfect first half of his life had involved rule over Scotland, he said, and the second perfect half would see him rule England. It was a personal matter to him that the nations under his rule not only tolerated each other but learned to love each other. Several years later he told Robert Cecil that anyone who hated Scots must also hate him: 'that nation cannot be hated by any that loves me'.[17] The king emotionally identified himself as the husband who was wedded to the whole island of Britain in a speech to the English Parliament in 1604:

> What God hath conjoyned then, let no man separate. I am the Husband, and all the whole Isle is my lawful Wife; I am the Head, and it is my Body; I am the Shepherd, and it is my flocke; I hope therefore no man will be so unreasonable as to thinke that I that am a Christian King

under the Gospel, should be a Polygamist and husband to two wives; that I being the Head, should have a diuided and monstrous Body.[18]

This highly personal concept was not an idea that many found attractive or could even understand.[19] It is just as well that King James did not elaborate on this occasion since it is suspected he was alluding to the ancient and specifically Scottish and Irish custom of the new ruler being ritually mated to the goddess who symbolised the land.[20] Sometimes James referred to his own supposed Gaelic lineage as a means of catapulting his claim of kingship stretching back unbroken into the remote past. He was equally adept at calling up genealogical links to the Welsh, Saxons, and others as circumstances demanded. But bluff English politicians did not make a receptive audience for royal Celtic mysticism. It was a clearly cynical ploy on the king's part since he was known to despise the barbarism of Scotland's Gaelic Highlands and Islands.

Some Scots saw the accession of King James VI to the English crown as the fulfilment of ancient prophecies. Prophetic verses had been manipulated by various hands throughout the sixteenth century as part of a propaganda war between the ruling dynasties and the nations of Scotland and England. The Stone of Scone, carried to London by Edward I in 1296, was said to have been engraved with a verse acting as a mystical time bomb proclaiming that, wherever the stone was taken, a Scot would eventually be crowned king.[21] Prophecies ascribed to the thirteenth-century seer True Thomas were used to bolster the Scots in their War of Independence against Edward I. His rhymes concerning a descendant of King Robert Bruce claiming the English throne were remembered on the death of Queen Elizabeth and taken more seriously, having been a subject for humour previously.[22] The old lore was believed by the educated as well as common folk, so the fulfilment of this prophecy through the person of James VI was proudly recalled by Scots such as John Spottiswood (d.1639), archbishop and chancellor of Scotland.[23]

Verses and ballads circulated to bolster James VI's historic right. Among the poems produced was one by the Irish poet Walter Quin, who arrived in Edinburgh in 1595, which boldly claimed that the king of Scots was worthy enough to claim the ancient throne of King Arthur.[24] Sir William Alexander (later Earl of Stirling) mentions a prophecy foretelling James uniting the whole island in the dedication to the king of his work the *Monarchicke Tragedies*. Intellectuals like the mathematician James Maxwell embraced the spirit of prophecy; all the more surprising given the fact he was a puritan Protestant and this branch of arcane knowledge had been decried as the work of demons by hard-line Protestants such as John Knox.[25] Among those who used Maxwell's material was the strange Scottish polymath Dr George Eglisham, who wove some of the material into verses that heralded King James as leading Britain into a glorious future, while his son Charles would triumphantly lead Christendom to victory against the heathen Turks. Eglisham claimed to have been one of the medics treating the king right at the end of his life and he stirred up massive controversy when he accused the favourite the Duke of Buckingham of poisoning him.[26]

James's accession in England was also linked with an ancient, hazy Britain of mythology and legend. Legends of supposedly Welsh origin were bandied about, including the claim that the king's accession was the fulfilment of a prophecy that a descendant of the ancient ruler Cadwaladr would one day rule all Britain. Imperial Rome was added to the mix: London was recast as Troy and featured in the lord mayor's show in 1605, where the theme was The Triumph of Reunited Britannia. On the silver coronation medal made in 1604 the king was described as 'James I, Caesar Augustus of Britain, Caesar the heir of Caesars.' Casting the new super-state of Britain as an empire put it on the same footing as the larger powers in Europe.

Another prophetic strain took its authority from the bible and was sanctioned even by severe Protestants, especially if it had anti-Catholic bias. But the Kirk frowned upon such dubious ancient oracles like Merlin as they smacked of diabolism. Nor did the strictly religious factions in Britain much fancy the overblown, poetic concept which predicted that King James would be the new Constantine, defeating the Turks, converting the Jews, and uniting all Christianity.[27] John Gordon, the Scottish born deacon of Sarum, preached that the re-establishment of the glorious, unified nation of Britain had been ordained by God. He said that the division of the island was evil and inspired by Satan and that any union must begin in the hearts of men. While King James may have said 'amen' to that, one can imagine the more sceptical English listening being appalled by the supposedly heavenly sanction of union. 'The name *Brit-an-iah* [Britannia],' Gordon exclaimed, 'was a propheticall name from the beginning, foreshewing that the covenant of God should be established in this Iland, at the appointed time by God.'[28]

The adjacent nations remained stubbornly different, with populations that did not regard each other fondly. Ireland was a separate kingdom legally subject to the English crown and only recently pacified. After a stormy relationship, the Acts of Union which tied Wales to England had been passed without major conflict in 1536 and 1543. Even Englishmen not overtly hostile to the Scots and unconcerned with the Scots at the court were indifferent to the British merger. But the king kept on trying. Even his common-sense observation that Scotland had often been used as a back door to attack England by devious European powers, and should therefore be drawn closer to England, was not enough to capture the hearts and minds of those who counted, though some English writers did see the benefit of severing the traditional Auld Alliance between Scotland and France. A mere few decades of wary peace between England and Scotland were not enough to create warmth between them. The fact that a king born in one country ruled another was a new phenomenon for England and Scotland, though fairly common in Europe, and the results there were not often permanent or happy.

Anti-Scottish feeling in England continued to be the subject of literature. A successful satire which targeted Scotland appeared in 1617 under the title of *A Perfect Description of the People and*

Country of Scotland. Usually ascribed to Sir Anthony Weldon (1583-1648), it seems to have been motivated by its author's sourness at the lack of advancement under King James I. The work outlines an Englishman's comedically appalled reaction to the northern nation while in the company of the king on his one and only homecoming journey north of the border in 1617. (Weldon's attack on the king, *The Court and Character of King James*, was also critical of the court.) There was common talk, Weldon said, that the horde of Scots would impoverish the nation; indeed, 'beggardly Scots (or Blue Caps)' became a byword. It was alleged that when some poorer Scots came to the king complaining of their lowly state, the king humorously told them not to worry, he would shortly make the English as poor as them. This he did, says Weldon, by depleting both himself and the nation in general.[29] Scots of the poorer sort were discouraged from migrating south by an order of the Privy Council in Edinburgh in 1611.

The *Perfect Description* scathingly attacks the king's native land, a country too good for the people who inhabit it and too bad for others to be bothered to conquer it. Although its air might begrudgingly admitted as wholesome, it was unfortunately polluted by the stink of its population. Even its clerics were illiterate, ignorant, and proud. Scotland's native creatures were singularly small, with the exception of the women, who were monstrous and only fit to be locked in cages, though no one in their right senses would want to carry them off. To be married to a Scot was likened to being 'tyed to a dead Carkasse and cast into a stinking ditch'. The tract was reprinted throughout the seventeenth century, a testament to the continuing trend of anti-Scottish animosity.

There were other humorous reflections of public contempt for the increased Scottish presence in England. One of these was the play *Eastward Ho!* (1605) which mentions the omnipresent Scots as a plague which might be encountered even in the New World across the Atlantic. The authorities rounded on the collaborative authors of the play, Ben Jonson, George Chapman, and John Marston. Punishment was not severe although a sentence of slit noses and ears was proposed at first. Jonson, who was of Scots ancestry, claimed that the offending passages were not his. He soon composed the masque *Hymenai* which contained positive comments on the union more in tune with the king's thinking. Nor was *Eastward Ho!* the only production of its kind to appear.

While few people in either realm were ready for complete integration, the king had other strategies. He fostered Anglo-Scottish integration in his own household and in the upper levels of society by encouraging families from both countries to marry. Some Scottish courtiers were quick to cotton on to the fact that marrying into the English upper classes was a fast track to success. Those upwardly mobile Scots who sought space at the top level of society in both nations were called 'amphibians' to reflect their ability to live in two worlds that were almost incompatible with each other. If a good many of them were paired off with suitably wealthy wives, many of these matches were second marriages and English wealth percolated north to bolster shakily financed Scottish estates.[30]

Balancing Scottish and English retainers in positions at court was a tricker matter. Some of Elizabeth's old advisers were kept on, but there was a marked influx of Scots in key positions under the new king. There were soon grumblings that these locusts from the north were becoming rich and insolent. There was an apparently disproportionate presence of Scots in key positions around the king, which stifled the ambitions of Englishmen who saw their pathway to success being blocked. One problem was that those Englishmen who might have expected reward at court had been held back by Elizabeth's tight fistedness and there was a scramble for preferment under the new regime. Scots may have held around forty per cent of the higher court offices over the course of King James I's reign.[31] Closest physically to the king were the staff of the bedchamber who controlled access to the king. In the middle of James's English reign in 1614, six out of the seven gentlemen of the bedchamber were still Scottish.[32] This imbalance had been in place from the beginning of his reign, although the king had tried to equalise numbers in the naive belief that it would make those Scots and English forced to work cheek by jowl begin to love each other. De Beaumont, the French ambassador, observed that the result was quite the opposite. The influx of Scots who flocked south to accompany their king as he assumed power in London was motivated as much by hope of riches as by loyalty to James. The king's falconer and barber (English born but Scottish raised), Sir Roger Aston, summed up the attitude when he answered the question about how he felt about his position coming back into England. He felt like 'a poore man wandring above forty years in a Wildernesse, and barren Soyle, and now arrived at the Land of Promise'.[33]

The atmosphere of the court was affected by the rise in honours doled out by the new king, which reflected the open-handed aspect of James's character. Whereas Queen Elizabeth was notoriously tight-fisted dispensing titles, her successor was prodigal. As the later seventeenth-century historian Arthur Wilson succinctly phrased it, knights swarmed in every corner. Elizabeth created 878 new knights during the whole of her reign, while the king made 906 knights in the first four months of his rule. One estimate states that James created 2,323 knights over the course of his reign.[34] Corruption was inevitable in such a large enterprise and the new title of baronetcy was offered for sale to bolster the crown's shaky finances. Other titles were gained by shady means. The Scots around the monarch were also blamed for the crown's financial woes. One MP spoke out against the Scots in 1610 and again four years later, wishing the king would send them home. He also darkly alluded to the Sicilian Vespers when the natives revolted against their French overlords.[35]

One reason perhaps why the venture to join two opposing countries together was doomed was that the king from a less powerful nation came to rule the greater one. The effort and enthusiasm that King James brought to the project to formally join his two kingdoms was immense, and had he succeeded, he would have been rightly recognised as a master nation-builder.[36] King James was possibly too flushed with success after surviving long battles with the warring nobles and the Kirk in Scotland and then winning the ultimate prize of England to appreciate that his union was unachievable. His attitude towards Scotland was also disingenuous to some degree. Despite his ongoing reliance on Scottish friends and a lingering fondness for his homeland, James was in fact ruthlessly Anglocentric when necessary and he recognised that any union would entail Scotland being very much the junior partner. Despite the lack of a political union, the union of crowns did, for a generation or two, dampen down the violent passions between the two countries, which was to the credit of the king. Later in the seventeenth century the peace between north and south was violently torn apart by bloody civil wars, and the notion of unity looked more distant than ever.

Chapter 10

The Nation's Second Scotsman

The Rise and Fall of Robert Carr

Between the death of Esmé Stuart, the Duke of Lennox, in 1583, and the next true favourite, Robert Carr, there was a space of twenty-two years. For much of that period the king concentrated on his marriage to Anne and their duty to provide royals heirs to his realms. But there is some information to suggest that the king did have personal contact with men after the exile and death of Lennox. The Englishman Thomas Fowler reported in the late 1580s that the king was believed to be overly influenced by young men who slept in his chamber. One of these, Alexander Lindsay, was 'the king's best beloved minion' and was afterwards created Lord Spynie.[1] Other contemporary sources use the same terminology and confirm that Lindsay was 'his nightly bed-fellow'. Lindsay caused jealousy among others because he was 'in great favour with his Majesty, and sometimes his bedfellow'.[2] Sandy, as he was affectionately known to the king, accompanied James on his marriage journey to Denmark and the king later returned the favour by encouraging him to marry a widow, Jean Lyon, setting a pattern whereby he actively sought to marry off his male favourites. In 1592 Lindsay fell out of royal favour when he was accused of being in league with the wild Earl of Bothwell. Although the charge came to nothing and he was formally restored to the king's favour, he never fully regained his trust. A son of the Earl of Crawford, his Lindsay kindred were notoriously riven by internecine violence. Lord Spynie tragically died in Edinburgh in 1607, accidently slain when he tried to intercede between his two brawling nephews.

It is difficult to determine whether there was personal intimacy between Lindsay and the king. The proximity of those trusted men who comprised the bedchamber together with the king's habit of being expressively loving to close associates disguises the facts about whether or not a sexual relationship was involved. After Lindsay, there is little evidence concerning close male favourites until King James encountered a young man named Philip Herbert, son of the Earl of Pembroke (who was afterwards created Earl of Montgomery). Nineteen-year-old Herbert was brought to the royal attention by Robert Cecil in May 1603. He seems to have been an unworthy recipient for the lavish attention which the king heaped on him. King James made him a gentleman of the privy chamber and knight of the Bath within a few months. Aside from his good looks, Herbert was a boorish and unsophisticated character with little to recommend him apart from a love of hunting which he shared with the king. But, in a pattern that the king was to repeat with subsequent favourites, he had honours and lands gifted to him and his huge debts were paid off. Montgomery showed scant appreciation for the sudden upturn in his fortune. He was finally discarded from his prime position as favourite when he was involved in an altercation with some Scots at Croydon races in 1611 which he had likely instigated.[3] Herbert became notorious for his ill temper and had violent outbursts, usually directed at his peers, including a bout of violence directed at the Earl of Southampton in 1610. Despite King James's roving eye fixing upon other young males, Herbert continued to be well treated and was offered further offices through the remainder of the king's reign. As with Spynie, King James keenly promoted an eligible bride for Montgomery. He was not jealous of the affections of his favourites and was well aware that they had to be suitably matched with ladies of good standing to ensure their long-term prosperity and standing in society.

There were other minor infatuations for the king at the time which appear even more transitory and unsuccessful. One of these was a young courtier named Henry Rich who did not reciprocate. In fact, he spat in disgust after the king had apparently slobbered over his face. The rebuff did not damage his long-term prospects and he became the Earl of Holland. Herbert's star was already on the wane when the king met and was immediately transfixed by the physical beauty of a newcomer who entered his life in 1607. Lord Thomas Howard was surprised at the young Scot's ability to 'win the Prince's affection … wonderously in a little time'.[4] The new man was Robert Carr, who was around twenty-two when he met the king and the king himself was twenty years older. What caught the royal eye was a youth who was, according to Thomas Howard, 'straight-limbed, well-favoured, strong-shouldered, and smooth-faced, with some sort of cunning and show of modesty; tho, God wot, he well knoweth when to shew his impudence'. Later in the seventeenth century he was described as 'rather well compacted than tall, his features comely and handsome rather than beautiful; the hair of his head flaxen, that of his face tinctured with yellow … In his own nature, of a gentle mind, and affable disposition'.[5] As with others he was fond of, James literally hung on Carr, leaning on his arm, pinching his cheeks, stroking his clothes.[6] As James's biographer David Harris Willson pointed out, if that was how the king behaved with him in public, the show of intimacy in private is liable to have gone a good deal further.

It is possibly appropriate that the first great favourite who dominated the life of King James through the first part of his reign in England was a Scotsman. Robert Carr (or Kerr) rose to great heights as the central romantic figure in the monarch's life between the years 1607 and 1615. In common with the man who eventually displaced him, he was a simple gentleman, but was soon raised to great heights through gifts and honours from the besotted ruler. The great favourites who came to favour before, as noted, had been established peers and courtiers. Esmé Stuart, the Duke of Lennox, and George Gordon, Marquess of Huntly, knew the system of reward and service at the royal court and used it to their own advantage, manipulating the king's emotions and naivety. Robert Carr did not fully comply with the rules of patronage expected from him as a suddenly elevated favourite and his refusal to recognise the limits of his own influence with the king would see him spectacularly fall from grace.

But before Carr came to the king's attention, there were others in England who temporarily caught his eye. The 'first Meteor' of that kind, according to the contemporary Sir Anthony Weldon, was another Scotsman, James Hay, a member of the Scots Guard who served the king of France. Weldon, a famously acidic observer of King James, spoke very highly of Hay. Generally beloved by all, of a fair demeanour, he was one who apparently knew the mind of the king more than others.[7] He was sent on many foreign diplomatic missions by the king and was highly rewarded, ending up as Earl of Carlisle, though his major failing was a lifelong profligacy with money. This extravagance made him the target of satire and indirect criticism towards the king; he was supposed, for example, to have spent the vast sum of £3,300 on a single dinner. (His more modest supper for the French ambassador in 1621 ran to a mere £500.) But many historians still regarded him positively. There was no suggestion, it seems, of a romantic link between Hay and the king, and his promotion does throw a positive light on King James's ability to recognise talent for its own sake, promoting deserving men who could assist his administration.

Carr came to the attention of the king entirely by accident and through Hay. The twenty-year-old was one of the contestants who were exercising on the tilting yard at Whitehall, as was traditional on King's Day (or Accession Day), 24 March 1607. Carr, who was serving as Hay's page, made ready to dismount and bring Hay's coat of arms to the king. At that moment the horse threw him, and his leg was broken. King James would have been familiar to some extent with the young man as the lad had been one of his pages of honour in Scotland several years before. The king now noted the extremely good-looking young man and was extremely concerned for his recovery. Soon he was visiting Carr as he recovered, and tried to teach him Latin. One commentator added that the king should have taught the 'Scotch lad' English also.[8] There was a paternal, schoolmasterly instinct in the king's relationship with younger men, irrespective of whether or not he had other impulses towards them.

Carr was the fifth son of an obscure and impoverished knight from the Scottish Borders. The sprawling, extended branches of the Kerrs were a notoriously warlike 'surname' who expended as much energy fighting local rivals (like the Scotts of Buccleuch) as battling the English when they chose to violate the border. Young Robert was hardly a typical representative of the volatile Kerr clan, whose local militarism caused the centralised Scottish authority headaches for decades right up to the 1590s. Yet the boy's father had been largely onside with the government for much of the king's reign. Sir Thomas Kerr (or Carr) had been among those men whom Esmé Stuart, Duke of Lennox, had persuaded the king to pardon after the death of the Earl of Morton. He had served as Warden of the Middle March on the border but had also become involved in the endemic factional strife of the Scottish nobility. Among Kerr's crimes was complicity in the raid at Stirling which resulted in the death of the previous Lennox, the king's grandfather. Thomas Kerr had been in exile and had suffered from abject poverty and struggled to support his large family. While he was abroad, the Earl of Morton purloined his treasure, which had been stored in Edinburgh Castle for safe keeping. He later had the satisfaction of attending the earl's execution.

Weldon noted the rise of Robert Carr and stated that he was very handsome, well-bred and (like many Scots) had spent a substantial time in France. He was held to be serious minded and only associated with those by whom he might be bettered.[9] In Scotland he had spent some time as a page at the court, in the household of the Earl of Dunbar. He came south when the king ascended to the English throne in 1603. There are contrary accounts of Carr's intelligence and interest in learning from contemporaries, along with conflicting assessments of his character. But he was neither as shrewd nor charismatic as the favourite who eventually displaced him, George Villiers. And the fact that he had to employ a friend to compose love letters to his eventual wife points more towards intellectual deficiency than lovestruck bashfulness.

The two most important men who looked suspiciously at the rise of Carr were Cecil and the king's own son Henry. There were rumours later which said he had a part in their untimely deaths, which is blatantly untrue. Yet, when these two died, the continued rise of Carr was assured. For a considerable time, he played his part well, modestly submitting himself entirely to the whims of the king in all matters. He followed James on his incessant rounds of countryside pursuits and dressed ostentatiously. Although James himself dressed conservatively, he liked his young favourites to dress in the height of fashion. Lord Thomas Howard noted, 'This young man doth much study all art and advice; he hath changed his tailors and tiremen [dressers] many times, and all to please the Prince.'[10] Carr also cannily distanced himself from more blatant money-grabbing Scots around court and surrounded himself with Englishmen, giving potential enemies one less weapon to beat him with.

Towards the end of 1607 Carr was made a Gentleman of the Bedchamber and was knighted. The next year the king contrived to give Sir Walter Raleigh's estate of Sherborne in Dorset to the young Scot, despite widespread opposition. The imprisoned Raleigh had tried to retain possession of the estate by transferring it to his wife, but the legality of the move was questioned, and the king sanctioned its confiscation, despite protests from Raleigh's family. Not without some embarrassment, he gifted the land to Robert Carr, who was also further enriched by the Scottish estate of Lord Maxwell in 1610. The sharp rise of the favourite, not linked with any known reciprocal service delivered to the king or state, may have alarmed some within the court. But the king was supreme in whom he chose to elevate and show favour to. There were worrying signs about the scope of the new king's favourites when wagging tongues suggested that he was trying to oust the king's foremost minister, Sir Robert Cecil.

In March 1611 Robert Carr was made Viscount Rochester (becoming the first Scot to gain a seat in the English House of Lords) and the following month he was made a Knight of the Garter. Further honours followed, including his appointment as keeper of Westminster and appointment to the Privy Council, then the role as Lord Treasurer of Scotland. Whatever the debatable personal credentials of Carr, he was in no sense equal to some of those roles into which he was thrust. But there was no doubt about the depth of the king's infatuation. He blatantly stated the terms of his possession of the favourite sometime later, writing in a letter to Carr, 'Remember, that all your being except your breathing and soul is from me.'

As the years progressed, some complacency perhaps entered Robert's attitude to this royal relationship. When it was reported, in December 1612, that he was temporarily in disgrace, Carr won his way back into the king's favour by being solicitous to him during an illness. The king made Robert Carr the Earl of Somerset in November 1613, and on Boxing Day 1613 Carr was married to Frances Howard in Whitehall, with the king paying for the whole celebration, despite the crown being chronically short of money. The following year saw Somerset at the peak of his power, appointed by King James as Lord Chamberlain. The king declared, 'that no man should marvayle that he bestowed a place so neere himself upon his frend, whom he loved above all men living'.[11]

But the end was in sight for the Scottish favourite. One problem was that his increased responsibilities as a husband demanded more revenue, and he was less diligent in his dealings with government business and more personally acquisitive. Carr's choice of wife also caused difficulties. This grew into a major crisis which may have culminated with actual murder. Frances was the daughter of Thomas Howard, Earl of Suffolk. When she was very young she had firstly married Robert Devereux, third Earl of Essex (son of Queen Elizabeth's executed favourite). But this marriage was never consummated and relations between the young couple became acrimonious. Many rumours began to circulate in 1613. Carr was rumoured to be the lover of the Countess of Essex. It was also said that the late Prince Henry had lost his virginity to the dazzlingly beautiful Frances and that this was the real reason behind his subsequent antipathy towards Robert Carr.[12] Henry hated Carr and did not try to disguise it. While the scheming Howard family actively encouraged the link with a daughter of their house as a means to re-establish their own power at court, she made an enemy with Carr's own favourite and close associate, Thomas Overbury.

Overbury was an accomplished English courtier whom Carr had first encountered in Scotland in 1601. Four or five years older than Carr, and from modest West Country roots, Overbury was not well regarded because of his overbearing manner. Sir Anthony Weldon said that Carr especially associated himself with Overbury and although the latter was a man of excellent parts and very witty, he was proud and rated himself too highly, looking down on others, and was infected with a kind of insolence.[13] His depth of arrogance was only matched by the rather more talented Sir Walter Raleigh. One acquaintance noted in 1612 that Overbury irritated and provoked almost everyone he came to know. At first, his good looks and manners won him attention and praise, including from Queen Anne who would later loathe him. Even Carr, his bosom associate, admitted that he never had a friend he didn't end up falling out with.

Why did Carr put up with him when all others, sooner or later, found Overbury intolerable? Inevitably, there are suggestions that the two men were lovers, though the evidence for this is circumstantial. Carr's close reliance on him was due to the fact that Overbury had brains and cunning, which compensated for his own shortage in those areas. The king was either unaware of the depth of Overbury's ambition and danger, or he disregarded him as inconsequential. But seeing Overbury up close in 1608, when he was appointed as his server at the royal table, soured King James toward him. Overbury egotistically blamed the king's loathing on the fact that James was jealous of the greater love which Carr had for him. He once suggested that Carr remind James that, as he was so much older than Robert, it was only natural that his favourite should find more solace in someone his own age. So far as we know, Carr sensibly refrained from transmitting this blunt message to the monarch.

On the credit side, Overbury like many others, turned his hand to poetry, though his efforts (like the king's) were deemed to be average. His poem 'The Wife' sets out those admirable characteristics which he believed should be foremost in any prospective character. Ben Jonson rated Overbury as a rising literary talent for a while, but his enthusiasm seems to have been misplaced, for the two men soon violently quarrelled and Overbury became his enemy. More successful was his series of pen portraits about character types found in the royal circle and in normal walks of life. These were collected and published as *Characters* in 1614, but owed a great deal of their success to his notoriety and posthumous fame.[14]

Overbury was knighted in 1608, and after a spell on the continent, he returned to court and became inseparable from Robert Carr, whom he strongly encouraged to aim for power and not just prominence at court. By doing so, and encouraging Carr to engage in political intrigue, he exposed a major flaw in the king's weakness for individual favourites. Carr recognised and relied on Overbury's greater ability to function in the political jungle at court. There was no doubting Overbury's ambition, but he still underestimated the subtle dangers which he was thrusting himself and Carr into. If inexperienced and powerful individuals close to the king could impose their own political agendas, it threatened to imbalance the legitimate machinery of Jacobean government. While political factions at the heart of the establishment were often primarily interested in aggrandizing themselves, at least they had experience and competence in wielding power. A favourite like Carr, who was being driven by Overbury's ambition, was a potentially more dangerous force. Worryingly, Overbury also had access to highly confidential government documents which Carr fed to him, requesting his assistance with the onerous mountain of paperwork which came with his responsibility as the king's right-hand man. Carr later claimed that the king knew about this arrangement and approved it. But it still appeared highly suspect, given Overbury's uncertain character, and people began to mutter that Carr ruled the king. Overbury, however, ruled Carr.

There was a minor crisis in 1611 when Overbury was banished from the court. Rather than being excluded because of his intrigues, records state that it was at the behest of Queen Anne. Anne became annoyed that Carr and Overbury had too much power over patronage, which lessened her own influence. She was annoyed when a property in Scotland she had intended to be presented to the Lord Chancellor of Scotland was granted instead to one of Carr's nominees. The men reciprocated her disdain in full measure. In May 1611 matters came to a head when the three encountered each other one evening at Greenwich Palace. Anne spied Carr and Overbury together in a garden below her window and broke into a fit of contemptible laughter at the sight of them. Possibly they were engaged in some strange activity. When they heard her, they responded in kind, and the outraged queen went to the king and said that she would return to Denmark if the pair went unpunished. A variation on the tale states that Overbury blatantly insulted Queen Anne.

Whatever the truth of events, King James was loathe at first to take any strong action. The Privy Council investigated, but James would not sanction anything that would overly offend Carr. The latter threatened to withdraw himself from court in protest when Overbury was sent away, but did not actually do so. Overbury was back in the bosom of the court after a few months out in the wilderness, [15] but he still had to swallow his pride and approach the queen for forgiveness, using Robert Cecil, the Lord Chamberlain, as intermediary. Whatever the truth of the story, Queen Anne's dislike of Robert Carr allegedly stretched back some time. There was a tradition that she was instrumental in his dismissal as a page of honour in Scotland, though his ineptness and inability to say grace in Latin may have been responsible.[16] Some contemporaries assign Anne's hatred to the supposition that he stole the king's affections from her, while others think she was alarmed by the accumulation of honours that Carr possessed. The latter seems more likely as it reflects concerns over her prerogative of influencing appointments to the king's household.

Carr and Overbury were soon part of a deadly romantic triangle which also included Frances Howard. Initially, Overbury did not believe there was anything serious between Howard and Carr and he even helped Carr draught love letters to her. He may have suspected that Carr was engaged in a casual fling rather than a real romance and perhaps saw it as an opportunity to cause dismay to her prominent family. When it became clear that Carr wanted to marry Frances, Overbury was incensed and warned him that she would be his ruin. He invariably (and bitchily) referred to Frances as 'that woman'. He acknowledged his own considerable part in the wooing: 'When you fell in Love with that Woman, as soon as you had wonne her by my Letters, ... then used your own for common Passages.'[17] The two friends had a furious argument in March 1613 which severely damaged their relationship, with Overbury demanding financial reward for the assistance he had given. Carr did not entirely cut ties with him, perhaps fearing that Overbury would cause him damage by revealing secrets if he entirely cut him loose.

While annulment proceedings between Essex and his wife proceeded, Carr colluded with the king in trying to get the troublesome Overbury removed. A plan to send him as ambassador to Moscow was scornfully refused when Overbury saw through the mission's purpose as a plan to get rid of him. After a modified offer to place him in a more congenial part of Europe was again turned down, he was sensationally arrested and thrown in prison. The legality of the king locking a man up for refusing to go abroad was not questioned at the time but was clearly doubtful. Overbury subsequently accused Carr of deceitfully advising him to resist these offers, though Carr refuted this. The major talking point at the time was what the imprisonment might mean for Carr since it was not widely known the two men had fallen out. Major gossip centred around the relationship of the Earl and Countess of Essex. When the authorities appointed a panel to decide whether or not to grant an annulment, Frances went through the humiliating but not unheard-of physical examination to determine whether or not she was a virgin. Essex was also accused of impotence by Frances, which he rejected, saying he was only incapable of performing with her, and the king appointed a commission of bishops to examine the evidence and ascertain whether a marriage termination could be granted. King James interfered with the legal process and intimidated the members, finally installing several more members to do his bidding when the commission was in a stalemate. By autumn (and thanks to royal intervention) the marriage was dissolved on 25 September 1613. Eleven days earlier, Sir Thomas Overbury died in the Tower of London, where he had been confined since April.

A few years later Carr was caught up in questions about Overbury's death, but for now he was most concerned by the king's fading affections and the rise of a rival, George Villiers. Carr, at the beginning of 1615, was in a foul and suspicious frame of mind with the king. James queried his behaviour and tried to restore their former good relations, but the fading favourite continued to act badly. The king wrote to Carr in early 1615 and asked him what more he could want from him. He also noted that Carr was displaying 'streams of unquietness, passion, fury and insolent pride, and a settled kind of induced obstinacy'. His complaints came to the king at all sorts of unreasonable hours, as if Carr was trying to vex him on purpose. Tellingly, and in a hurt fashion, the king accuses him of refusing to sleep in the royal bedchamber, despite the king imploring him to do so many hundreds of times. James shows all the sentiment of a spurned lover. He is forced to write 'from the infinite grief of a deeply wounded heart,' and reproaches himself 'for raising a man so high as might make him presume to pierce my ears with such speeches'. He reminds Carr that all he had came from him. 'God is my judge, my love hath been infinite towards you; and only the strength of any affection towards you hath made me to bear these things and bridle my passion.'[18]

A second letter, a few months later, contained more warnings and less love. King James sternly advised that he had been needlessly troubled by his desperate letters. When James made a point of sending Villiers to Somerset in an act of reconciliation, the new man humbly requested to be Carr's servant and creature, saying he would only seek preferment through him and would be as faithful a servant as Carr ever had. But Carr harshly rebuffed him and replied, 'I will have none of your service, and you shall have none of my favour. I will, if I can, break your necke, and of that be confident.'[19] In July 1615 Somerset, grudgingly seeing the writing on the wall, tried to safeguard his future by arranging a pardon against any future charges for himself, but he was unsuccessful.[20] His refusal to fully accept that the king was enamoured with his new favourite in the end ensured that he was totally eclipsed. Had he accommodated Villiers he could have remained as Lord Chamberlain and a member of the Privy Council.

Rumours about possible poisoning of Overbury began to seriously circulate in July 1615. The circumstances of the death were not questioned for some time and the matter evolved into a historical whodunit to rival the Gowrie Conspiracy. Carr may well have intrigued to put Overbury in the Tower, but his wife was rumoured to be the primary hand behind his death.[21] The motive was Overbury's opposition of her second marriage and the trouble he was now causing Carr by threatening to reveal the incriminating correspondence between them. With a reputation as a scheming adulteress, Frances was painted as a plotter who corrupted a band of associates to help her kill Sir Thomas by an especially malicious, slow death when she might easily have killed him quickly. Her alleged employment of witchcraft against Overbury (and possibly against her first husband in making him impotent), added another combustible element to the scandal and her reputation. It was believed that she had also attempted to use strange potions against her first husband.

The authorities rounded up those who had been in contact with Overbury while he was locked up. These included Sir Gervase Elwes, Lieutenant of the Tower, who was questioned and revealed that he had wind of poisons being sent in to be used on Sir Thomas, some of them concealed in jellies and tarts. Convinced that no one would believe the truth that the Countess of Essex was behind the poisoning campaign, he kept the information to himself while dealing with each doctored item that was intended for Overbury. This evidence was eventually brought before the king and an investigation started. It was revealed that Lady Frances had tried to pay a certain Sir David Wood, 'an ill-looked red-bearded Scot', £1,000 to assassinate Overbury, though he had wisely refused this commission. He advised that he might be willing to torture him for that amount but wouldn't countenance murder and ending up swinging from Tyburn Tree for any lady's pleasure.[22] Frances had also asked a witch named 'Cunning Mary' to kill her unwanted spouse. An associate then revealed that Frances had paid him a sum of money to poison Overbury, and further blackened her name by saying that he had acted as a go-between in the adulterous relationship between her and Carr when Frances was still married to the Earl of Essex.

After the discovery of adulterated foods being fed to Overbury, the fatal dose of poison was administered by an enema. The hapless official Gervase Elwes and an associate of the countess, Mrs Anne Turner, were hanged along with several others. Frances and Carr were arrested, and pressure put upon them to plead guilty. By doing so, less sordid details involving the king might come out in court. Frances duly admitted her guilt and was treated with some consideration in court. Somerset, who may only have known the poisoning details after the fact, defiantly stated that he was not guilty. The evidence against him which emerged appeared circumstantial and fell some way short of proving guilt. There was, for instance, the account of an apothecary who stated that he witnessed Carr's cold lack of concern when he informed him multiple times that Overbury was gravely and possibly mortally ill. Carr denied meeting the man more than once, and, besides, had information from Overbury himself that he had been taking emetics to try to improve his health. It was true also that he dissuaded Overbury's father from petitioning the king directly to ask for his son's release, saying that it would best come from him, a request which he failed to follow up. But again, this only shows that he was indifferent to the fate of his former friend rather than responsible for his death. More suspiciously, Carr sought to destroy some of the correspondence between various parties involved in the matter. He had his own property ransacked to find letters from his former friend and paid a servant of Overbury £30 for letters he had sent to him in prison and which he then destroyed.[23] Despite these precautions, Carr characteristically fumbled the clean-up operation. Excerpts from surviving letters fell into the hands of those prosecuting him. Sir Francis Bacon wrote to the king and detailed precisely which parts he would use to blacken both the name of Carr and the memory of Overbury: 'First, I shall read some passages of Overbury's letters, namely these: "Is this the fruit of nine years' love, common secrets, and common dangers?" In another letter: "Do not drive me to extremity to do that which you and I shall be sorry for."'[24]

Carr's desperation to destroy evidence may have been motivated by a wish to protect his heavily pregnant wife as much as self-preservation. When Overbury died, few people voiced regret, though Robert Carr did so, though the sentiment may have been dishonest. When he did find out about the poisoning, he did his best to frustrate attempts by the authorities to uncover the truth and also destroyed evidence which was harmful to his wife. Overbury himself had seemed confident of release in the weeks leading up to his death, after going to the trouble of apologising to the Howard family for any past offence he may have caused them. However, he was also threatening to reveal incriminating secrets about Carr and his wife during the same period.

At the start of November 1615 Carr was placed in the Tower of London and his wife was placed under house arrest in London. The rumour mill intensified towards the end of the year. It was being said that Carr had poisoned Overbury after consulting a wizard who said that one man posed a serious threat to him. He refused to name the man but showed Carr a mirror in which Thomas Overbury's image magically appeared.[25] There were also wild conspiracy tales which said that the Earl of Somerset and his wife were ultimately planning to wipe out all members of the royal family with poison. Frances gave birth to a daughter at the beginning of December, but she and her husband were still kept apart and were periodically questioned by the authorities. If there was doubt that Carr was involved in the death, there was also a question mark over the method of the victim's disposal. One lurid tale suggests that the final murderous act was the unfortunate prisoner being smothered.[26] But a natural death from consumption was proposed by at least one apothecary and one doctor who treated him.[27] Sir Thomas had been ill for some time, suffering from fever, vomiting and other symptoms. He had been treated by the reputable Swiss doctor Mayerne, whose treatments included opening wounds deliberately in patients' backs to effect a cure. Building on this, one modern author wonders whether such an open wound in a man already ill and living in unsanitary conditions may have led to septicaemia. Complications from diabetes is yet another possibility.[28] The coroner's inquest concluded that Overbury died of natural causes. Based on the fact that the body corrupted remarkably quickly, or perhaps as a result of deliberate misinformation, it was initially believed that Overbury had died from natural causes of his own making. The historian Arthur Wilson commented several decades later, 'And to kill him again after death, they brand him with the scandall of a lascivious life, giving out that he died of the Pox.'[29]

Rumour magnified the implications of the scandal of poisoning. A man named James Franklin hinted that Overbury's death was linked to the alleged poisoning of Prince Henry in 1612, something that Carr and others were linked to at different times. King James was appalled by the circumstances of the plot and anxious to distance himself from any incipient scandal, but he agreed to an investigation into the matter following the details revealed by Sir Gervase Elwes; especially that there were important people involved. He went to the council table and 'kneeling down there, desired God to lay a Curse upon him and his posterity forever, if he were consenting to Overburies death'.[30] One valid reason that gave fuel to the rumour of state involvement in Overbury's end was the fact that the deceased knew more state secrets than the Privy Council, thanks to the weakness of Carr and the laxness of King James.

While Carr still languished in the Tower of London in January 1616, King James met Sir Francis Bacon, the Attorney General, to discuss the case. He sought assurances that Carr would be found guilty if he was brought to trial, for the Crown would be cast in an ill light if he was acquitted. James also expressed his concern that the proceedings might lead to difficulties for himself, though he did not specify what these might be. It was a fortuitous coincidence that Carr was causing problems for the king when it became clear that he and his wife had some involvement in Overbury's demise. Several observers believed that Carr and Frances were made scapegoats for the death because the king wanted rid of them. Whatever the truth of this, the keen-eyed predators in Whitehall had sensed Carr's end was nigh and told tales about him to the king, which James listened to. Foreign observers looked on in rapt fascination. Weldon accuses the king of being disingenuously and overly affectionate to Somerset at the end when he knew that he was done with him forever. According to Weldon, who was a witness to the scene, it appeared as if Somerset's star was more rising than falling. During a meeting at Royston House prior to his arrest, the earl kissed the king's hand and was rewarded by James slobbering his cheek, saying he would neither eat nor sleep after he left until he came again. As soon as Somerset did depart to London, King James said to all present, 'Now the Deil go with thee, for I shall never see his face more.'[31]

When Carr understood that the protection he expected from the king would not be forthcoming he desperately tried to blackmail him. The disclosures that Carr had (or thought he had) which would lead to the monarch getting the charges dropped are not now known. James stated in a letter to the new man in charge of the Tower of London that Carr was 'laying an aspiration upon me of being in some sorte accessorie to his crime'.[32] James was rightly worried about how much of his private life with Carr might possibly leak out. When Carr was arrested in 1615 his correspondence was seized by the Lord Chief Justice, Edward Coke. Among the papers were letters that the king had written to Carr. These were returned to James, but Coke read them and was apparently shocked by the sexual content of one letter at least.[33]

Frances was transferred to the Tower in April 1616. Robert Carr, however, still maintained his innocence and King James was also left pondering the difficulty of how he should handle the Somersets if and when the case reached the trial stage. He favoured ceasing the legal proceedings before the verdict was brought, which would give him the opportunity to pardon Carr and his wife. There was huge interest in the trials of husband and wife on 24 and 25 May, with places of public entertainment closed and the public galleries congested. Frances was treated with some deference and her dignified demeanour in court was remarked upon. Carr was soberly dressed and subdued when he appeared. His face was pale, his beard long and his eyes sunken. He had refused to admit guilt as an accessory to the poisoning, despite being cajoled by various state emissaries to the Tower. An offer of leniency by the king if he admitted guilt was twice refused. When his wife was brought to court, Robert Carr advised that he would not attend his own trial and would have to be physically dragged there. One commentator spun a tale which says that the Earl of Somerset was hoodwinked into submitting to the trial by a royal promise that it was a formality and he would be acquitted.[34] No such devious ploy seems to have been undertaken by King James. On the day of the favourite's trial the king was highly agitated but determined to see the dirty business through. The prosecution suggested that Carr had colluded in the poisoning plot on account of his fear that Overbury would reveal damaging political secrets against him, and also that he bore a grudge against him for obstructing his romance with Frances, Countess of Essex. The Earl of Essex was a conspicuous, gloating presence in the court room during the proceedings. He had pressed for his former wife to be executed. Although the evidence against Carr – in so far as the incomplete record can be judged now – falls short of proof of guilt, Carr was shown in a damaging light, dishonest and disloyal to his former friend. Overbury, according to one of his servants, was highly suspicious of the earl, writing to him, 'If I die, my blood lie upon you.'[35]

Overbury wrote numerous missives asking for his friend's help to release him from the Tower and their tone became ever more desperate. In the end he resorted to barely veiled threats, once writing,

'All I intreat of you is, that you will free me from this place, and that we may part friends. Drive me not to extremities, lest I should say something that you and I both repent.' Even more alarmingly, he also admitted that he was compiling a document detailing his life and deeds with Carr.[36] What effect did such loaded words have on Robert Carr and his protective wife Frances?

Carr admitted sending food to Overbury, but denied it was adulterated. More damning was his destroying the correspondence of some others implicated in Overbury's death. But the poorly educated earl did himself no favours when he provided a rambling and erratic defence of himself. In common with other accused people in that period, he did not hear the evidence against him until he was standing to hear it in the dock. It was no surprise that he was found guilty.

The sentences of death against him and his wife were commuted, but the couple were kept in the Tower. There was a surprising amount of sympathy for Carr at court, even among his enemies. His estates were forfeited to the Crown, but he was left with an extremely generous allowance. Carr was eventually released, despite the fact that the king had sworn he would never pardon anyone who was guilty of Overbury's death, and the former favourite maintained his innocence. Following his pardon in October 1624, little more was heard from Carr. Unlike the favourite who replaced him, Buckingham, he had no redeeming features or any definable talent that would have been useful in the service of the new monarch, King Charles I. Yet strangely, he made contact with Buckingham in 1628, soliciting aid for himself in the role of his 'unfortunate predecessor'. Buckingham, after initial reluctance, had a reportedly good-humoured meeting with Carr in London in August 1628. Who knows what tales of the late king and his habits may have been discussed there. Further contact was curtailed by Buckingham's assassination shortly afterwards.

Some writers have treated Somerset with sympathy, seeing him as merely misguided in comparison with the man who displaced him in the king's affections and accrued too much corrupting power to himself. In line with the sexist attitudes of the age, the prime villain in many people's eyes was the beautiful, but deadly and sexually rapacious Frances Howard, Countess of Essex and then Countess of Somerset, who ruined two high-ranking men (three if you include Overbury) with her deviousness. There was even a spitefully malicious anagram game which played on the names of the guilty parties and pointed the finger of blame at the countess:

>Francis Howarde
>*Car finds a whore*
>Thomas Overburie
>*O! O! A busie murther*[37]

The king's part in the Overbury affair did not, in the end, do him the substantial damage which it might have done. Nobody at the time or since has proven convincingly he had any culpability in the man's death, even though he can be blamed for incarcerating Overbury for insufficient reason. Yet the atmosphere of dishonesty and sleaze which tarred the careers of Sir Thomas Overbury and Robert Carr, Earl of Somerset, engendered unease among many even if it did not lead to direct criticism of the king. The communication between the king and the Lord Chancellor, Francis Bacon, deals with the implications of the trial and the ramifications of a possible pardon for Carr. There is no agonising, nor even a mention, of whether he was in fact guilty or innocent. This icy ability to disassociate himself from death and from justice was an old, worrying trait of the king, forged in the deadly atmosphere of Scotland. Here was the ruler who barely blinking an eye when the young Earl of Moray was slaughtered by the Earl of Huntly in 1592. At least one writer who studied the evidence about Overbury's death in the nineteenth century concluded that the king was the sponsor of his death, with the collusion of the royal doctor, Mayerne, who was conspicuously absent from giving evidence at the trial of Frances or Carr.[38]

Carr's final years were obscure and largely free from public drama. He had a minor brush with the authorities in 1629 when he was accused of distributing a pamphlet which was critical of the monarchy, but he escaped punishment. Four years later (and a year after the death of Frances), King Charles harried him about a jewel which was supposedly royal property and there was also digging into the earl's finances a few years later. He died in relative obscurity in July 1645 and left an only child, Anne, who became the wife of the first Duke of Bedford.

It is difficult to disagree with the conclusion that Carr was unsuited to the power which he and Overbury overwhelmingly craved.[39] He and Frances also seem to have brought out the worst in each other. The easy going, genial groom was a very different character from the sniping, bitter man who threw away all that the king had gifted him. Had he been more clear-sighted, King James might have been thankful that Robert Carr was not politically astute enough to take full advantage of the enormous opportunities that his position afforded him. More insight still would have prevented the king in giving so much reward to a favourite who little deserved it. James appears to have treated him with remarkable forbearance even during his prosecution when it appeared a possibility that the former favourite would unleash damaging information about him (though Carr did not explicitly threaten to do so). It is hard to credit Carr with the capability of engineering the death by poisoning of Thomas Overbury by himself, let alone murdering Prince Henry (or even Robert Cecil, as another story said) by the same means. In the end, his petulant behaviour as he fell from grace showed the true mark of the man.

Chapter 11

Steenie

George Villiers, Duke of Buckingham

The man who ended his life as the immensely rich Duke of Buckingham was, in the words of one commentator, the greatest subject that England ever had. Titles, wealth, and influence were heaped on him to an extent that even he felt was incredible and he was duly thankful to the source of this abundance, King James I. With some awe, he acknowledged that James had filled his purse and given him a profusion of houses and lands, so that his shoulders could not bear the weight of any more gifts.

The king, contemporaries acknowledged, loved George Villiers beyond all measure, even beyond the excessive love he squandered on the previous favourite, Somerset. Sir John Oglander wrote that James 'loved young men, his favourites, better than women, loving them beyond the love of men to women. I never saw any fond husband make so much or so great dalliance over his beautiful spouse as I have seen King James over his favourites, especially the Duke of Buckingham.'[1] An Italian ambassador noted that that the king gave much trust in conducting affairs to Buckingham, 'who has given him all his heart, who will not eat, sup or remain an hour without him and considers him his whole joy'.[2] To console himself when Villiers was absent, the king wore his miniature portrait beneath his clothes. More than twice his age when they met in August 1614, there was again some element of paternal love on the king's part for Buckingham, though it was both complicated and all consuming. Buckingham had been carefully selected to catch the king's attention and counterbalance existing factions then in favour with the monarch by astute political operators. But there is no doubt that Buckingham himself loved the king, though it seems impossible that his feelings matched the emotional incandescence which James felt for him. It was a long-lasting ardour. Late in his life (in December 1623) James wrote passionately and dramatically to Villiers that 'I desire only to live in this world for your sake, and that I had rather live banished in any part of the earth with you than live a sorrowful widow's life without you ... God bless you, my sweet child and wife, and grant that ye may ever be a comfort to your dear dad and husband.'[3]

George Villiers was the fourth son from a reasonably prominent Leicestershire family, born in 1592. His lowly pecking order within the family and resultant lack of prospects about inheriting either wealth or position prepared him for a life where he had to make the most of whatever opportunities materialised. His father, an MP and minor landowner, had died early, which caused financial peril for his mother and the whole family. He was neither a great scholar nor blessed with any accomplishments that were useful for advancement beyond a winning manner and a pleasant personality. His formidable mother Mary had a chequered past which included trying to defraud her elderly second husband when he was in his final illness. Mary was to remain very close to her son through the course of his career. She had been unkindly characterised by a modern historian as 'perhaps the most objectionable of the whole set of female dragons pestering the court at this time'.[4] As Frances Howard was a key player in the upward mobility of Robert Carr, so Mary Villiers was a keen driving force in the career of her son. Wilful upper-class women of the age who had ambition had to pin their ambitions onto men.

Villiers became attached to the household of one of the king's close associates, Sir Roger Aston, and tried to marry the latter's daughter Ann not long after Sir Roger died in 1612, though his poverty prevented it. Villiers intruded into the royal presence several years later when James was on one of his frequent visits to the country houses of the aristocracy. The young man, serving as a cupbearer, immediately caught the monarch's eye. As he was carrying food through the hall in the royal presence, he had a scuffle with another servant. The king's current favourite, Robert Carr, Earl of Somerset, demanded he have his ears cut, the standard brutal punishment for violence in the king's presence, but King James immediately pardoned him. Villiers' sponsors had calculated the young man's appeal correctly; he was just the type the king liked. Young George was naturally good looking, but mild and gentle in manner, innately elegant, with a delicacy that bordered on enchantment. Those who plucked the young man forward and thrust him in front of the king also ensured that he was given, in place of his one threadbare suit, an outfit which dazzled in its magnificence. And, of course, the king was enchanted. He was ready for someone new to make a profound difference in his life. His difficulties with Somerset and attempts to keep him in line were proving exhausting. The queen was distant from him and the prospects of building the reticent Prince Charles into a worthy successor must also have been a cause for concern.

Carr initially protested when the king wanted to make Villiers a Groom of the Bedchamber, saying that he wanted the post for his own nephew. For the time being the upstart was relegated to the minor post of cupbearer, but Carr's star was already on the wane. Villiers found wealthy sponsors who gave him the necessary backing, which enabled him to function at court, hoping to set him up as a potential replacement to the Scot. His placement was associated with a plan by the faction opposed to the alliance which might have resulted in a match between Prince Charles and a Spanish infanta. The resultant concord with the primary force of the Catholic Church in Europe alarmed some in England who were suspicious of what they perceived as the king's lax adherence to the strictures of Protestantism. The Archbishop of Canterbury, George Abbot, solicited the help of allies to place Villiers as Gentleman of the Bedchamber. Unlike Somerset, therefore, Buckingham's intrusion into the king's inner circle was achieved through astute political engineering rather than an accidental happening.

The powers of patronage and influence tangled up in the prominence of favourites under the king were immense and generated intrigue and powerful political strategy. Insider assistance was required to make it happen. The king and queen were no longer on intimate terms, though there was a residual fondness between them. In most things, James would not defer to the opinion of Ann, but he did listen to her when she recommended new recruits to his household. This deference to her was a cynical ploy of the king to give the illusion that his wife had some influence over his court. Although she was friendly with Abbot, the queen warned him openly about his intention to insert this new young man into the inner circle. She told the prelate that, once he was in place, 'the first persons that he will plague must be you that labour for him … The king will teach him to despise and hardly entreat us all, that he may seem to be beholden to none but himself.'[5] 'Noble queen,' Abbot replied, 'how like a prophetess did you speak.'

Perhaps swayed by assurances that Villiers was more even tempered (and malleable) than Somerset, Anne was persuaded to introduce upstart into the king's presence on St George's Day 1615. This was despite her observation that she been 'bitten with favourites both in England and Scotland' (which suggests she knew about her husband's proclivities early in their marriage). Asking the prince to lend her his sword, Anne presented this to the king with the intention of getting him to knight Villiers on the spot. But a moment of comedy ensued when the king became alarmed by the sight of the unsheathed rapier and the ceremony was almost abandoned. However, in honour of St George, James went along with the ploy and made the unknown youth a new knight. Sir George was then appointed Gentleman of the Bedchamber, despite the dissuasion of Somerset who was watching the event from the wings. Happily for the new knight, he was also awarded a pension of £1,000 per year.

The new man impressed all with his gentle manner, good humour and elegance. As inwardly beautiful as he was outwardly, one clerical admirer gushed. His striking effeminacy and beauty certainly made him stand out from the crowd of retainers, with his childlike face, and long, slender legs. Villiers had dark-chestnut hair, clear skin, dark-blue eyes and a golden-brown beard, and was eminently appealing to the eye. He also dressed to accentuate his slim figure. Gentle manners and the ability to put all at their ease were additional gifts which aided his progress and won him plenty of admirers. Despite his own best intentions, Bishop John Williams was overcome by Villiers' charm. Several years later, a courtier named Simonds d'Ewes found himself distractedly staring at Villiers in fascination for fully thirty minutes, fascinated despite himself by the aura of this favourite. D'Ewes noted several examples of the king's infatuation for Villiers in his diary. There was the instance of the king spontaneously blurting out to Villiers, 'By God, George, I love thee dearly.' Another time, Villiers entered the royal presence and James fell wordlessly upon his neck. More selfishly, he once begged Villiers not to pull a rotten tooth in case is spoiled his looks. On another occasion, he swore that never had one loved another like he loved George Villiers.[6] Simonds also records a conversation with a friend in 1622 when they discussed the frequency of sodomy in the city of London. They wondered that God did not punish this sin and said surely there would be some terrible punishment for its prevalence, especially as they had probable cause to fear, since it was 'a sinne in the prince [King James]'.[7]

Another man bedazzled by George Villiers was William Laud, who would become Archbishop of Canterbury in 1633. Acting as Villiers' private confessor brought the two men into prolonged personal contact. Laud alludes several times in his diary to close but unspecified proximity to Villiers. On one occasion in June 1621, he wrote vaguely about Villiers being pleased to enter 'a near respect' with him, then carefully adds, 'The particulars are not for paper.' If there was any doubt about his feelings, he relates a dream he had in 1625 where the Duke of Buckingham (as Villiers became) entered his bed and behaved with 'great kindness' towards him. There was a guilty end to the homoerotic dream as he admitted that many people then entered the chamber and witnessed them. He had another intense dream about the same subject soon afterwards.[8]

But the existing favourite was certainly not a fan of the newcomer. While Somerset floundered in the awareness that his position was slipping away fast and recognised that Villiers was the man who was going to replace him as the primary favourite of the king, James himself counselled him to mend his ways and return to his former placid and reasonable self. While this was undoubtedly apt advice, he was being disingenuous to a degree by not honestly addressing what was alarmingly plain to a man fast fading from the royal horizon. And yet, King James honestly endeavoured to think the best of those he loved and cherished most. His attempt to reconcile the two men and foster a connection between them was doomed to be disastrous. When the king arranged for Villiers to go Somerset and humbly ask for his guidance and support at court, he was vocally rebuffed. While violence was threatened by Carr on that occasion, it was not delivered. A greater threat to the new man came when he was on his way back south from Scotland, following the king's visit there in 1616. A wild relative of the ousted favourite journeyed from Ferniehurst in the Borders to Carlisle with the intention of slaughtering Villiers as the royal party reached the town. He was betrayed by someone he had confided in and was imprisoned, though he was eventually released.[9]

The gap that Villiers now filled, and which ensured his victory over his rival, was a physical one. It is likely that he sealed his ascendancy by giving himself physically to the king, possibly as early as August 1615, at Farnham Castle in Hampshire. Everyone close to court sensed the level of the monarch's immediate infatuation. Sir Anthony Weldon blatantly recorded in his memoirs that 'in his passion of love to his new Favourite ... the King was more impatient than any woman to enjoy her love.'[10] Did this signify physical consummation between the king and the new favourite? There seems to be evidence to support this from George Villiers himself. Many years later he wondered whether the king now loved him better that that time at Farnham Castle in August 1615, 'where the bed's head could not be found between the master and his dog'.[11] One of the king's quirks was to designate those whom he liked by familiar nicknames, and so Villiers became 'Steenie'. This Scottish diminutive of the name Stephen was odd, of course, because it was not George Villiers' given name. It is peculiarly apt that King James combined theology with carnal desire when he chose this pet name, for it came from the *Acts of the Apostles* and referred to St Stephen: 'And all that sat in the council, looking steadfastly on him, saw his face as it had been the face of an angel.'[12] The king became quite open in his love for George Villiers. He told the Privy Council in 1617:

> I, James, am neither a god nor an angel, but a man like any other. Therefore I act like a man, and confess to loving those dear to me more than other men. You may be sure that I love the Earl of Buckingham more than anyone else, and more than you who are here assembled. I wish to speak in my own behalf, and not to have it thought to be a defect, for Jesus Christ did the same, and therefore I cannot be blamed. Christ had His John and I have my George.[13]

Despite the high pitch of royal passion, Villers knew there may always be upstarts and was determined not to be replaced as he had replaced Robert Carr. Midway through his career as a favourite there is evidence that he thwarted the rise of at least one rival, alarmed at the interest the king began to show another young man in 1622. This was Arthur Brett, a cousin of Buckingham, who was a Groom of the Bedchamber. The king's roving eye in this case was noted in correspondence between two Scottish earls and must have been common knowledge. Contrary to his usual generous and easy manner, Villiers told the king off for looking so blatantly at Brett and threatened the young man.[14] The danger of Brett was both political and personal, since it seems that he was thrust forward into the king's attention at the behest of the scheming Earl of Middlesex. Another pretty upstart named Monson (who was sponsored by the Howard family, old allies of Robert Carr) was similarly unsuccessful. Despite being tarted up and washed with 'posset curd' each day, the king was unimpressed by his manufactured prettiness. He bluntly told Monson that he did not like his forwardness in constantly presenting himself and the youth was banished from the royal presence.

There were swarms of hopefuls on the make at court, some of whom were young, gay and pretty. The extent to which they disrupted the business of government is debatable, but they constituted a distraction at least. Many of these fringe characters tried to attach themselves to Villiers' coat tails. When king James published his meditation on the Lord's Prayer in 1619, he recognised in the preface that Villiers was continually active in his service, though he was hampered by 'the uncessant swarme of suitors importunately hanging upon you without disrupture'. By taking on the constant stream of supplicants who were magnetically attracted to the king, he deflected much of the tiresome attention but also soon became a powerful conduit of patronage himself.

There is no doubt that George Villiers was, for much of the time, an effective personal secretary to the king and took on a lot of laborious work travelling to and from the king, between his various country retreats where he was hunting and London. Buckingham was certainly loyal to the king until the last few years of his reign at least when, in conjunction with the heir Prince Charles, he began to pursue his own foreign and domestic policies. The extent of the physical relationship between the king can be judged against the liaisons that Villiers had with women, though his sexuality seems to have been fluid. Court gossip points to a number of connections with ladies at court, including the married Lucy Percy, wife of Lord Doncaster.

King James was never physically jealous with his favourites, nor demanded exclusivity when it can to partners, and happily saw Villiers married, as he had done with Somerset. Villiers' appreciation of women was marked throughout his life, and he even attempted to seduce Anne of Austria, the queen regnant of France, while finalising the negotiations of the marriage of King Charles I to Henrietta Maria.[15] But this side of Villiers' character, and other aspects, was magnified by Puritan and anti-royalist enemies throughout his life, and soon after his death. From opponents we have the story of him spoiling the solemnity of a christening by leering and winking at young women in the congregation when the priest mentioned weaknesses of the flesh. And there is also the odd rumour that he and King James frequented an upmarket brothel run by the notorious madam Donna Hollandia. If the visit actually took place, the impetus may have been titillation rather than any carnal indulgence with ladies.

Villiers' marriage to Katherine Manners, daughter of the Earl of Rutland, was amiable and successful, and his wife was genuinely in love with him. The king took a delight in the company of Buckingham's wife and especially his young daughter Mary (known as Mall), playing with her for hours and lavishing more attention on her than he had on his own children. The Villiers family became the king's own surrogate family. There were unpleasant rumours that the king had an inappropriate interest in Mall, which was picked up by the French ambassador, Count Leveneur de Tillières. Although the ambassador disbelieved this malicious tale, he did report that the king inappropriately touched a niece of Buckingham, though this was also hearsay. The tales may have been prompted by the fact the king allowed the children to play in his own bedchamber, though with their nurse present. The royal residences were swarmed by the Buckingham offspring: 'little ones would dance up and down the privy Lodgings like Pharies'.[16] The French ambassador was scathing about other indicators of decadence around the English court. James was purposeless, he said, and lost in wine much of the time. He was 'devoted to nothingness ... plunging himself deeper into vice of every kind'. The Frenchman concluded that King James was leading a 'filthy and scandalous life'.[17] Another time he said plainly that he believed that Buckingham had bewitched the king.

Advancement for Villiers was quick and spectacular. When the king appointed him as Master of the Horse he successfully used the position to rapidly improve the equine holdings of the royal stable and proved himself an adaptable project manager in the role. Soon after he was appointed to the Order of the Garter, James made him simultaneously Baron Whaddon and Viscount Villiers. Substantial gifts of property augmented his standing and his fortune throughout the year. A more personal gift was a miniature painting of the king with his heart in his hand. At the beginning of 1617 he was made the Earl of Buckingham and his ascendancy was sealed. When he became Lord Admiral of England at the beginning of 1619, he immediately showed his versatility by tackling the problems of waste and corruption which were endemic within the navy. Buckingham planned to introduce two new ships to the fleet each year. One of the first of these was named by the king *Buckingham's Entrance*, which must have cause widespread amusement since it was quickly renamed *Happy Entrance*. The pinnacle of his rewards came in May 1623 when he was made Duke of Buckingham, the only non-royal duke and only the second one in England. The last non-royal duke had been created in 1551.

Many of the young man's immediate family were soon also ennobled. His mother, Mary Villiers, and his sister, Susan Feilding, both became countesses. Mary was a strong personality who sought advancement for her whole brood and became a favourite of the king, despite her Catholicism. George's brother, John Villiers, was created Viscount Purbeck, and another brother, Christopher, became Earl of Anglesey. Nieces, in-laws and more obscure relatives also rose.

The honours system was notably dishonest during James' reign, but the scale of good fortune showered on Villiers' entire kindred was unusual. Both the king and Sir Francis Bacon carefully tutored the meteoric new duke in the subtleties of statecraft and Buckingham adapted quickly to the art of surviving and thriving at the royal court. One thing difficult to manage for an inexperienced courtier was the sustained and heavy attacks from factions which represented the interests of old and established aristocratic families. The Howard family, which included the Earl of Suffolk, was one such formidable grouping, but Buckingham successfully created his own court alliances to neutralise the threat from this source and Suffolk was deposed from his position of Lord Treasurer. He was able to consolidate his role and assist the king closely with the shaping of his policies, both domestic and foreign. Through patronage and deft handling of men, both important and lesser, he was able to create a very wide circle of influence in the court. Generous to those who were indebted to him or who did him favours, he was cold and vengeful against those whom he perceived had acted against him. He also became an astute player of the political patronage game, learning the craft from a number of mentors, including Sir Francis Bacon. Bacon, ironically, came to rely on Buckingham's patronage and was finally disgraced with his tacit approval. Bacon had taken the new man into his confidence when following the king's difficult mission of ensuring that Robert Carr was found guilty of Overbury's murder but not actually put to death. Villiers took advantage of this opening and seems to have used Bacon's sexuality to win further favour. Sir Francis, in his mid-fifties, wrote excitedly about a letter he had received from young Villiers which had kindled a flame in him that would never be extinguished.

The surviving letters between James and Buckingham show a profound connection between two men who were bound up in a complex relationship. The same paternal language aimed at former favourites was used again by the king for Steenie, but the king overwhelmed George with a wide array of familiar, possessive terms. King James addressed his protégé variously as his child, wife, his boy, Steenie, of course, sweetheart and 'gossop' (meaning godson). In several letters (written in 1620 and 1621), James refers to him as 'my only sweet and dear child'.[18] In one letter he termed Buckingham 'my bastard brat'. Buckingham in turn often called himself the king's servant, slave, or dog.

Buckingham seemed happily content during the early years as a favourite simply to go with the flow of accruing resources from the monarch and assisting family and friends to climb socially, as well as using his new powers to extend his influence into new areas. He acted as the king's messenger and representative with the ambassador of Spain and other important figures, but he soon evolved into a more active figure who became embroiled in murkier political manoeuvrings. This inevitably polarised opinion about him. He was drawn into the messy European struggle which ensued when King James's son-in-law Frederick, the Elector Palatine, accepted the crown of Bohemia and was then deposed by Catholic forces, paving the way for the Thirty Years War. His reputation further declined when he became tainted by accusations of corruption involving the system of court patronage. The king was obliged to go before the House of Lords and defend Buckingham, saying he was beset by people clamouring for preferment from all sides. In a warning to his listeners (and, more mildly, also to Buckingham), he stated that, if push came to shove and Buckingham was indeed guilty of misdeed, he might revert to being plain George Villiers. But there was no blatant wrongdoing, apart perhaps for Buckingham on occasion not being as discriminating as required when dealing with financial business. Critics continued to circle Buckingham, concerned with the sale of titles and other matters, but he weathered the storm. In the end, Francis Bacon, as Lord Chancellor, was made to take the brunt of the tide of opinion against establishment dishonesty when he was charged with corruption and made to resign his office, then landed with a huge fine. His crime of accepting bribes from litigants was hardly unique in the higher tiers of government and he became a target for enemies when he conspicuously fell into debt.

Buckingham managed the king's business and furthered his own agenda successfully, thanks to a stubborn element in his personality which earned him the nickname of the 'White Mule'. As with his reorganisation of the navy, Buckingham got a firm grip on the king's Bedchamber, reorganising it and gaining even more control over the central mechanism of the king's household. By 1622 he was in control of the Bedchamber along with Prince Charles. Although the two became close confederates, their initial relationship was strained. The insecure prince was still coming to terms with the shock of being elevated to heir to the throne following the unexpected death of his brother, Henry. Unsure of himself and rather immature at sixteen, he was in awe of his father and threatened by this new favourite who was eight years older than him. The two squabbled like siblings over the matter of a ring at one of their initial meetings. In May 1616 Charles directed a jet of water at the rival for his father's affections and had his ears boxed twice by James. The king forced the pair of them together since he could never stand ill-feeling among his nearest and dearest. Buckingham finally won over Charles with a magnificent 'Prince's Feast' in June. Despite their different characters, it has been wondered whether Villiers was accepted into the king's immediate family as a substitute for the deceased and dearly loved Prince Henry.[19]

After their friendship was cemented, the strangest episode Charles and Villiers embarked upon was an adventure to Spain, undertaken to finalise the marriage negotiations between Charles and the Infanta Maria. The Spanish were dragging their heels over the negotiations and Charles hoped that he could conclude the match by being personally present in Spain. King James was initially against the journey, but was browbeaten into giving his permission, on the condition that Buckingham accompanied the prince on his ill-advised trip. Dressed in disguise, including false beards, Buckingham and Charles were in high spirits when they set off. They even called themselves by pseudonyms, prompting the now reconciled king to scribe a poem about the jape, 'Off Jacke, and Tom', in which he links his escapade with the undercover adventures of King James V of Scotland and also with his own overseas jaunt to Denmark. Addressing Charles, he wrote, 'Thie grandsire greate, thie ffather to were thine examples.'

The English pair travelled to Paris and then on to Spain completely undetected. But the astonished Spanish got the wrong end of the stick and hopefully assumed that Prince Charles had come to convert to Catholicism. Then the marriage negotiations dragged on for months. As it became clear that Charles and Buckingham would be delayed for an extended period in Madrid, King James began to fret and told them the news 'hath strukken me dead. I fear it shall very much shorten my days'. An agreement of sorts was concluded, and the pair of adventurers arrived back in England towards the end of the year to widespread relief and celebration. The jubilation was largely due to the fact that the adventurers had not brought the infanta back with them.

But the general feeling against the Spanish and against Buckingham was growing. The Spanish themselves began to drip poisonous accusations against Buckingham that were so effective at one stage that the king believed them, exclaiming that he was the unhappiest man alive, to be treated with such ingratitude by those who were dearest to him.[20] James's suspicious nature and credulity were worked upon well by expert Iberian propagandists. The Spanish insinuated that Charles and Buckingham would force the king to abdicate and be confined to Theobalds House, a propaganda tale aimed at countering the two men most in favour of war with Spain.[21] The Spanish priest Padre Maestro had private meetings with King James and spun an incredible story which said that Buckingham planned to overthrow him, then marry off his own daughter to Frederick and Elizabeth's son and so secure the kingdom for his posterity. The king was so concerned about the possibility that he summoned the Lords of Council before them and made them swear that they knew nothing of any allegation that Buckingham was plotting against him. When Buckingham sensed the king turn against him, he pressed James to reveal the reason and the king burst into tears. Shocked, Buckingham declared his innocence and love and eventually conquered the king's suspicions. When Buckingham fell gravely ill in May 1624, the king's full feelings for him returned and their relationship was restored. The duke's recovery was slow, and he was left lean and discoloured. When he was well enough to appear again before King James, the monarch showered him with a hundred kisses.

The relationship between king and duke may have ceased being physical for several years before the king's demise.[22] An interesting indicator of possible intimacy was the recent discovery of a hidden passage at the king's mansion of Apethorpe, dated 1622-24, linking the royal bedchamber with the duke's apartments. It was at Apethorpe where the king first encountered Villiers in 1614. The end of the physical relationship was largely due to the king's failing health.

A useful side effect of this breach in physical relations may have been that it allowed Prince Charles to draw a veil over the past sexual history of James and Buckingham, and the two formed a tight political bond which moved policy away from the pacifism which King James had long espoused. While the king attempted to resist the growing national tide of feeling for war by telling Parliament that it would inevitably be an expensive prospect, Buckingham and Charles persisted in moved the nation closer to conflict. Buckingham and Prince Charles spoke to Parliament in February 1624 after their less than successful Spanish mission and entered into full sabre-rattling mode, strongly urging war against Spain. Buckingham certainly threatened to withdraw affection from the king if he did not accept the need to alter his foreign policy in favour of a more warlike stance.

In the period from the mid-1620s until his death, Buckingham's reputation fluctuated. He was well regarded on his return from Spain with Charles in 1624, but his less than glorious handling of English attacks on Spain and the lack of any real gains from alliance with the Dutch Republic in late 1625 did not enhance his reputation. Another setback was his handling of an expedition in 1627 to relieve the siege of La Rochelle, which resulted in the death of 5,000 English troops. The mounting cost of war, once English troops engaged in the Low Countries, was alarming to powerful men in England, especially when set against the duke's personal prodigal spending record. This and his lack of military experience made him a target for high-profile attacks, with criticisms further motivated by jealousy and his reputed homosexuality. The assault on his character was relentless and savage, though mostly anonymous. One poem memorably likened him to a capon, a castrated rooster. It seems that supernatural forces were also gathering against the duke. A freak storm and whirlwind which assaulted London on 12 June 1626 was so powerful that it demolished churchyard walls and tumbled corpses out of their graves. Keen observers saw significance in the fact that the London mansion which suffered the most damage that day was Buckingham's most lavish property, York House.

Despite the fates ranged against him, and the suspicions that he was guilty of hastening the end of King James, in early 1625 Buckingham retained his position under King Charles I and his influence was no less than previously. His power was perceived by some as being equal to the king's and he was also resented for having been born a commoner. The Venetian ambassador reported to his countrymen that George Villiers 'seems naturally modest, affable, kind and courteous, and deserving of the good fortune'. The Italian was plainly baffled by the English class system, writing that the people here 'cannot endure that one born a simple gentleman, a rank slightly esteemed ... should be the sole access to the Court, the sole means of favour, in fact one might say the King himself ... who has given him all his heart, who will not eat, sup or remain an hour without him and considers him his whole joy.'[23]

Criticism of Buckingham had to be formulated in a circumspect fashion because of his immense power within the establishment. His unpopularity gave some commentators the excuse to target his close physical relationship with king and use it as a weapon against him. The anonymous poem 'The Warre of the Gods' (1623) portrays King James as Jupiter drunk on nectar given to him by the upstart 'white fayst boy' whose influence is so great that the other gods plot to 'scurdge his arse'. The allusions to sodomy are clear.[24] Villiers was undoubtedly extremely unpopular in his final days. A popular jingle summed up public sentiment: 'Who rules the kingdom? The king. Who rules the king? The duke. Who rules the duke? The devil.' There are echoes here of the years earlier jingles that mocked the previous favourite, Robert Carr, and his associate, Overbury.

There were plenty willing to attack Buckingham for leading the king astray sexually and monopolizing power in the court. Buckingham, together with Prince Charles, was strongly opposed to the power of Spain and in tune with the sabre rattlers who wanted English engagement in continental warfare. In this he was on the same side as notable aristocrats such as the Earl of Southampton (who was Shakespeare's patron), who viewed national pride and aristocratic purpose as being fuelled by proud aggression against European enemies. Buckingham's determination to pursue an aggressive anti-Spanish policy can be seen in the ruthless way he caused the ruin of

Lionel Cranfield, Earl of Middlesex, his close associate and Lord Treasurer, who opposed the policy. In 1624 Buckingham forced the king to break Cranfield, who was stripped of his offices and penalised with a massive fine. Severely reduced in power himself as he entered the last months of his life, King James could only manage to reduce the financial penalty imposed upon Middlesex.[25] The fact that Charles and Buckingham were effectively draining away his control over the nation in the last few months of his life did not escape the king. He felt dejected and deserted by the two men he relied on most in life. On one occasion he poignantly told Prince Charles, however seriously, that he would give him the reins of government and devote all his remaining energies to merely staying alive, a hope that was not fulfilled.[26]

The controversial role that Buckingham may have played in the death of King James is discussed in the next chapter. Suspicion about his killing King James was just one accusation against him. The Puritan Alexander Leighton roundly cursed Villiers for his 'Masses, Murders, Poisons, Treasons, Venery, & Venifices', all part of 'his Jesuited tricks', even though he was not a Catholic. Villiers appeared genuinely affected by the death of the king and he was entrusted by the new monarch Charles I with a high degree of trust in negotiating the complex politics relating to England's relationship with Spain, France, and other European powers. Charles had told the tearful duke that, in himself, he had 'found another that will no less cherish you'.

But the tide of opinion continued to turn against Buckingham and he became widely despised by high and low alike. In 1626 the MP Sir John Elliot was sent to the Tower for comparing him to the evil Sejanus, adviser to the emperor Tiberius. Common people were openly satirical about him. Three fiddlers from Middlesex were arrested in 1627 for singing ribald ballads against Villiers. The following year, there were rumours saying he would be jailed in the Tower of London. An informal occult industry centred around foreseeing the manner of Villiers' demise. People made anagrams of his name in a crude fortune telling attempt to see how the fates would punish him.

One chronogram pinned his dark fate down to the year 1628: 'Thy numerous name with this year doth agree, But twenty-nine, Heaven grant thou never see!' His portrait was seen to topple from the wall shortly before his demise, signalling his own fall. The aristocratic (and insane) prophetess Lady Eleanor Davies annoyed King Charles by repeatedly stating that Buckingham would not live past August.[27] A posthumous story appeared (in 1652) claimed that the spectre of Buckingham's father, dressed in Elizabethan garb, appeared to a man named Towse and gave warning that his son would die unless he followed instructions given to the man. Buckingham met the man, but apparently would not follow the ghostly advice.[28] Villiers himself became a supernatural symbol, resurrected as a warning for many decades after his death whenever an unpopular figure was seen as similarly hoarding too much influence with successive rulers. It was inevitable that the great power he accumulated would breed commensurate loathing. Even Robert Cecil, a very different character, was vilified when he died. But the hate campaign against George Villiers started before he died and lingered long afterwards.

Some friends who were mindful of his great unpopularity asked Villiers to wear mail or similar protective clothing, but through bravado or confidence he refused. But did he privately gauge the powerful feelings of violence gathering against him? During his last meeting with King Charles he is said to have been very solemn and embraced him fervently. There was a story that he was once separated from his company and met a man who had evil intentions toward him. Instead of killing him, the would-be assassin was won over by his manner and later reported the duke was nothing like the person he was reported to be. On his way to Portsmouth from London, his friend Sir John Goring had sent him a letter advising him to change his route because his life was in danger. He ignored the warning and travelled on regardless. Further on, an old lady accosted the travelling party and said there was a plot in the next town to murder the duke and his nephew begged him to let him wear his clothing as a decoy, but Villiers would not hear of it. There was a real scare when the duke's coach was mobbed by angry sailors on 17 August. They were furious they had not been paid their wages. One sailor tried to enter the coach, but Buckingham leapt out, grabbed the man and had him imprisoned. There was further trouble after the man was released for fear of reprisals, against the will of the duke, who later recaptured him, sparking another riot by the mariners.

On 22 August he was fatally stabbed by a man while staying at an inn in Portsmouth. The assassin was named John Fenton and he fled into the kitchens. The people in the inn thought the murderer was a foreigner and started to cry 'Frenchman', which the real assassin comically misheard as his own name and gave himself up on the assumption that his identity was known. He was executed a month later, but many applauded his actions. The duke was only thirty-five years old.

His mother, Mary, a strong character, took the news of his death calmly. It is said she too had a premonition of it. Soon after he heard about the news, King Charles threw himself on his bed and cried pitifully. But it was notable that the duke was not replaced by anyone with the same wide-ranging powers. Charles did not concentrate all his hopes or love in the hand of one powerful favourite. In this and many other things he was the opposite of his father. Charles was not prone to overindulging in food or alcohol and opposed foul language and immoral behaviour. He was also conspicuously devoted to his wife.

The question remains as to whether King Charles believed that Buckingham was indeed his father's lover. Would he have remained close to Buckingham, and indeed trusted him as his right-hand man and trusted advisor, if he had seriously countenanced the possibility of a relationship between his father and the favourite? To be a successful king entails stowing unpleasant information to the back of the mind if it runs counter to the business of successfully maintaining sovereignty. When he became king, the uncertain and diffident Charles I needed George Villiers, Duke of Buckingham, or believed that he did. The spell that Villiers cast over him was as complete as that which he used on James I, though the terms of their close relationship were different.

Chapter 12

The Forerunner of Revenge

The Death of King James

In March 1625 King James went into what proved to be a final decline. His health had begun to deteriorate several years earlier as he reached his fiftieth year, with possible signs of premature senility. In 1616 his arthritis and gout caused him weakness and swelling in his legs for months on end. Pain spread to all his joints and particularly affected him in the winter. His spirits were also affected, and he became morose and depressed. Following the death of Queen Anne, and possibly partly because of it, King James was simultaneously seriously affected by 'the stone', gout and arthritis, vomiting and diarrhoea. He was seriously ill for eight days and caused serious concern to doctors treating him. For a period after his recovery, he had to be carried in a litter by servants like some ancient potentate. But in periods of good health the king seemed to fool himself that he was well, overindulging in fruit and in alcohol, scoffing at the advice of the medical profession. (One doctor noted in 1623 that 'he laughs at medicine'.) Even towards the end he was reportedly not following medical advice.[1] The Swiss physician Theodore Turquet de Mayerne had noted, when James was in great pain, 'it tortures him with violent movements, his mind is tossed as well, thus augmenting the evil. He demands relief from pain without considering the causes of his illness.'[2]

With the king's ageing came a lessening of his will and concentration on the affairs of state. A large part of his power was delegated to Buckingham. He became more fearful of death at times and more indulgent of his own bad habits. His drinking and overeating became worse, and it was keenly noted by his subjects and by foreign observers. The Venetian ambassador Alvise Vallaresso noted:

> All good sentiments are clearly dead in the king. He is too blinded in disordered self-love and his wish for quiet and pleasure, too agitated by constant mistrust of everyone, tyrannised over by perpetual fear of his life, tenacious of his authority as against the Parliament and jealous of his son's obedience, all accidents and causes of his almost desperate infirmity of mind.[3]

The king's notoriously poor personal hygiene may also have made him more susceptible to illness. Despite all this, to some it seemed like he might reign for many more years, but things changed. He had been crippled with gout in November 1623 and was again ill at the end of 1624, more or less confined to his quarters and very melancholy. James had to be carried indoors by two servants because of his immobility, necessitating the internal doorways to be widened. The king came to his final place of rest, Theobalds House, north of London, on 28 February. Already subject to fainting, gout and arthritis, he contracted a serious fever. The latter was ascribed to tertian ague, linked to malaria, which was not generally deemed to be fatal by itself. The illnesses continued for around three weeks, with the fever striking the king on the 6 March. His favourite Buckingham was on his way to France to finish negotiations for the marriage of Prince Charles and Henrietta Maria, but rushed back to his master's bedside. The treatment given a week later was a plaster or poultice which had been strongly advised by Buckingham and his mother. This plaster was supposed to work into the king's stomach to quell the fever. Witnesses examined after the king's death said that plasters were reapplied to the king after doctors removed the first one. Royal surgeon Gilbert Penrose stated that the king became worse after the plaster was applied to him, but the facts around the poultice treatment are disputed, with some testimony saying that Buckingham delayed sending for it, and the impatient king dispatched a man to fetch it himself.

A second treatment was a julep drink, or posset, which the old king could only manage a few sips of.[4] It was stated that the king was unhappy with this potion, exclaiming, 'They gave me warm drink that makes me burn and roast so, and would have given more.' The Scottish doctor James Chambers also heard the king say, in agony, 'Will you murder or slay me?' The king's personal doctors refused to countenance their own treatment until these unofficial remedies were stopped. Some of the medics stated outright that the king was being poisoned. A number of doctors saw the king in his last few weeks, possibly as many as nine.[5] If they were generally in unanimity about his condition, it seems they did not offer a decisive and effective course of treatment. Nor did they muster the collective authority to forestall unofficial treatment given to the monarch.

There is confusion in the records concerning the way in which these unofficial treatments were administered. One story says that Buckingham advised the king to try out the medicine on a servant who was ill, but this was not done as the man was not present. Contrary to the evidence stating that King James was suspicious of these potions, it was also said that he responded angrily when told that the things were administered to him without sound medical opinion and the duke meant him harm. 'They are worse than devils that say it,' he is alleged to have said.[6]

One doctor, Dr John Craig, protested so loudly about the treatment that he was sent away. He later told the inquiry into the king's death that it had been said within the royal chamber, 'that which was given to the King by the Duke was as bad as poison'. But Craig denied that he had voiced this himself. (Craig had been a principal court doctor during the latter part of the king's Scottish reign and migrated with him to England.) King Charles was displeased that Craig was blatantly implicating Buckingham. A delegation of doctors had allegedly complained to Charles about the interference of Buckingham, which Charles had done nothing to stop.[7]

James was well enough to play cards with Buckingham on 11 March. He seemed better again on 18 and 19 March, and when Buckingham returned to his side on 21 March, having been away for a few days, he was well enough to take a few steps out of bed.[8] But he soon suffered a relapse, and this was followed by a stroke which left his jaw loose, and he struggled to cope with a surge of phlegm. Though he had become speechless, James, characteristically signalled for the comfort of a book to be brought to him; but he had little time left to indulge in literature. Soon he was assaulted by a dreadful bout of dysentery. One version of events states that the doctors were thrown from the sick chamber by the outraged Buckingham around this time, and Buckingham's mother begged the king to clear her and her son of the charges of poisoning that were already being whispered against them.

The fevers were prolonged, but the king rallied slightly. Then the final downturn began on 24 March when he had a terrible convulsion and James quietly accepted the news that he should prepare for death. The medical report following his death states that he suffered a fit which endured for twenty hours and left him in a deep sleep. Further symptoms attacked the monarch, including violent, continuous diarrhoea. After a final violent bout of dysentery, the king succumbed to death on 27 March.

A sanitised version of his end included a touching adherence to religious observance and the peaceful and saintly rising of the king to a seated position, just long enough to utter his last words, '*Veni, Domine Jesu*', before relapsing into oblivion. This version was partly promoted by another of the king's personal physicians, the eminent and elderly Sir William Paddy, who arrived at the royal bedside on the day before his death. Paddy realised there was nothing more that could be done for the monarch. Archbishop George Abbot and another bishop, John Williams, spiritually supported the king and he seemed reconciled to his end.

Some other courtiers reported, falsely, that the king left some pertinent and wise advice for his son Charles, thus giving a smooth transfer of power to his successor.[9] Yet another fabulous tale states that the dying king placidly told his favourite, several days before the end, 'Steenie, I am willing to die but I am sorry I must leave the world before I have done for thee [what] my love intended.'[10] When he eventually succumbed to death, the duke was weeping so much that he could not see to close the monarch's eyes. What else, one wonders, could the king have given to Villiers that he had not already received.

The Privy Council met soon afterwards and proclaimed his son King Charles. It was the first time for almost eighty years that the throne had passed directly from father to son and heir. From Theobalds, a messenger was sent to London to break the news. Charles and Buckingham reached London a short time later and Archbishop Laud was told of the death shortly before ascending into the pulpit to give his address at the evening service. Just as he was starting to speak, he was interrupted by piteous sobs coming from the pews. He looked down and saw that Buckingham was responsible and he was obliged to stop his sermon. King Charles and Buckingham later spent two hours locked away from the world in personal grief. Buckingham had a relapse in health soon afterwards, possibly brought on by his grieving.

There were soon persistent rumours that James's death had been hastened by poison. The large number of people who were coming and going confused the events which later investigation tried to establish. Remarkably, two foreign agents were said to have been present in Theobalds House during the king's final days. They reported to their spymaster, Jean Baptiste Van Male, in the Spanish Netherlands that there were 'strange tragedies' around the royal sickbed. As well as noting the odd plasters and potions, they had wider fears regarding the implication of the king's demise for the whole of Christendom.[11] Most particularly, this was linked with the sinister machinations of the Duke of Buckingham, who would be freed to unleash all his sinister policies.

Some of the king's attendants also pointed the finger at Buckingham and his mother for being directly complicit in the king's death. The House of Commons impeached Buckingham for causing the king's death in 1626. Mr Wandesford, prosecuting Buckingham, stated that there was something malignant about the poultice applied to the king's person. At least one of the two treatments devised by Remington, either the plaster or the posset, were composed of a secret recipe based on mithridate, a complex formula comprising at least fifty ingredients.[12] After taking two drinks of the posset from Buckingham, King James refused a third. When he had a relapse, he said it was not from any ordinary cause but 'it is that which I had from Buckingham'. A different source states that the king blamed his suffering health on the black plaster and powder given to him and he gladly pulled the plaster off, along with the skin it was attached to.[13]

Buckingham told a different story regarding the drink. He said the king asked him what he had taken for his own recent fever and Buckingham had recommended the posset. According to some, the concoction was a harmless blend of milk, ale, hartshorn and marigold. He stated to the enquiry that the Earl of Warwick's physician had prescribed the drink and the plaster to him. Yet Buckingham was cautious, he said, of procuring these items for the king himself; the king commanded Buckingham's own servant to bring him the remedies. Does this show a genuine concern for the king or a foresight that he might be blamed for unauthorised treatment? Even experienced doctors sometimes hesitated when the life of a monarch hung in the balance. Perceived failure, incompetence, or charges of deliberate malice might put them in mortal danger. When, in 1453, Henry VI was sick, his doctors thought it was not safe to administer anything to him without the express consent of the Privy Council.[14]

Buckingham did not make the case for his innocence any better by driving away the king's physicians at the point of his sword. It was unfortunate for the king that one of the chief medical men responsible for his health, the Swiss Mayerne, was abroad when James fell seriously ill. Before his departure he had left detailed instructions about how to manage the king's health, including the sensible advice that there should be a panel of five eminent medics jointly in charge of treating any illness of the king.[15] Unfortunately, this was not strictly followed at the end. Mayerne's attention may not have made any significant difference as the king's lifestyle choices and disdain of treatment had already pushed him past the point of no return. Mayerne was a wealthy practitioner with an international reputation and clientele on the Continent. He had links to the court of James's daughter Elizabeth and was himself a baron in Switzerland.[16] He had treated Prince Henry in his last illness and had also been one of the physicians who visited the fever-ridden Thomas Overbury in the Tower of London prior to his death by poisoning.

An enquiry into the source of the suspect medication revealed that it had been sourced from Dr John Remington, of Dunmow in Essex. Buckingham had paid this practitioner handsomely in the past for treatments, despite the fact that the man had no medical training. Buckingham's patronage of unorthodox physicians may have raised some eyebrows, but he had made light of it previously, even to the king himself. He advised Bishop Laud in 1624 that he had consulted a man who had offered him an odd remedy to cure illnesses in himself and his brother. During the same period, he was involved with another notorious quack doctor, John Lambe, a convicted witch and rapist. Ironically, Lambe was stoned to death by a mob in 1628, shortly before Buckingham met his own death, partly on account of his own crimes, but also perhaps because of his association with the duke. A popular rhyme at the time hoped the duke's death would follow this man's: 'Let Charles and George do what they can, the Duke shall die like Doctor Lambe.' Ominously, on the day when Lambe was murdered, Villiers' portrait fell from its frame in the High Commission chamber in Lambeth Palace.

In a letter to King James, Villiers confessed that he had paid yet another, anonymous healer, who he called 'my divill', the enormous sum of £400 for his services. A concoction from this source had been sent to his majesty 'to preserve you from al sicknes ver herafter'.[17] His association with the notorious Lambe allowed George Eglisham to claim that the duke publicly consorted with the ringleader of witches. Evidence concerning King James's death also heard about a mysterious Irishman named Piers Butler who implied he had given

Buckingham a magical amulet that would protect him from harm and who supposedly dealt in occult potions. There was a suggestion that he used toad venom, and this may have been added to medicine given to the king. He may have been Buckingham's elusive devil. A man with a chameleon-like reputation (alchemist, poisoner or medic), Butler was as enigmatic as another character in the mystery of the king's death, the Scotsman named Eglisham.

Among other things, George Eglisham was a medic who may have treated the king at some stage. Shortly after the king's death he produced a work entitled *Prodromus Vindictae*, or *The Forerunner of Revenge*, in different versions published in Europe, which sought to convince readers that Buckingham had engineered the deaths of the king and his great friend the Marquis of Hamilton. Eglisham, who had his own religious agenda, states that Buckingham had wind of the displeasure of both the king and Hamilton regarding his misadventures in Spain. According to Eglisham, King James was administered a white powder by Buckingham on the Monday evening before he died, when all his doctors were dining. He refused to swallow it at first, but eventually took it with some wine and immediately became violently ill. In the midst of severe stomach pains, he cried out, 'Would to God I had never taken it! It will cost me my life.' Buckingham's mother likewise later applied the poisonous plaster to the king's body when the doctors were not present. After the king passed away, Buckingham tried to persuade the doctors that the white powder was not noxious, but they refused to sign anything.[18]

Eglisham had to flee into exile to escape the commotion his allegations caused. His work sparked great consternation in Britain, despite the fact that he was acknowledged to be an ardent Catholic convert. There is also no surviving proof that he was actually an officially appointed doctor to the king as he claimed to be. Among other sensational claims in his book, he accused Buckingham of authoring a hit-list of people he wanted killed in London. A document placed before Parliament spoke about Buckingham's 'fowle and unchristian like carriage about the kinge towards his ende'. Parliament was dismissed before the matter could be properly assessed and when it was recalled in 1628, the matter was still under consideration when Buckingham himself died. Some people gave credit to the allegations, including David Calderwood, author of the *History of the Kirk of Scotland*. In the latter work the minister informed his readers of dreadful storms throughout Scotland at the end of March which he linked to the news reaching the nation of the death of the king. He also tells a bizarre tale that Buckingham took a pig into the sick chamber and performed a mock baptism on it and chased it up and down the room. Some thought the crude profanity was to make the king laugh, 'But it was said by manie that heard of it, that it was plaine magicke.'[19]

Eglisham's probable libel was later utilised for political purposes. In 1648 the imprisoned King Charles I was accused by Parliament of allowing the Duke of Buckingham and his mother to murder his father. The rumours surrounding 'plasters and potions' were certainly not the invention of Eglisham. Remarkably, a spy reported to the Dutch representative of the Spanish Netherlands on 25 March, two days before the king's death, that these things had been administered to James and brought him to the point of extremity.[20] *The Forerunner of Revenge* alleges that Buckingham broke with the king by wrecking the Anglo-Spanish peace and destroying the chances of the marriage between Charles and the infanta. Buckingham, Eglisham wrote, was stung by the king's criticism and wanted to forcibly retire him to some hunting park so he could act as the evil power behind the throne of King Charles. When it became clear that James was wise to his opposition, the only recourse left to him was to kill the king.

Eglisham outlived Buckingham and died a natural death in exile in the 1630s, despite claims that he was assassinated on royal orders. He certainly enjoyed a colourful career in Europe, dabbling in medicine, teaching, plus lecturing in philosophy, and moving in circles close to the French court. There are indications that he enjoyed controversy, since we know that he quarrelled with Jesuit authorities in Rouen and was not highly thought of by the secular staff at the University of Paris.[21]

But some of the information he gives regarding the king and Hamilton may be true. It seems that he was distantly related to the Hamilton family, which may explain his hostility to Buckingham (if we believe the tale that the latter caused his death). The pamphlet's account of Hamilton's corpse can be verified through other sources. It seems that his body swelled up and assumed a strange colour some fifteen hours after his death. Rumours swirled soon afterwards, compounded with the likely false tale that he had converted to Catholicism on his deathbed.[22] Eglisham attended Hamilton at the very end of his life and was rumoured to have engineered a last-minute Catholic conversion. The fallout over his part in this event may have been the underlying reason why Eglisham fled abroad, not his fear of repercussions for exposing the poisoning of the king. In his tract, Eglisham firmly paints Buckingham as the villain in the Scottish nobleman's death. Buckingham hated Hamilton after he refused to agree to the marriage of his eldest son to Buckingham's niece. A low born man, unnaturally raised to great heights artificially by a besotted monarch, Buckingham was jealous of the true nobility of Hamilton.

The controversy about whether Buckingham poisoned King James was a powerful element in the fierce contest between monarchists and revolutionary republicans in the decades after 1625. Eglisham's pamphlet was reprinted several times after 1642 in the Civil War period and radical figures used the allegations of complicity in his father's death as one reason for breaking off negotiations with the embattled King Charles I. It was ironic that a pamphlet accusing a king of helping to murder his father and written by a Scottish Catholic was used by puritan English Protestants as a weapon to help kill the second king. On a wider level, the discussion of the king's death was examined as if it could afford a clue into the moral decay of the House of Stuart, and historians of all shades discussed it for many generations. Literal minded Victorian writers, who had little time for the embarrassing credulity of their predecessors, largely came to the conclusion that the whole event was a baseless conspiracy. This was reasonable, but it failed to take into account the fact that the 'rumour' was very widely believed for a long time and was indeed a potent story, whether or not it was actually true.²³

One of the more curious manifestations of the rumour was a tract published in 1642 titled *Strange Apparitions, or The Ghost of King James*. This presented a dialogue between the ghosts of King James and the Duke of Buckingham, and also featured the figures of Dr Eglisham and the Marquis of Hamilton. Hamilton accuses Buckingham of killing both himself and King James and forcing the doctor to flee to the Netherlands, where he was stabbed to death on Buckingham's instigation. Buckingham quails before his fellow ghosts: 'My liege, I cannot discourse as long as they are present, they do behold me with such threatening looks; and your Majesty hath a disturbed brow, as if you were offended by your servant Buckingham.' Although Buckingham denies the misdeeds, the doctor calls him to order and accuses him of Hamilton's death. The king's ghost exclaims that he believes that angels would sooner be corrupted than Buckingham. But the doctor accuses him of killing the king to hide his own behaviour and to replace him on the throne with his son Charles. At last Buckingham confesses, but he will not reveal those others who conspired with him in the foul deed.²⁴

So, did Buckingham actually kill King James? His biographer, Roger Lockyer, thinks there was no deliberate malice involved in the medicines he administered, although the concoctions may indeed have been potentially harmful.²⁵ There was an official Latin report on the king's cause of death and various medical conditions which does not raise any suspicions whatever that the death may have been caused by poison or by any kind of foul play.²⁶ Some modern reassessments suggest that the king was indeed poisoned. One modern toxicologist, Dr John Henry, examined the evidence and suggested that James I died from the effects of iconite, a derivative of wolfsbane.²⁷ Buckingham did go against the agreed practice among the king's doctors that only they should administer medicine to his majesty and that any drugs should be produced exclusively by the royal apothecary. His own evidence stressed his reluctance to procure medicine for the king and insisted that James spurred him on to procure it. He also insisted that it be tried first on James Palmer, a gentleman of the bedchamber who himself was suffering from a similar ague. Buckingham distanced himself from formulating the medicine, though he had tried them himself when previously ill, saying that they had been recommended to him by the Earl of Warwick. Tellingly, he omitted the fact that he had admitted Dr Remington into Theobalds House and he had treated the king at the beginning of March.[28] The doctors who examined the king's corpse could find no conclusive evidence of poisoning. Among those who denied the charges against poisoning was another royal doctor, William Harvey, in 1618.[29]

The tangled facts seem to suggest that Buckingham acted out of goodwill by suggesting the potion and the plaster remedies for the king. There was no real reason why he would have wanted the king's death, despite suggestions to the contrary. In the end the charges against him were as ridiculous as the alternative suggestion that King James was in fact murdered by the Jesuits. There were other variants in the tales. Sir Anthony Weldon says that a Spanish agent maliciously sent a Jesuit to the king with the warning that Buckingham meant to slay him, though whether by poison, pistol, or dagger he could not tell. King James upbraided the favourite when they next met, saying, 'Steenie, Steenie, wilt thou kill me?' When Buckingham asked who had said so, the king was quiet. Buckingham soon learned from a former associate of Somerset that the king bore him great malice now.[30]

The many outlandish details added to tales of Buckingham murdering King James strengthen the implausibility of his guilt. Did Buckingham introduce a pig into the death chamber and blasphemously christen it? Did he foully kick a royal servant at the bedside of the dying monarch? Most likely not, in both cases. But, by working in tandem with Prince Charles, in an effort to break the peace with Spain and promote war, Buckingham had effectively neutralised the king in the end. As an independent, effective ruler he was killed. One writer has stated that this was a true political tragedy: at the point when James was capable of putting the weight of his English political experience to lasting use to help foment a European peace, he was rendered powerless.[31] Whether the duo of Buckingham and Charles would have wanted to or could actually depose King James is another matter, and very likely only the product of fevered imaginations.

The deaths of many monarchs were shrouded in mystery and suspicion. Every royal favourite in Tudor and Stuart times seems to have been accused of poisoning. James's grandson King Charles II died suddenly in 1685 and some thought his death (probably from apoplexy) was due to poison. Royal deaths were closely scrutinised because royalty was next to divinity, and the supernatural was frequently attendant when kings passed on. Prophetic and fateful signs signalled preordained and possibly strangely accomplished royal deaths.

The Venetian source who stated that King James was given advance notice of his own demise as early as 1622 via a dream messenger, his grim old childhood tutor George Buchanan, was not alone.[32] That dream correctly prophesied that he would suffer through ice and fire, referring to his fever and chills before death. Buchanan must have been busily pursuing the king in his afterlife since variations of the dream tale are found in several sources. A Mr Downham reported that the terrifying old scholar appeared to the king in a dream in 1619. Buchanan seemed to check the king severely and James tried to pacify him, but the old man recited some verses regarding his doom which the king was able to repeat verbatim next morning.[33] In 1626 Buckingham's distant relative Edmund Bolton resurrected the ghost of Buchanan in a printed defence of his kinsman which stated the king dreamt that Buchanan came to him and said that 'death would come when his carbuncle should boil with burning fire'. This was explained when it was discovered that the old highway that ran where Theobalds House was built was named Carbuncle Street.[34] Even the death of Queen Elizabeth was attended by strange irregularity. A former lady-in-waiting to the queen, Elizabeth Southwell, related uncanny circumstances about the queen's last days which appeared in a manuscript several years after her death.[35]

King James's embalmed body travelled with great dignity in procession from Theobalds House and reached London at dusk on 4 April. It lay in state at Denmark House for a month. The royal coffin was topped with a magnificently attired wooden effigy of the king. His funeral process took place on 7 May, travelling from Denmark House to Westminster, and it was one of the most lavish ceremonies witnessed in the Stuart Age. It was estimated that in excess of 5,000 people took part in the procession that day. Another contemporary estimates there were 8,000 mourners.[36] The entire funeral proceedings cost more than double the amount which had sent off Queen Elizabeth (typical for her spendthrift successor).

Various controversies obviously attended the sombre ceremonials. Leading Scottish clerics refused to dress in robes which suggested they condoned Anglicanism. The Venetian ambassador was hoodwinked into not marching and was mortified when he saw two French representatives in the solemn parade. King Charles walked behind the bier as the principal mourner and was praised for his attendance and his bearing. Quite a distance back, the Duke of Buckingham proceeded, as if conscious not to usurp the authority of the royals, nor draw undue attention to himself. A profusion of banners and flags accompanied the remains of the king. One of the four inscriptions on the hearse bore James's favoured motto, *Beati Pacifici*, 'blessed are the peacemakers', celebrating royal justice and his aim for peace within Christendom.

Chapter 13

Solomon Weighed

Reputation and Legacy

John Williams, Bishop of Lincoln and Lord Keeper of the Great Seal, gave the funeral oration in Westminster Abbey on 7 May. Making a parallel between the late King James and King Solomon, he said the king of Israel and the king of Great Britain were linked by great deeds, eloquence, and wisdom. Both were twice crowned, both had a hard upbringing, both writers of prose and verse, both unparalleled in eloquence and intelligence.[1] James himself would have been extremely pleased at such praise. But whether he was, in the bible's words about Solomon, 'a Miracle of Kings and a King of Miracles', is rather more contentious.

The image of James Stuart as a magisterial dispenser of wise justice was also fostered by himself. This is the posthumous version of the king by Rubens which sprawls across the ceiling of the banqueting hall in the Palace of Westminster. Whether it was a true reflection of his talents is debatable. Dubious also was the bishop's praise of James's warlike skills. As an international statesman, he seriously over-estimated his own capacity and was not given respect as a serious figure. His attempts to bridge the difference between the monolithic Catholic and Protestant churches may have been laudable to some but was as naïve as his attempt to force Scotland and England into one political state, and it caused alarm in the British Isles.

The king's reputation as a peacemaker stands up better than some other aspects of his life, in some respects. Whether striving to end the murderous blood feuds in his native land or decreeing against the widespread practice of duelling as soon as he came to England, James showed himself genuinely concerned with the level of damaging violence in society. But his forced pacification of the Borders and West Highlands of Scotland was not without brutality, and his placement of Protestant settlers in Ireland had troubling historical consequences. The entry of England into the wars of Europe, which James I had adamantly resisted, was a failure that could not be avoided since it was brought into being by the combined will of the nation and through the impetus of Buckingham, Charles and the majority of the establishment figures in England. James was too ill and distracted at the end of his reign to resist it. The conflict cost the lives of some 20,000 men from the British Isles.[2]

It is ironic that King James was castigated more for his pantomimic image after his death than for his actual habits, much less than his occasionally subtle statesmanship. Sir Antony Weldon and his ilk must be congratulated for the powerful caricature of the king they created, which has persisted to the present day. The dirty, slovenly, frequently drunk king is portrayed not so much as a man but as a grotesquely overgrown schoolboy who had never recovered from his traumatic upbringing. There is a bit of truth in the slander, but only some. More truthful are those who criticise James for over-spending and nearly ruining the monarchy financially. While Robert Cecil may have defended him by claiming that a king should be bountiful, he fought a running battle against James's continuous extravagance, and while it is fair to admit that King James had a far greater financial outlay because of his wife and children – unlike the childless Queen Elizabeth – he treated the treasury with careless abandon. But even in his native land, before the burden of family spending became a factor, he was living well beyond his means. He confessed to Chancellor Maitland in 1591 that he had 'offended the whole country for prodigal giving'. The king's idea of an endlessly bountiful England was just one aspect of his misreading of the southern nation. And, if England did not fully understand James Stuart, James Stuart certainly did not understand

England. The opposite is true for Scotland. When he boasted that he could govern Scotland remotely from London via the action of his pen, he was speaking the truth. It was no mean feat and certainly something that his son, Charles I, lamentably failed to do.

Milder critics than his contemporaries have damned James with faint praise. Among these is the towering eighteenth-century philosopher and historian David Hume. According to Hume:

> In all history, it would be difficult to find a reign less illustrious, yet more unspotted and unblemished, than that of James ... No prince, so little enterprising and so inoffensive, was ever so much exposed to the opposite extremes of calumny and flattery, of satire and panegyric ... his intentions were just; but more adapted to the conduct of private life than to the government of kingdoms ... And, upon the whole, it may be pronounced of his character, that all his qualities were sullied with weakness and embellished by humanity.[3]

It has to be admitted that his actions did not help him to claim enduring praise after his death. His standing was not assisted by his own productions in prose and verse. Few in the colourful era of Restoration Britain or in the age of dandies in the eighteenth century had much time for the king's overworked literature and his didactic thinking. A major failure was his dishonesty in dealing with those who did not share his own religious opinions, which naturally centred around the conviction that all should admit that he was a divinely appointed ruler. Calvinists, Catholics and others suspected King James, with good reason. He was castigated by those writers with Puritan instincts, such as Lucy Hutchinson (1620-1681), who firmly blamed him for sowing the seeds which caused the conflagrations of civil wars in the mid-seventeenth century. According to her, it was not just a matter of policy that he was guilty of: cowardly folly in the king went hand-in-hand with wickedness and vindictiveness.

The matter of the king's same-sex relationships is clouded by modern perceptions and the complex social perceptions of it in his own age. Gay sex may have been condemned, but it was in fact widely, if quietly, accepted as a fact, and there were hardly any prosecutions for sodomy.[4] Some aspects of same sex activity, especially submissive ones, were certainly frowned upon and used as means of castigating those who took part in those acts. But some men in power, even kings, were able to participate in non-secretive same-sex relationships without attracting the stigma that King James did. King William III (who reigned 1689-1702) escaped the degree of negativity that James suffered although he also cultivated favourites and had homosexual relationships. He avoided censure because of his powerful militaristic image and reputation.[5] The distrust of James and his favourites centred around the imbalance which their rapid promotions caused to the working of the royal court. Not only were the privileges of the old factions overturned by Carr and Villiers, which may have been no bad thing in itself, there was a dangerous lack of effective counterbalance against these untried and basically self-serving upstarts.

It is obvious that he enjoyed physical relationships with Villiers and Carr, and probably also with Esmé Stuart and others. Yet, no matter how effusive he was with these men in public, and gushingly emotional in his letters, he was also secretive when he thought it best served his interests. Suspicion was one of the hallmarks of James Stuart, an urge to keep enemies and even doubtful allies on the back foot. He could lie outright to once-beloved supporters, such as the time he assured the Earl of Morton of his loyalty shortly before the nobleman was executed. He was also guarded at times with his favourites. In 1622 he advised Villiers not to write to him again, probably in some sort of panic at having said too much of a personal nature in previous missives. The following year he fretted to Villiers again that the Duke of Lennox was peering over his shoulder when he was reading letters from him.

Which of the other aspects of King James's character that we can look at to pin him down? For those who believe that the child is the father of the man, he remains indeed the royal orphan, the

Cradle King of his own description, who miraculously survived the vicissitudes of a savage Caledonian background, congratulating himself on his self-taught kingcraft. Behind this façade is the small boy terrified by the learned spectre of George Buchanan who came back to persecute him as the shadows of mortality gathered around him. The most powerful ghost to appear in his reign was not the king's supposed ancestor Macbeth in Shakespeare's play, but his own monstrous pedagogue who terrorised his schooldays and beyond. Buchanan's ghost, or rather his influential castigation of the tyranny of kings, was an element in the rise of those forces which gathered against and toppled Charles I later in the seventeenth century. So powerful was the malignant intellectual spirit of George Buchanan that the university of Oxford tried to exorcise it, in July 1683, by having his works burnt by the public hangman. The spirit of King James may have enjoyed some measure of vicarious, literary revenge on Buchanan's ghost via the appearance of a 19th-century chapbook, *The Witty and Entertaining Exploits of George Buchanan*, which portrayed the fearsome polymath as a wise-cracking court fool.

What about the king's contention that he was never a bloodthirsty man? He was certainly not compulsively violent in comparison with monarchs like Henry VIII, but he was ruthless when it suited him, as in the case of Sir Walter Raleigh, or, more damningly, his own cousin Arbella. Possibly more instructive than those two seemingly rare public acts of ruthlessness are those equally cold (but also uncommon) merciless acts against lowly subjects. In these cases, there is a clear intersection between the James as a king and a private individual. The first episode involved Francis Tennant, a merchant of Edinburgh, who appeared before the Scottish authorities in 1600, charged with composing a seditious *pasquinade* about the king. Details about his satirical ballad are unknown, but it seems unlikely to have been connected to the contemporary events of the Gowrie Conspiracy, for Francis stated in his defence that he had circulated the letters containing the offensive material three years before. His defence foundered mainly because the Crown raised against him a statute that extended the death penalty to those who wrote or were caught reading any slanderous writings or speeches against the king.

Two letters of Tennant's were produced for the jury. These, he confessed, were his and he was sentenced on 23 September to be taken to the cross at Edinburgh and there to have his tongue torn out by the root and a paper affixed to his head stating that he was the author of 'wild and seditious pasquils'. Then he was to be taken to the gallows and hanged.[6] An eighteenth-century editor of criminal proceedings in Scotland says Tennant's trial was one 'which must leave an indelible stain on the character of King James VI'.[7] But the intriguing case is incompletely recorded. The only notice which the scrupulous Pitcairn found in contemporary records was in the diary of Robert Birrell, who notes an execution on 8 October 1600 of a man named Francis Kinnaird. This man was guilty of producing writing which contained treasons against the king including 'cokklentis', which may mean cuckolding.[8] Is this a reference to the supposed dalliance of Queen Anne with Alexander, Master of Ruthven? The most popular slander against his majesty was the 'Signor Davie' nickname which assigned paternity to Riccio, his mother's secretary. An English mariner named John Dickson, who was executed in Edinburgh in August 1596 for slandering the monarch, may well have repeated the parental slur, or else alluded to his sexuality. Sensitivity on these subjects was enshrined by an Act of Parliament in 1585, which made it treasonous to slander the king. An Act in 1596 extended the punishment to include any slander against the king's parents or progenitors.

Tennant's execution takes a darker significance in light of the fact that he was an erstwhile associate of the lawless Earl of Bothwell. He had taken the king's bribe on one occasion to deliver the earl into his hands, but decided to return his loyalty to Bothwell and revealed the deceit. Not only did the peer escape on that occasion, he ultimately fled to Europe in a ship belonging to the same Francis Tennant. The motives for royal revenge ran deep in this case, it seemed, and a further incentive in the political execution was the opportunity it gave King James to confiscate Tennant's considerable wealth following his death. Bothwell may have used the common rumours about the king – his supposed bastardy and his homosexuality – which had been rife for years. In 1592 James had complained to the ministers of Edinburgh about parties that were openly conspiring against him. He showed them intercepted documents, including verses written by Bothwell's associate Captain Hackerston 'calling him Davie's sonne, a bougerer, one that left his wife all night *intactam*'.[9]

In April of the following year and in the same burgh, a town officer named Archibald Cornwall was charged with selling satirical likenesses of the king, which were displayed on the public gallows. He too was sentenced to death.[10] These cases point towards a hardened attitude from an oversensitive ruler. It was to his credit perhaps that the opening of the golden gates of the English kingship mellowed his reactions to serious opposition. Was it easier for him to accept that he was the victim of a widespread Catholic conspiracy in the Gunpowder Plot than to tolerate the sniggering accusations that he was the bastard of an Italian minstrel or a sodomite? The paranoia of self-importance would have chimed with the confirmation that he was a prime Popish target, just as he was convinced that Satan had him in first place as his personal enemy.

The competence of the king's rule in England is complicated by the unclear inheritance which he had from Elizabeth I. The myth of the glittering, purposeful and popular *Gloriana*, was promoted by the great queen herself, but her sure touch in government was faltering by the 1590s. Corruption was rife at court, the country was heavily taxed, and many in the top tier of society were frustrated by the concentration of power in too few hands (a situation which led to the failed rebellion by the Earl of Essex in 1601). The poor administration of the monarch made a 17th-century writer compare the government to 'a sluttish housewife, who swept the house but left the dust behind the door'.[11] These problems were compounded by James facing some unique difficulties which Elizabeth never encountered. He ruled three nation states with three different parliaments and their own identities. Unity was also threatened by the fact that a significant minority of people under his rule spoke no English. It's also estimated that, in the year 1600, up to a third of the population of the British Isles and Ireland was still non-Protestant.

Despite his failings, James VI and I was arguably no more dishonest than many rulers, before and since. But his dissembling policies on religion and other subjects stored up long-term trouble for his successors. He was laughably puffed up by the pride he took in his motley ancestry, claiming descent from a dubiously wide range of ancient worthies, from King Arthur to Brutus and beyond, yet there were others who encouraged him in this and seemed to believe it also. The dogmatic, darker side of his royal self-importance was his insistence on the Divine Right of Kings. The partial victory of the Kirk in Scotland, insisting 'no bishops, no king', was storing up trouble for his son, King Charles I, in his confrontation with Presbyterianism decades later. In England, his dishonest handling of the concerns of Catholics and Puritans alike also stored up trouble for times ahead. The will and the instinct which manoeuvred him successfully through the dark landscape of Scotland in his adult years was dissolved by his lethargy as the ruler of England. Such political energy as he did have was expended in pointless battles against Parliament or achieving impossible dreams such as the creation of a British state. In his early years in England, James admitted that it would take him years to master the complexities ruling the larger nation of England. It was something he never achieved and he allowed his indolence to overcome his ambition.

The writing had been on the wall even as he happily journeyed south in 1603 to claim his long-awaited throne. An 'honest plain' Scotsman with a prophetical expression observed him as he passed and announced that 'this people [England] will spoyl a gud King'.[12] James was a willing accomplice in his own decline into royal nonentity. Neither he nor Scotland was every truly itself again after he retired south to bask in his long-anticipated inheritance. Yet, if King James VI and I was indeed the 'complicated neurotic', as one modern writer describes him, then he was not far out of tune with most of humanity in his own day and ours.

Illustration Sources

1.	*The Gowrie conspiracy and its Official Narrative*, Samuel Cowan, 1902.
2.	*Newes from Scotland*, 1591. Criminal Trials in Scotland, Robert Pitcairn, 1833.
3, 4.	*The Secret History of King James the First*, Walter Scott, 1811.
5. 6.	*The Lennox*, William Fraser, 1874.
7.	*History of the House of Douglas*, Herbert Maxwell, 1902.
8.	Portrait in private collection.
9.	Engraving by Jan Luyken (*c.* 1700).
10, 11.	*King's Favourite, The Love Story of Robert Carr and Lady Essex*, Philip Gibbs, 1890.
12, 13, 14, 15.	*James VI & I*, T. F. Henderson, 1904.
16.	*Master Robert Bruce, Minister in the Kirk of Edinburgh*, D. C. MacNicoll, 1907.
17.	*Five Stuart Princesses*, Robert R. Rait, 1902.
18.	*The Progresses, Processions and Magnificent Festivities of King James*, John Nichols, London, 1838.
19.	*Surgundo*, Charles Kirkpatrick Sharpe, 1837.
20.	*Arbella Stuart, A Biography*, B. C. Hardy, 1913.
21.	*A Life of Mary, Queen of Scots*, Agnes Strickland, 1903.
22.	*Lives of the Queens of England*, Agnes Strickland, ed. Rosalie Kaufman, 1894.

Notes and References

Introduction

1. Letter to Queen Mary's secretary, 15 August 1584, Ashton (1969), p2.
2. *Basilkon Doron*, in King James (2010), p51.
3. Thomson (1970), p5.
4. Willson, (1963), p165.
5. Akrigg (1984), p3.
6. Capps and Carlin (2007).

Chapter 1: Buchanan's Boy – *Early Years*

1. Weldon in the 1640s (1817), p55.
2. Thomson (1970), p8.
3. Herries (1836). p79.
4. Pitcairn (1833), p333.
5. Thomson (1970), p12. For a variation, see Osborne (1811), p231.
6. Matusiak (2015), p1. Napoleon was another historical leader born with a caul.
7. Westwood (1985), pp30-1.
8. Heanley (1931), p37.
9. Wilson (1891), p165, first published 1848.
10. *Corona Regia*, ed. Sutton (2011).
11. *Calendar of State Papers*, Venetian, vol. 17 (London, 1911), pp444-5.
12. Henry Killigrew to Francis Walsingham, 30 June 1574, Edinburgh. *Calendar of State Papers Scotland*, vol. 5 (1907), p13.

13. Peters *etc.* (2021).
14. M. de Fontenay, letter to Queen Mary's Secretary, 15 August 1584. Ashton (1969), p2.
15. Bingham (1968), p125.
16. Weldon (1817), p55.
17. Bellany and Cogswell (2015), p36.
18. Harris (2014), p47.
19. Furdell (2001), p108.
20. *Basilkon Doron*, in King James (2010), p39, 41.
21. Bingham (1968), p19.
22. *Basilkon Doron*, in King James (2010), p41.
23. Bingham (1968), 45, citing letter of countess of Lennox to Cecil, 22 July 1562. See Fraser, vol. 1 (1874), 388, referring to him not abiding solitude.

Chapter 2: First Loves – *Esmé Stuart and the Earl of Huntly*

1. Bingham (1968), p119.
2. Cust (1891), p88.
3. Melville (1842), pp76-7.
4. Bergeron (1999), p37.
5. Young (2000), p10.
6. Moysie (1830), p26.
7. Cust (1891), p92.
8. Widdrington to Walsingham, 4 May, 15 May, Bain, vol. 1 (Edinburgh, 1894), pp82-3.
9. Calderwood, vol. 3 (1843), p642.
10. Young (2000), 41. Also Wilson (1963), p36.
11. Young (2000), p40.
12. Calderwood, vol. 3 (1843), p463. Melville (1842), p81.
13. Bingham (1968), p145.
14. *Historie of King James the Sext* (1825), pp292-4.
15. Spottiswoode, vol. 2 (1851), p290.
16. Bergeron (1999), p42.

17. Reid (2017), p37.
18. Reprinted in Bergeron (1999), pp220-9.
19. Reid (2017), p38.
20. Anonymous letter to Thomas Randolph, cited in Reid (2017), p53.
21. Bergeron (1999), p38.
22. Young (2000), pp40-41.
23. Bergeron (1999), p52.
24. Ruth Grant (2017), p59.
25. Grant (2017), p62.
26. Akrigg (1984), pp89-91.
27. Akrigg (1984), p148.

Chapter 3: The Devil on the Forth – *King James and Witchcraft*

1. Normand and Roberts (2000), p4.
2. Larner (1981), pp1-3.
3. Maxwell-Stuart (2001), p141.
4. Kallestrup (2018), p139.
5. Williams (1970), p17.
6. Maxwell-Stuart (2001), p143.
7. Normand and Roberts (2000), p135.
8. Normand and Roberts (2000), pp309-26.
9. Maxwell-Stuart (2001), pp146-7.
10. Normand and Roberts (2000), p162.
11. Murray (1918), p321.
12. Bain, vol. 1 (1894), pp486-9.
13. Murray (1921), pp56-59.
14. Sandys (1621), p250.
15. Normand and Roberts (2000), pp39-49.
16. Loomis (2010), p91, 94.
17. Bellany and Cogswell (2015), p186.
18. Carr (2013), p34.

19. Normand and Roberts (2000), p163.
20. Normand and Roberts (2000), p213, 260.
21. Brock (2016), p44.
22. Arthur H. Williamson (1994), pp192-3.
23. Larner (1981), p70.
24. Kittredge (1912), p16.
25. Willson (1963), p309.
26. Letter to Robert Cecil, 10 October 1605. Akrigg (1984), p268.
27. Akrigg (1984), pp265-6.
28. Arthur Wilson (1653), p111.
29. Robert Ashton (1969), pp154-5.
30. Elmer, Peter (2016), p39.
31. Letter of John Chamberlain to Sir Dudley Carleton, 12 October 1616. Williams, vol. 1 (1848), p427.

Chapter 4: Above the Black Turnpike – *The Gowrie Conspiracy*

1. Harleian Misc., vol. 3 (1745), pp77-8.
2. Pitcairn, vol, 2 (1833), p171.
3. Pitcairn, vol, 2 (1833), p184.
4. Panton (1812), p174.
5. Pitcairn, vol. 2 (1833), p75.
6. Pitcairn, vol. 2 (1833), p175.
7. Arbuckle 2, pp100-1.
8. In evidence given at Perth on 22 August. Pitcairn, vol, 2 (1833), 149, pp174-9.
9. Pitcairn, vol. 2 (1833), p182.
10. Arbuckle 1 (1957), p13.
11. Arbuckle 2 (1957), p99.
12. Calderwood, vol. 6 (1845), p85.
13. Macnicol (1907), pp186-7.
14. Pitcairn, vol. 2 (1833), pp218-19.
15. Arbuckle 1 (1957), p3.
16. Birrell (1798), p52.

17. Goodall, (1957), p21. Williams (1970), p62. Young (2000), p22.
18. Arbuckle 2 (1957), p108.
19. Letter of Sir William Bowes to Cecil, Arbuckle 2 (1957), pp97-8.
20. Dunn-Hensley (2017), pp60-1.
21. Letter of Scrope to Cecil, 15 August 1600. Bain, vol. 2 (1894), 1220. Letter of Sir Henry Neville to Mr Winwood, 15 November 1600. Pitcairn. vol. 2 (1833), p316.
22. Lang (1902), pp132-3.
23. Chambers, vol. 2 (1827), 186-91. Lang (1902), p2.
24. Williams (1970), p63.
25. Melville (1842), p487.
26. Arbuckle 2 (1957), p89.
27. Osborne (1811), p277.
28. Weldon (1817), p3.
29. Based on a version of the event published at Copenhagen in 1601. Craigie (1908).
30. Wormald (2017), p205.
31. Melville (1842), pp485-6.
32. Calderwood, vol. 6 (1845), pp49-50.
33. Chambers, vol. 2 (1827), p80.

Chapter 5: Two Mothers, One Wife – *Elizabeth, Mary, Anne*

1. M. de Fontenay, letter to Mary's secretary, 15 August 1584. Ashton (1969), p1.
2. Rait and Cameron (1927), pp101-2.
3. Harington, vol. 1 (1804), p369.
4. Melville (1827), p159.
5. Peyton (1811), p342.
6. Susan Doran (2005), p26.
7. Ashton (1969), pp6-8.
8. Akrigg (1984), p71.
9. Cited Doran (2005), p208.
10. Akrigg (1962), p1.

11. Neller (1995), p16.
12. Loomis (2010), p37.
13. Dunn-Hensley (2017), p4.
14. Williams (1970), p13.
15. Stevenson (1879), p260.
16. Dunn-Hensley (2017), p28.
17. Meikle (2019), p175.
18. Williams (1970), pp53-55.
19. Letter from Sir Thomas Edmonds to the Earl of Shrewsbury, 16 June 1603. Ashton, (1969), pp92-93.
20. Peyton (1811), p339.
21. Akrigg (1984), p286.
22. Young (2000), p82.
23. Roper (2003), p56.

Chapter 6: A Family Man – *The King's Children and Cousin*

1. Simonds d'Ewes, vol. 1 (1856), p46.
2. Akrigg (1962), p129.
3. Simonds d'Ewes, vol. 1 (1856), p48.
4. Peyton (1811), p345.
5. Osborne (1811), p264.
6. Weldon (1817), p26.
7. Sanderson (1811), p252.
8. Wilson (1653), p63.
9. Simonds d'Ewes, vol. 1 (1856), p47.
10. Somerset (1997), p390.
11. Simonds d'Ewes, vol. 1 (1856), p91.
12. Burnet (1823), p19.
13. Ashton (1969), p219.
14. Akrigg (1962), p141.
15. Hodgkin (1902), p86.
16. Bergeron (1999), p22.
17. Durant (1978), p11.

18. Bradley, vol. 1 (1889), p91.
19. Hardy (1913), p85.
20. Bradley, vol. 1 (1889), p94.
21. Hardy (1913), p104.
22. Bradley, vol. 2 (1889), p136.
23. *Calendar Manuscripts, Hatfield House* (1930), p65.
24. Durant (1978), p131.
25. Durant (1978), p128.
26. Hardy (1913), p254.

Chapter 7: Shadows at the King's Right Hand – *Royal Associates and the Path to the English Crown*

1. Gajda (2012), p37.
2. Letter of King James to Cecil, October 1605. Akrigg (1984), p260.
3. Mears (1995), p59.
4. Wilson (1653), p2.
5. De Lisle (2007), p72.
6. De Lisle (2007), p180.
7. Reported back to Cecil by the Earl of Dunbar, April 1609. *Calendar Manuscripts, Salisbury* (1970), p47.
8. Wilson (1653), p61.
9. Bruce (1861), p67.
10. King James (2010), p37.
11. Anne Somerset (1997), p24.
12. Wilson (1653), p3.

Chapter 8: The King at Leisure – *Poetry and the Hunt*

1. Verweij (2014), p112.
2. Lewis (1944), p120.
3. Bawcutt (2001).
4. Dunnigan (2002), p79.

5. Ashton 1969), pp8-10.
6. Bell (1857), pp72-5.
7. Scott (1911), vol. 1, p365.
8. Ashton (1969), p6.
9. Willson (1963), p182.
10. King James (2010), p56.
11. Letter of Horatio Busino, 22 December 1617. *Calendar of State Papers, Venice*, 15 (1909), p79.
12. Stewart (2003), p179.
13. *Calendar of State Papers*, vol. 10 (1967), p53.

Chapter 9: Lion Versus Unicorn – *The Ill-Made Marriage of Scotland and England*

1. Melville (1842), pp171-2.
2. Michael (1990), p21.
3. Brown (1994), p64.
4. Williamson (1994), p211.
5. King James (2010), p59.
6. Spelman (1985), p175.
7. Levack (1987), p179.
8. Brown (1993), pp87-88.
9. King James (2010), pp161-2.
10. *Calendar State Papers, Venice*, 10 (1900), p94.
11. Wormald (1992), p39.
12. 'A tract on the succession', quoted in Levack (1987), p35.
13. Akrigg (1962), pp51-53.
14. Waurechen (2011), p63.
15. Wormald, Jenny (1994), p20.
16. Jenny Wormald (1992), p188.
17. Letter of James I to Robert Cecil, 6 December 1610. *Calendar Manuscripts, Salisbury* (1970), p265.
18. 19 March 1604, King James (2010), p136.
19. Jenny Wormald (1996), p149.

20. Enright (1976), pp31-35.
21. Wilson (1653), p5.
22. Murray (1991), xl-xli.
23. Spottiswood, vol. 1 (1847), pp93.
24. Willson (1963), p141.
25. Arthur Williamson (1994), pp200-3.
26. Bellany and Cogswell (2015), p107.
27. Levack (1987), p108.
28. Gordon (1604), p24.
29. Weldon (1817), p18.
30. Kishlansky (1997), p47.
31. Harris (2014), p66.
32. Brown (1993), p10.
33. Weldon (1817), p3.
34. Ashton, (1969) p105. Burgess, Wymer, Lawrence (2006), xiii. Akrigg (1962), p233, gives a variant figure for knights in the king's first year (838).
35. John Joskyns. Letter from Sir John Chamberlain to Sir Dudley Carleton, June 1614. Folkestone, vol 1, (1848), p320.
36. Levack (1987), p180.

Chapter 10: The Nation's Second Scotsman – *The Rise and Fall of Robert Carr*

1. Young (2000), p42.
2. Melville (1842), p220.
3. Akrigg (1962), p52.
4. Young (2000), p42.
5. Wilson (1653), p83.
6. Harington (1804), pp392–7.
7. Weldon (1817), p7.
8. Harrington (1804), p395.
9. Weldon (1817), p20.
10. Somerset (1997), p59.

11. Letter of John Chamberlain cited by Akrigg (1962), p178.
12. D'Ewes, vol 1 (1845), p90.
13. Weldon (1817), p20.
14. Somerset (1997), p71.
15. Seddon (1970), p51.
16. Williams (1970), p133.
17. Bergeron (1999), p76.
18. Bergeron (1999), pp85-6.
19. Weldon (1817), p19.
20. Akrigg (1962), p189.
21. Seddon (1970), p60.
22. D'Ewes, vol. 1 (1845), p71.
23. Akrigg (1962), p191.
24. Bergeron, (1999), p79.
25. Somerset (1997), p353.
26. D'Ewes, 1 (1845), p86.
27. Amos (1846), p167, 169.
28. Somerset (1997), p229, 232-3, 239.
29. Wilson (1653), p73.
30. Wilson (1653), pp89-90.
31. Weldon (1817), p32. Slightly different version in Amos (1846), p34.
32. Akrigg (1962), p200.
33. Somerset (1997), p61.
34. Somerset (1997), p389.
35. Amos (1846), p81.
36. Bergeron (1999), pp74-5.
37. Bellany (1994), p290.
38. Amos (1846), p493.
39. Seddon (1970), p68.

Chapter 11: Steenie – George Villiers, *Duke of Buckingham*

1. Bergeron (1999), p107.
2. Young (2000), p33.

Notes and References

3. Bergeron (2000), p138.
4. Akrigg (1962), p215.
5. Lockyer (1981), p19.
6. Young (2000), p44.
7. Young (2000), p50.
8. Bergeron (2000), p103.
9. Sanderson (1811), p262.
10. Weldon (1817), p29.
11. Bergeron (2000), p111.
12. Acts 6:15.
13. Bergeron (2000), p104.
14. Lockyer (1981), p122.
15. Lockyer (1981), p240.
16. Wilson (1653), p147.
17. Young (2000), pp60-62.
18. Akrigg (1984), p376.
19. Bergeron (2000), p113.
20. Lockyer (1981), p195.
21. Reported in letter from Thomas Locke to Sir Dudley Carleton, May 1624. Ashton (1969), p269.
22. Young (2000), p97.
23. *Calendar State Papers, Venice* 17 (1911), p439.
24. Young (2000), p54.
25. Akrigg (1962), p101.
26. Willson (1963), p441.
27. Lockyer (1981), p452.
28. D'Ewes, vol 1 (1845), p389.

Chapter 12: The Forerunner of Revenge – *The Death of King James*

1. D'Ewes, vol 1 (1845), p263.
2. Willson (1963), p378.
3. Willson (1963), p428.

4. Lockyer (1981), p234.
5. Wooley (2017), p200.
6. Riddell (1928), p32.
7. Bellany and Cogswell, (2015), p222.
8. Wooley (2017), p202.
9. Bellany and Cogswell, (2015), p28.
10. Bellany and Cogswell, (2015), p429.
11. Wooley (2017), p204.
12. Wooley (2017), p201.
13. Weldon (1817), p54.
14. Riddell (1928), p31.
15. Bellany and Cogswell (2015), p34.
16. Furdell (2001), p104.
17. Bellany and Cogswell (2015), p86.
18. 'Account of a tract' (1825).
19. Calderwood, vol. 8 (1849), pp632-3.
20. Bellany and Cogswell (2015), p68.
21. Bellany and Cogswell (2015), p95.
22. Bellany and Cogswell (2015), p72.
23. Bellany and Cogswell (2015), xxvi, p524.
24. *Harleian Miscellany*, vol. 5 (1810), pp211-15.
25. Lockyer (1981), p234.
26. Bellany and Cogswell, (2015), p35.
27. Wooley (2017), pp291-3.
28. Bellany and Cogswell, (2015), p528.
29. Furdell, (2001), p107.
30. Weldon (1817), pp48-50.
31. Ashton (1969), p254.
32. *Calendar State Papers, Venice*, vol. 17 (1911), pp444-5.
33. Letter of Rev Joseph Mead to Sir Martin Stuteville, 30 March 1622. Folkestone, vol. 2 (1848), p301.
34. Bellany and Cogswell (2015), p277.
35. Loomis (2010), pp83-118.
36. D'Ewes, vol. 2 (1845), p267.

Chapter 13: Solomon Weighed – *Reputation and Legacy*

1. Ashton (1969), pp19-21.
2. Young (2000), p102.
3. Hume (1803), pp662-3.
4. Bergeron (1999), p38.
5. Young (2000), p155.
6. Arnot (1812), pp69-71.
7. Pitcairn, vol. 2 (1833), p332.
8. Craigie (1950), p208.
9. Calderwood, vol. 5 (1844), p171.
10. Arnot (1812), pp72-3.
11. Seel (2005), p28.
12. Wilson (1653), p3.

Bibliography

'Account of a tract concerning the death of King James I,' *The Belfast Magazine and Literary Journal* 1, No. 6 (July 1825), pp575-578.

Akrigg, G. P. V., *Jacobean Pageant or, The Court of King James I* (Cambridge, Massachusetts, 1962).

Akrigg, G. P. V., (ed.), *Letters of James VI & I* (Berkeley, 1984).

Amos, Andrew, *The Great Oyer of Poisoning: The Trial of the Earl of Somerset for the Poisoning of Sir Thomas Overbury* (London, 1846).

Arbuckle, W. F., 'The "Gowrie Conspiracy"': part 1, *The Scottish Historical Review* 36, No. 121, Part 1 (April 1957), pp1-24, Part 2, Vol. 36, No. 122, Part 2 (October 1957), pp89-110.

Arnott, Hugo, *Celebrated Criminal Trials in Scotland, from AD 1536 to 1784* (Glasgow, 1812).

Ashton, Robert (ed.), *James I By His Contemporaries* (London, 1969).

Bain, Joseph (ed.), *The Border Papers*, 2 vols. (Edinburgh, 1894).

Bawcutt, Priscilla, 'James VI's Castalian Band: a modern myth,' *The Scottish Historical Review* 80, no, 210 (Oct. 2001), pp251-9.

Bell, Robert (ed.), *Ancient Poems, Ballads and Songs of the English Peasantry* (London, 1857).

Bellany, Alastair, 'Railinge rhymes and vaunting verse: libellous politics in Early Stuart England, 1603-1628,' in *Culture and Politics in Early Stuart England*, ed. Kevin Sharpe and Peter Lake (Basingstoke, 1994), pp285-310.

Bellany, Alastair James and Cogswell, Thomas, *The Murder of King James I* (New Haven, 2015).

Bergeron, David M., *King James and Letters of Homoerotic Desire* (Iowa City, 1999).

Bingham, Caroline, *The Making of a King* (London, 1968).

Birrell, Robert, *The Diary of Robert Birrell*, in *Fragments of Scottish History* (Edinburgh, 1798).

Bradley, Emily, *Life of the Lady Arabella Stuart*, 2 vols. (London, 1889).

Brock, Michelle D., *Satan and the Scots, The Devil in Post Reformation Scotland*, (London, 2016).

Brown, Keith M., *Kingdom or Province? Scotland and the Regal Union, 1603-1715* (London, 1993).

Brown, Keith M., 'The vanishing emperor: British kingship and its decline, 1603-1707,' in Scots and Britons, *Scottish Political Thought and the Union of 1603*, ed. Roger A. Mason (Cambridge, 1994), pp58-88.

Bruce, John (ed.), *Correspondence of King James VI of Scotland with Sir Robert Cecil and Others in England* (London, 1861).

Burgess, Glenn, Wymer, Rowland, Lawrence, Jason, *The Accession of James I, Historical and Cultural Consequences* (Basingstoke, 2006).

Burnet, Gilbert, *Bishop Burnet's History of His Own Time*, vol. 1 (Oxford, 1823).

Calderwood, David, *The History of the Kirk of* Scotland, 8 vols. (Edinburgh, 1842-49).

Calendar of the Manuscripts of the Most Honourable Marquess of Salisbury, Preserved at Hatfield House, Hertfordshire, Part 15 (London, 1930).

Calendar of the Manuscripts of the Most Honourable Marquess of Salisbury, Part 21 (London, 1970).

Calendar of State Papers, 1619-1623, vol. 10 (1858, rep. Nendeln, 1967).

Calendars of State Papers and Manuscripts, Venice, 1603-1607, vol. 10, ed. Horatio F. Brown (London, 1900).

Calendars of State Papers and Manuscripts, Venice, 1617-1619, vol. 15, ed. A. B. Hinds (London, 1909).

Calendar of State Papers, Venice, 1621-23, vol. 17, ed. A. B. Hinds (London, 1911).

Calendar of State Papers Relating to Scotland and Mary, Queen of Scots, 1574-1581, vol. 5, ed. William K. Boyd (Edinburgh, 1907).

Capps, Donald and Carlin, Nathan Steven, 'The homosexual tendencies of King James: should this matter to bible readers today?' *Pastoral Psychology* 55 (2007), pp667-99.

Carr, Victoria, 'The Countess of Angus's escape from the North Berwick witch-hunt,' in *Scottish Witches and Witch-Hunters*, ed. Julian Goodacre (London, 2013), pp34-48.

Chambers, Robert, *The Picture of Scotland*, 2 vols. (Edinburgh, 1827).

Cogswell, Thomas, *James I, The Phoenix* King (London, 2017).

Collingwood, Bruce J., 'Observations on the trial and death of William Earl of Gowrie, A.D. 1584, and on their connection with the Gowrie conspiracy, A.D. 1600.' *Archaeologia* 33(1849), 143-173.

Corona Regia (1615), hypertext edition ed. Dana F. Sutton philological. bham.ac.uk/corona/ (2011).

Cowan, Samuel, *The Gowrie Conspiracy and its Official Narrative* (London, 1902).

Cowan, Samuel (ed.), *The Ruthven Family Papers, The Ruthven Version of the Conspiracy and Assassination at Gowrie House, Perth, 5th August 1600* (London, 1912).

Craigie, James (ed.), *The Basilicon Doron of King James VI*, vol. 2 (Edinburgh, 1950).

Craigie, W. A. (ed.), *Skotland's Rímur, Icelandic Ballads on the Gowrie Conspiracy* (Oxford, 1908).

Croft, Pauline, *King James* (Basingstoke, 2003).

Cromarty, George Mackenzie, Earl of, *An Historical Account of the Conspiracies of the Earls of Gowry and Logan of Restalrig Against King James VI* (Edinburgh, 1713).

Cust, Lady Elizabeth, *Some Account of the Stuarts of Aubigny, in France, 1422-1672* (London, 1891).

D'Ewes, Simonds, *The Autobiography and Correspondence of Sir Simonds D'Ewes,* 2 vols. (London, 1845).

De Lisle, Leanda, *After Elizabeth, The Rise of James of Scotland and the Struggle for the Throne of England* (London, 2007).

Doran, Susan, 'Loving and affectionate cousins? The relationship between Elizabeth I of England and James VI of Scotland 1586-1603,' in *Tudor England and its Neighbours*, ed. Susan Doran and Glenn Richardson (Basingstoke, 2005), pp203-34.

Dunn-Hensley, Susan, *Anna of Denmark and Henrietta Maria, Virgins, Witches and Catholic Queens* (London, 2017).

Dunnigan, Sarah M., *Eros and Poetry at the Courts of Mary Queen of Scots and James VI* (Basingstoke, 2002).

Durant, David N., *Arbella Stuart, A Rival to the Queen* (London, 1978).

Elmer, Peter, *Witchcraft, Witch-Hunting, and Politics in Early Modern England* (Oxford, 2016).

Enright, Michael, 'King James and his island: an archaic kingship belief?' *The Scottish Historical Review* 55, no. 159, part 1 (April 1976), pp29-40.

Fraser, William, *The* Lennox, 2 vols. (Edinburgh, 1874).

Furdell, Elizabeth Lane, *The Royal Doctors 1485-1714: Medical Personnel and the Tudor and Stuart Courts* (Rochester, New York, 2001).

Gajda, Alexandra, *The Earl of Essex and Late Elizabethan Political Culture* (Oxford, 2012).

Galloway, Bruce R., and Levack, Brian P. (ed.), *The Jacobean Union – Six Tracts* (Edinburgh, 1985).

Goodacre, Julian, 'John Knox on demonology and Witchcraft,' *Archiv für Reformationsgeschichte,* 96 (2005), pp221-245.

Goodall, Archibald L. 'The Health of James the Sixth of Scotland and First of England,' *Medical History*, 1 (1) (January 1957), pp17-27.

Gordon, John, *Enōtikon or A Sermon on the Vnion of Great Brittani* (1604), Early English Books Online: quod.lib.umich.edu/

Grant, Ruth, 'Friendship, politics and religion: George Gordon, Sixth Earl of Huntly and King James VI, 1581–1595', in Miles Kerr-Peterson & Steven Reid (ed.), *James VI and Noble Power* (Abingdon, 2017), pp57–90.

Hardy, B.C., *Arbella Stuart, A Biography* (London, 1913).

The Harleian Miscellany, vol. 3 (London, 1745).

The Harleian Miscellany, vol. 5 (London, 1810).

Harington, Sir John, *Nugæ Antiquæ*, vol. 1 (London, 1804).

Harris, *Rebellion, Britain's First Stuart Kings, 1567-1642* (Oxford, 2014).

Heanley, K., 'Claims James I was impostor. Infant's body discovered in wall of Edinburgh Castle has caused conjecture,' *Macleans Magazine* (1 September 1931), p37.

Herries, John Maxwell, *Historical Memoirs of the Reign of Mary, Queen of Scots, and a Portion of the Reign of King James the Sixth* (Edinburgh, 1836).

The Historie and Life of King James the Sext: Being an Account of the Affairs of Scotland, from the year 1566 to the year 1596 (Edinburgh, 1825).

Hodgkin, R. H., 'Elizabeth of Bohemia,' in *Five Stuart Princesses*, ed. Robert S. Rait (London, 1902), pp47-164.

Hume, David, *The History of England, from the Invasion of Julius Caesar to the Revolution in 1688*, vol. 6 (London, 1803).

James, King, VI and I, *Political Writings*, ed. Johann Somerville (Cambridge, 2010).

Kallestrup, Louise Nyholm, '"Kind in words and deeds, but false in their hearts": fear of evil conspiracy in late-sixteenth-century Denmark,' in *Cultures of Witchcraft in Europe from the Middle Ages to the Present, Essays in Honour of Willem de Blécourt*, ed. Jonathan Barry, Owen Davies and Cornelie Usborne (London, 2018), pp137-54.

Kishlansky, Mark, *A Monarchy Transformed, Britain 1603-1714* (London, 1997).

Kittredge, George Lyman, 'English witchcraft and James the First,' in *Studies in the History of Religions Presented to Crawford Howell Toy*, ed. David Gordon Lyon and George Foot Moore (New York, 1912), pp1-65.

Lang, Andrew, *James VI and the Gowrie Mystery* (London, 1902).

Larner, Christina, *Enemies of God: The Witch-Hunt in Scotland* (London, 1981).

Levack, Brian P., *The Formation of the British State: England, Scotland and the Union, 1603-1707* (Oxford, 1987).

Lewis, C. S., *English Literature in the Sixteenth Century, Excluding Drama* (Cambridge, 1944).

Lockyer, Roger, *Buckingham: The Life and Political Career of George Villiers, First Duke of Buckingham, 1592-1628* (London, 1981).

The Life and Historie and King James the Sext (Edinburgh, 1804).

Loomis, Catherine, *The Death of Elizabeth I: Remembering and Reconstructing the Virgin Queen* (Basingstoke, 2010).

Lynch, Michael, 'Queen Mary's triumph: the baptismal celebrations at Stirling in December 1566,' *The Scottish Historical Review* 187, part 1 (April 1990), pp1-21.

Macnicol, D. C., *Master Robert Bruce, Minister in the Kirk of Edinburgh* (Edinburgh, 1907).

Matusiak, John, *James I: Scotland's King of England* (Stroud, 2015).

Maxwell-Stuart, P. G., *Satan's Conspiracy: Magic and Witchcraft in Sixteenth Century Scotland* (East Linton, 2001).

Mears, Natalie, '*Regnum Cecilianum*' A Cecilian perspective of the Court,' in *The Reign of Elizabeth I, Court and Culture in the Last Decade*, ed. John Guy (Cambridge, 1995), pp46-64.

Meikle, Maureen M., 'Once a Dane, always a Dane? Anna of Denmark's foreign relations and intercessions as queen consort of Scotland and England, 1588-1619,' *The Court Historian*, 24:2 (2019), pp168-80.

Melville, James, *The Autobiography and Diary of Mr James Melvill, With A Continuation of the Diary* (Edinburgh, 1842).

Melville, *Sir James, of Halhill, Memoirs of His Own Life* (Edinburgh, 1827).

Moysie, David, *Memoirs of the Affairs of Scotland, 1577-1603* (Edinburgh, 1830).

James A. H. Murray, *The Romance and Prophecies of Thomas of Erceldoune* (1875, reprinted Felinfach, 1991).

Murray, Margaret, 'The "Devil" of North Berwick,' *The Scottish Historical Review* 15, no. 60 (July 1918), pp310-321.

Murray, Margaret, *The Witch-Cult in Western Europe* (London, 1921).

Neller, Howard, *The Right to Be King, The Succession to the Crown of England, 1603-1714* (Basingstoke, 1995).

Normand, Lawrence and Roberts, Gareth, *Witchcraft in Early Modern Scotland* (Liverpool, 2000).

Osborne, Francis, *Traditionall Memorialls on the Raigne of King James the First*, in *The Secret History of the Court of King James the First*, ed. Sir Walter Scott, vol. 1 (Edinburgh, 1811), pp123-289.

Panton, William, *A Dissertation on that Portion of Scottish History Termed the Gowry Conspiracy* (Perth, 1812).

Paul, Sir James Balfour, *The Scots Peerage*, vol. 4 (Edinburgh, 1907).

Peters, Timothy, Garrard, Peter, Ganensan, Vijeya, Stephenson, John, 'The nature of King James VI/I's medical conditions: new approaches to the diagnosis,' *History of Psychiatry* 23:3 (January 2021), pp277-90.

Peyton, Sir Edward, 'The Divine Catastrophe of the Kingly Family of the House of Stuarts,' in *The Secret History of King James the First*, ed. Sir Walter Scott, vol. 2, (Edinburgh, 1811), pp301-466.

Pitcairn, *Ancient Criminal Trials in Scotland*, vol. 2 (Edinburgh, 1833).

Rait, Robert S. and Camerson, Annie I. (ed.), *King James's Secret: Negotiations Between Elizabeth and James VI Relating to the Execution of Mary Queen of Scots, from the Warrenden Papers* (London, 1927).

Reid, Steven J., 'Of Bairns and Bearded Men: James VI and the Ruthven Raid', in Miles Kerr-Peterson and Steven J. Reid, ed., *James VI and Noble Power in Scotland, c. 1578-1603* (London, 2017), pp32-56.

Riddell, William Renwick, 'The death of King James I – A medico-legal study,' *Journal of Criminal Law and Criminology*, Issue 1, 19 (May 1928), pp30-35.

Roper, Louis H., 'Unmasquing the connections between Jacobean politics and policy: the circle of Anna of Denmark and the beginning of the English empire, 1614-18,' in *High and Mighty Queens' of Early Modern England: Realities and Representations*, ed. Carole

Levin, Jo Eldridge Carney, Debra Barrett-Graves (Basingstoke, 2003), pp45-60.

Roughead, William, *The Riddle of the Ruthven and Other Studies* (Edinburgh, 1919).

Sanderson, Sir William, *Aulicus Coquinariae: or a vindication in answer to a pamphlet entituled 'The Court and Character of King James'* (1650, rep. in *The Secret Court of James the First*, ed. Walter Scott, vol. 2 (Edinburgh, 1811), pp91-298.

Sandys, George, *The Relation of a Journey Begun An. Dom. 1610, in Four Books* (London, 1621).

Scott, Rev. James, *A History of the Life and Death of John, Earl of Gowrie, With Preliminary Dissertations* (Edinburgh, 1818).

Scott, Walter (ed.), *The Secret History of the Court of James the First*, 2 vols. (Edinburgh, 1811).

Seddon, P. R., 'Robert Carr, Earl of Somerset,' *Renaissance and Modern Studies* 14, issue 1 (1970), pp48-68.

Seel, Graham E., *The Early Stuart Kings, 1603-1642* (London, 2005).

Somerset, Anne, *Unnatural Murder, Poison at the Court of James I* (London, 1997).

Spelman, Sir Henry, 'Of the Union,' in *The Jacobean Union, Six Tracts of 1604*, ed. Bruce R. Galloway and Brian P. Levack (Edinburgh, 1985), pp160-83.

Spottiswoode, John, *The History of the Church of Scotland*, 3 vols. (1655, reprinted Edinburgh, 1847-51).

Stevenson, Joseph, 'Gleanings among old records: Anne of Denmark, Queen of Great Britain,' *The Month and Catholic Review* 35 (1879), pp256-65.

Stewart, Alan, *The Cradle King, A Life of King James VI and I* (London, 2003).

Thomson, George Malcolm, *A Kind of Justice, Two Studies in Treason* (London, 1970).

Verweij, S., '"Book, go thy ways": the publication, reading, and reception of James VI/I's early poetic works,' *Huntingdon Library Quarterly* 77 (2) (2014), pp111-31.

Watson, Geoffrey, *Bothwell and the Witches* (London, 1975).

Waurechen, Sarah Katerina, *Talking Scot: English Perceptions of the Scots During the Regal Union*, Unpublished PhD Thesis (Ontario, 2011).

Weldon, Sir Anthony, *The Court and Character of King James the First* (1650, reprinted London, 1817).

Westwood, Jennifer, *Albion, A Guide to Legendary Britain* (London, 1985).

Williams, Edith Carleton, *Anne of Denmark* (London), 1970.

Williams, Robert Folkestone, *The Court and Times of James the First*, 2 vols. (London, 1848).

Williamson, Arthur A., 'Number and national consciousness: the Edinburgh mathematicians and Scottish political culture at the union of crowns,' in *Scots and Britons, Scottish political Thought and the Union of 1603*, ed. Roger A. Mason (Cambridge, 1994), pp187-212.

Willson, David Harris, *King James VI and I* (1956, reprinted London, 1963).

Wilson, Arthur, *The History of Great Britain, Being the Life and Reign of King James the First* (London, 1653).

Wilson, Daniel, *Memorials of Edinburgh in the Olden* Time, 2 vols. (2nd edn., Edinburgh, 1891).

Wooley, Benjamin, *The King's Assassin: The Fatal Affair of George Villiers and James I* (London, 2017).

Wormald, Jenny, 'The creation of Britain: multiple kingdoms or core and colonies?', *Transactions of the Royal Historical Society* 2 (1992), pp175-94.

Wormald, Jenny, 'The Gowrie conspiracy: do we need to wait until the Day of Judgement?', in *James VI and Noble Power in Scotland 1578-1603*, ed. Miles Kerr-Peterson and Steven J. Reid (London, 2017), pp194-206.

Wormald, Jenny, 'James VI, James I and the Identity of Britain,' in *The British Problem, c. 1534-1707, State Formation in the Atlantic Archipelago*, ed. Brendan Bradshaw and John Morrill (London, 1996), pp148-71.

Wormald, Jenny, 'The union of 1603,' in *Scots and Britons, Scottish Political Thought and the Union of 1603*, ed. Roger A. Mason (Cambridge, 1994), pp17-40.

Young, Michael B., *King James and the History of Homosexuality* (New York, 2000).